Communications
in Computer and Information Science 274

Gabriela Csurka   Martin Kraus
Leonid Mestetskiy   Paul Richard
José Braz (Eds.)

Computer Vision, Imaging and Computer Graphics

Theory and Applications

International Joint Conference, VISIGRAPP 2011
Vilamoura, Portugal, March 5-7, 2011
Revised Selected Papers

 Springer

Volume Editors

Gabriela Csurka
Xerox Research Centre Europe, Meylan, France
E-mail: gabriela.csurka@xrce.xerox.com

Martin Kraus
Aalborg University, Denmark
E-mail: martin@create.aau.dk

Leonid Mestetskiy
Moscow State University, Russia
E-mail: mestlm@mail.ru

Paul Richard
University of Angers, France
E-mail: paul.richard@istia.univ-angers.fr

José Braz
Escola Superior de Tecnologia do IPS, Setúbal, Portugal
E-mail: jbraz@est.ips.pt

ISSN 1865-0929   e-ISSN 1865-0937
ISBN 978-3-642-32349-2   e-ISBN 978-3-642-32350-8
DOI 10.1007/978-3-642-32350-8
Springer Heidelberg Dordrecht London New York

Library of Congress Control Number: 2012952222

CR Subject Classification (1998): I.3, I.5, H.2.8, I.3.7, I.2.10, I.3.1, I.4

Typesetting: Camera-ready by author, data conversion by Scientific Publishing Services, Chennai, India

Printed on acid-free paper

Springer is part of Springer Science+Business Media (www.springer.com)

Preface

This book includes extended versions of the selected papers from VISIGRAPP 2011, the International Joint Conference on Computer Vision, Imaging and Computer Graphics Theory and Applications, which was held in Vilamoura, Algarve, Portugal, during March 5–7, 2011 and organized by the Institute for Systems and Technologies of Information, Control and Communication (INSTICC).

VISIGRAPP comprises four conferences, namely, the International Conference on Computer Vision Theory and Applications (VISAPP), the International Conference on Computer Graphics Theory and Applications (GRAPP), the International Conference on Imaging Theory and Applications (IMAGAPP), and the International Conference on Information Visualization Theory and Applications (IVAPP).

VISIGRAPP received a total of 405 paper submissions from more than 50 countries. After a rigorous double-blind evaluation, only 14% of the papers were accepted and published as full papers. These numbers clearly show that this conference is aiming at high quality standards and is now an established venue for researchers in the broad fields of computer vision, computer graphics, and image analysis and information visualization. From the set of full papers, 15 were selected for inclusion in this book. The selection process was based on quantitative and qualitative evaluation results provided by the Program Committee reviewers as well as the feedback on paper presentations provided by the Session Chairs during the conference. After selection, the accepted papers were further revised and extended by the authors. Our gratitude goes to all contributors and reviewers, without whom this book would not have been possible.

Additionally 84 papers were accepted for short presentations and 49 were accepted for poster presentations. These works were not considered for the present book selection process.

VISIGRAPP 2011 included four invited keynote lectures, presented by internationally renowned researchers, whom we would like to thank for their contribution to reinforce the overall quality of the conference, namely, in alphabetical order: Brian A. Barsky (University of California, Berkeley, USA), Vittorio Ferrari (ETH Zurich, Switzerland), Carlos González-Morcillo (University of Castilla-La Mancha, Spain) and Joost van de Weijer (Autonomous University of Barcelona, Spain).

We wish to thank all those who supported VISIGRAPP and helped to organize the conference. On behalf of the Conference Organizing Committee, we would like to especially thank the authors, whose work was the essential part of the conference and contributed to a very successful event. We would also like to thank the members of the Program Committee, whose expertise and diligence were instrumental to ensuring the quality of the final contributions. We also wish to thank all the members of the Organizing Committee whose work and commitment were invaluable. Last but not least, we would like to thank Springer for their collaboration in getting this book to print.

October 2011

Gabriela Csurka
Martin Kraus
Leonid Mestetskiy
Paul Richard
José Braz

Organization

Conference Chair

José Braz   Escola Superior de Tecnologia de Setúbal, Portugal

Program Co-chairs

GRAPP

Paul Richard   Laboratoire D'ingénierie des Systèmes Automatisés - LISA, France

IMAGAPP

Gabriela Csurka   Xerox Research Centre Europe, France

IVAPP

Martin Kraus   Aalborg University, Denmark

VISAPP

Leonid Mestetskiy   Moscow State University, Russian Federation

Organizing Committee

Sérgio Brissos	INSTICC, Portugal
Helder Coelhas	INSTICC, Portugal
Andreia Costa	INSTICC, Portugal
Patrícia Duarte	INSTICC, Portugal
Bruno Encarnação	INSTICC, Portugal
Liliana Medina	INSTICC, Portugal
Carla Mota	INSTICC, Portugal
Raquel Pedrosa	INSTICC, Portugal
Vitor Pedrosa	INSTICC, Portugal
Daniel Pereira	INSTICC, Portugal
José Varela	INSTICC, Portugal
Pedro Varela	INSTICC, Portugal

GRAPP Program Committee

Tomi Aarnio, Finland
Francisco Abad, Spain
Marco Agus, Italy
Marco Attene, Italy
Dolors Ayala, Spain
Sergei Azernikov, USA
Rafael Bidarra, The Netherlands
Jiri Bittner, Czech Republic
Manfred Bogen, Germany
Kadi Bouatouch, France
Willem F. Bronsvoort,
   The Netherlands
Stephen Brooks, Canada
Patrick Callet, France
Pedro Cano, Spain
Thanh Tung Cao, Singapore
Maria Beatriz Carmo, Portugal
L.G. Casado, Spain
Teresa Chambel, Portugal
Hwan-gue Cho, Korea, Republic of
Ana Paula Cláudio, Portugal
Sabine Coquillart, France
António Cardoso Costa, Portugal
Victor Debelov, Russian Federation
John Dingliana, Ireland
Sasa Divjak, Slovenia
David Duce, UK
Arjan Egges, The Netherlands
Petr Felkel, Czech Republic
Jie-Qing Feng, China
Fernando Nunes Ferreira, Portugal
Luiz Henrique de Figueiredo, Brazil
Martin Fuchs, USA
Ioannis Fudos, Greece
Alejandro García-Alonso, Spain
Marina Gavrilova, Canada
Miguel Gea, Spain
Mashhuda Glencross, UK
Stephane Gobron, Switzerland
Jérôme Grosjean, France
Jean-Yves Guillemaut, UK
Peter Hall, UK
Vlastimil Havran, Czech Republic

Nancy Hitschfeld, Chile
Toby Howard, UK
Andres Iglesias, Spain
Insung Ihm, Korea, Republic of
Jiri Janacek, Czech Republic
Frederik Jansen, The Netherlands
Juan J. Jimenez-Delgado, Spain
Robert Joan-Arinyo, Spain
Andrew Johnson, USA
Chris Joslin, Canada
Marcelo Kallmann, USA
Josef Kohout, Czech Republic
Martin Kraus, Denmark
Marc Erich Latoschik, Germany
Miguel Leitão, Portugal
Heinz U. Lemke, Germany
Suresh Lodha, USA
Adriano Lopes, Portugal
Steve Maddock, UK
Joaquim Madeira, Portugal
Claus B. Madsen, Denmark
Nadia Magnenat-Thalmann,
   Switzerland
Michael Manzke, Ireland
Ramon Molla, Spain
Guillaume Moreau, France
David Mould, Canada
Gennadiy Nikishkov, Japan
Marc Olano, USA
Samir Otmane, France
Georgios Papaioannou, Greece
Alexander Pasko, UK
Giuseppe Patané, Italy
Daniel Patel, Norway
João Pereira, Portugal
Steve Pettifer, UK
Dimitri Plemenos, France
Anna Puig, Spain
Enrico Puppo, Italy
Werner Purgathofer, Austria
Paul Richard, France
María Cecilia Rivara, Chile
Inmaculada Rodríguez, Spain

Przemyslaw Rokita, Poland
Manuel Próspero dos Santos, Portugal
Rafael J. Segura, Spain
Alexei Sourin, Singapore
A. Augusto Sousa, Portugal
Frank Steinicke, Germany
Veronica Sundstedt, Sweden
Jie Tang, China
Matthias Teschner, Germany
Walid Tizani, UK

Juan Carlos Torres, Spain
Alain Trémeau, France
Anna Ursyn, USA
Luiz Velho, Brazil
Andreas Weber, Germany
Daniel Weiskopf, Germany
Alexander Wilkie, Czech Republic
Burkhard Wuensche, New Zealand
Lihua You, UK
Jianmin Zheng, Singapore

GRAPP Auxiliary Reviewers

Thomas Auzinger, Austria
Ben van Basten, The Netherlands
Daniela Giorgi, Italy
Olle Hilborn, Sweden
Yazhou Huang, USA
Petar Jercic, Sweden

Stefan Jeschke, Austria
Endre M. Lidal, Norway
Stephan Mantler, Austria
Veronika Solteszova, Norway
Andreas Vasilakis, Greece

IMAGAPP Program Committee

Amr Abdel-Dayem, Canada
Constantino Carlos Reyes Aldasoro,
    UK
Emmanuel Audenaert, Belgium
Xiao Bai, China
Reneta Barneva, USA
Arrate Muñoz Barrutia, Spain
Sebastiano Battiato, Italy
Hugues Benoit-Cattin, France
Franco Bertora, Italy
Djamal Boukerroui, France
Marleen de Bruijne, Denmark
Teof lo de Campos, UK
Xianbin Cao, China
Gustavo Carneiro, Portugal
Vinod Chandran, Australia
Chin-Chen Chang, Taiwan
Jocelyn Chanussot, France
Samuel Cheng, USA
Hocine Cherif , France
Laurent Cohen, France
Gabriela Csurka, France

Aysegul Cuhadar, Canada
Jérôme Darbon, France
Emmanuel Dellandréa, France
David Demirdjian, USA
Jorge Dias, Portugal
Jana Dittmann, Germany
Patrick Dubois, France
Mahmoud El-Sakka, Canada
Zhigang Fan, USA
Ivar Farup, Norway
GianLuca Foresti, Italy
Miguel A. Garcia-Ruiz, Mexico
Jordi Gonzàlez, Spain
Manuel González-Hidalgo, Spain
Bernard Gosselin, Belgium
Nikos Grammalidis, Greece
Christos Grecos, UK
Raouf Hamzaoui, UK
Allan Hanbury, Austria
Alex Pappachen James, Australia
Xiaoyi Jiang, Germany
Zhong Jin, China

Martin Kampel, Austria
Etienne Kerre, Belgium
Jana Kludas, Switzerland
Syoji Kobashi, Japan
Ville Kolehmainen, Finland
Andreas Koschan, USA
Maria Kunkel, Germany
Fatih Kurugollu, UK
Slimane Larabi, Algeria
Tong-Yee Lee, Taiwan
Sebastien Lefevre, France
Chang-Tsun Li, UK
Xuelong Li, China
Daw-Tung Dalton Lin, Taiwan
Xiuwen Liu, USA
Alexander Loui, USA
Rastislav Lukac, USA
Javier Melenchón, Spain
Jean Meunier, Canada
Rafael Molina, Spain
Luce Morin, France
Henning Müller, Switzerland
Peter Nillius, Sweden
Francisco Perales, Spain

Ana Reis, Portugal
Alessandro Rizzi, Italy
Mário Forjaz Secca, Portugal
Fiorella Sgallari, Italy
Dinggang Shen, USA
Sandra Skaff, France
Bogdan Smolka, Poland
Ömer Muhammet Soysal, USA
Liana Stanescu, Romania
Sabine Süsstrunk, Switzerland
Tamás Szirányi, Hungary
Yi Tang, China
Sabina Tangaro, Italy
João Manuel R.S. Tavares, Portugal
Nipon Theera-Umpon, Thailand
Shoji Tominaga, Japan
Georgios Triantafyllidis, Greece
Joost van de Weijer, Spain
Pingkun Yan, USA
Shan Yu, France
Yizhou Yu, USA
Jun Zhang, China
Peter Zolliker, Switzerland

IMAGAPP Auxiliary Reviewers

Bahadir Gunturk, USA

Bei Li, USA

IVAPP Program Committee

Huub van de Wetering,
   The Netherlands
Maria Beatriz Carmo, Portugal
Wei Chen, China
Chi-Wing Fu, Singapore
David Gotz, USA
Pheng-Ann Heng, China
Danny Holten, The Netherlands
Seokhee Hong, Australia
Tony Huang, Australia
Jessie Kennedy, UK
Andreas Kerren, Sweden

Martin Kraus, Denmark
Peter Lindstrom, USA
Lars Linsen, Germany
Giuseppe Liotta, Italy
Shixia Liu, China
Ketan Mane, USA
Krešimir Matkovic, Austria
Silvia Miksch, Austria
Klaus Mueller, USA
Luis Gustavo Nonato, Brazil
Steffen Oeltze, Germany
Benoît Otjacques, Luxembourg

Alex Pang, USA
Margit Pohl, Austria
Aidan Slingsby, UK
Shigeo Takahashi, Japan
Chaoli Wang, USA

Matt Ward, USA
Tino Weinkauf, USA
Jonathan Woodring, USA
Xiaoru Yuan, China

IVAPP Auxiliary Reviewers

Daniel Cernea, Germany
Maria Cristina Ferreira de Oliveira,
  Brazil

Fernando Paulovich, Brazil
Qiong Wang, China
Wang Weiming, China

VISAPP Program Committee

Amr Abdel-Dayem, Canada
Jörgen Ahlberg, Sweden
Sileye Ba, France
Arrate Muñoz Barrutia, Spain
Sebastiano Battiato, Italy
Olga Bellon, Brazil
Diego Borro, Spain
Adrian Bors, UK
Alain Boucher, Vietnam
Roger Boyle, UK
Marleen de Bruijne, Denmark
Pedro Latorre Carmona, Spain
M. Emre Celebi, USA
Ronald Chung, China
Carlos Correa, USA
Guido de Croon, The Netherlands
Gabriela Csurka, France
Fabio Cuzzolin, UK
Dima Damen, UK
Roy Davies, UK
Kenneth Dawson-Howe, Ireland
Jorge Dias, Portugal
Grigori Evreinov, Finland
Giovanni Maria Farinella, Italy
Gernot A. Fink, Germany
Robert Fisher, UK
David Fofi, France
Tyler Folsom, USA
Roberto Fraile, UK
Yun Fu, USA

Antonios Gasteratos, Greece
Basilios Gatos, Greece
Manuel Grana, Spain
Jiro Gyoba, Japan
Anders Heyden, Sweden
Hsi-Chin Hsin, Taiwan
Fay Huang, Taiwan
Xiaolei (Sharon) Huang, USA
Sae Hwang, USA
Kevin (Jiancheng) Jia, USA
Anastasios Kesidis, Greece
Nahum Kiryati, Israel
Dimitrios Kosmopoulos, Greece
Constantine Kotropoulos, Greece
Michal Kozubek, Czech Republic
Arjan Kuijper, Germany
Paul W.H. Kwan, Australia
Andreas Lanitis, Cyprus
Reiner Lenz, Sweden
Baoxin Li, USA
Chang-Tsun Li, UK
Jing Li, UK
Weihong Li, USA
Xuelong Li, China
Ang Li-minn, Malaysia
Rastislav Lukac, USA
Pere Millan Marco, Spain
Brendan Mccane, New Zealand
Gerard Medioni, USA
Jaime Melendez, Spain

J.P. Mellor, USA
Leonid Mestetskiy, Russian Federation
Washington Mio, USA
Pradit Mittrapiyanuruk, Thailand
Ali Mohammad-Djafari, France
DavideMoroni, Italy
Stefan Müller-Schneiders, Germany
Vittorio Murino, Italy
Lazaros Nalpantidis, Greece
Heinrich Niemann, Germany
Mark Nixon, UK
Charalambos Poullis, Cyprus
Bogdan Raducanu, Spain
Elisa Ricci, Italy
Mariano Rivera, Mexico
Jarek Rossignac, USA
Adrian Rusu, USA
Ovidio Salvetti, Italy
Xiaowei Shao, Japan
Lik-Kwan Shark, UK
Li Shen, USA

Maryam Shokri, Canada
Chang Shu, Canada
NH Siddique, UK
Luciano Silva, Brazil
José Martínez Sotoca, Spain
Joachim Stahl, USA
Filippo Stanco, Italy
Changming Sun, Australia
Shamik Sural, India
Ryszard Tadeusiewicz, Poland
Yi Tang, China
Jean-philippe Tarel, France
Muriel Visani, France
Frank Wallhoff, Germany
Tiangong Wei, New Zealand
Christian Wöhler, Germany
Stefan Wörz, Germany
Jianmin Zheng, Singapore
Ying Zheng, UK
Yun Zhu, USA
Zhigang Zhu, USA

VISAPP Auxiliary Reviewers

Hugo Álvarez, Spain
Rubisley Lemes, Brazil
Giovanni Puglisi, Italy

Jan Richarz, Germany
Jairo Sanchez, Spain
Maurício Pamplona Segundo, Brazil

Invited Speakers

Carlos González-Morcillo   University of Castilla-La Mancha, Spain
Vittorio Ferrari   ETH Zurich, Switzerland
Brian A. Barsky   University of California, Berkeley, USA
Joost van de Weijer   Autonomous University of Barcelona, Spain

Table of Contents

Invited Speaker

Using Expert Knowledge for Distributed Rendering Optimization   3
   Carlos Glez-Morcillo and David Vallejo

Part I: Computer Graphics Theory and Applications

Dual Spherical Spline and Its Application in Tool Path Planing for
5-Axis Flank Milling   19
   Yayun Zhou, Jörg Schulze, and Stefan Schäffler

Estimating Outdoor Illumination Conditions Based on Detection of
Dynamic Shadows.   33
   Claus B. Madsen and Brajesh B. Lal

Feature-First Hole Filling Strategy for 3D Meshes   53
   Hanh T.-M. Ngo and Won-Sook Lee

Inhomogeneous Axial Deformation for Orthopedic Surgery Planning   69
   Sergei Azernikov

Modelling of 3D Objects Using Unconstrained and Uncalibrated Images
Taken with a Handheld Camera   86
   Minh Hoang Nguyen, Burkhard Wünsche, Patrice Delmas, and
   Christof Lutteroth

Part II: Imaging Theory and Applications

Blind Image Deconvolution of Linear Motion Blur 105
   Florian Brusius, Ulrich Schwanecke, and Peter Barth

Part III: Information Visualization Theory and Applications

Human Centered Design in Practice: A Case Study with the Ontology
Visualization Tool Knoocks 123
   Simone Kriglstein and Günter Wallner

SmoothScroll: A Multi-scale, Multi-layer Slider 142
   Michael Wörner and Thomas Ertl

Part IV: Computer Vision Theory and Applications

Palm Shape Comparison for Person Recognition 157
  Irina Bakina

Bioinformatics-Motivated Approach to Stereo Matching.............. 172
  *Jesus Martinez-del-Rincon, Jerome Thevenon, Romain Dieny, and
  Jean-Christophe Nebel*

Hierarchical Grid-Based People Tracking with Multi-camera Setup 187
  Lili Chen, Giorgio Panin, and Alois Knoll

The Spiral Facets: A Compact 3D Facial Mesh Surface Representation
and Its Applications... 203
  *Naoufel Werghi, Harish Bhaskar, Mohamed Khamis Naqbi,
  Youssef Meguebli, and Haykel Boukadida*

REFA: A Robust E-HOG for Feature Analysis for Local Description of
Interest Points... 225
  Manuel Grand-brochier, Christophe Tilmant, and Michel Dhome

Mutual On-Line Learning for Detection and Tracking in High-Resolution
Images 240
  David Hurych, Karel Zimmermann, and Tomáš Svoboda

Computational Framework for Symmetry Classification of Repetitive
Patterns 257
  M. Agustí-Melchor, Á. Rodas-Jordá, and J.M. Valiente-González

Author Index... 271

Invited Speaker

Using Expert Knowledge for Distributed Rendering Optimization

Carlos Glez-Morcillo and David Vallejo

University of Castilla-La Mancha, Paseo de la Universidad 4, 13170 Ciudad Real, Spain
{Carlos.Gonzalez,David.Vallejo}@uclm.es

Abstract. The generation of virtual images, which do not differ from those taken from the real world, from an abstract description of a 3D scene is defined as Photorealistic Image Synthesis. Since achieving greater realism is the ultimate goal, the rendering of a single image may take hours or days even on powerful computers. To face this challenge, in this work we discuss the potential benefits of combining the use of expert knowledge and the adoption of a multi-agent architecture in order to optimize the rendering of complex 3D scenes. Within this context, we apply novel techniques based on the use of expert knowledge to distribute the different work units in which the input scene is divided in a balanced way, to automatically generate the rendering engine setting parameters, and to optimize the configuration of the rendering parameters given by the user. The conducted experiments demonstrate that our approach can drastically reduce the rendering time with unnoticeable quality loss.

1 Introduction

The goal of Photorealistic Image Synthesis is to obtain computer-generated images which do not differ from those taken from the real world [16]. This is a complex process composed of several steps, such as 3D modeling, set up of materials and textures, allocation of virtual lights, and rendering. Within this context, rendering algorithms simulate the light behavior to produce the resulting 2D images [17]. The more complex and accurate the rendering algorithm is, the more real the result looks like. Although these algorithms are highly optimized, the rendering stage is often considered as a bottleneck due to the huge amount of time needed just to generate one single image. Depending on the rendering algorithm and the scene characteristics, the generation of one high-quality image may take hours or even days. That is why one of the remaining challenges of Photorealistic Rendering is dealing with high computational demands.

For instance, the James Cameron's famous film *Avatar*, the highest-grossing film of all time, took an average rendering time of 40 hours per frame. Since the movie lasts 2 hours approximately, more than 216 thousand frames were rendered. These frames must be generated twice because of stereoscopy (one frame per eye). In total, the film was estimated to spent around 2 thousand CPU years by one single computer. Attending to these figures, one of the possible solutions to this problem consists in using a significant number of computers to render the full movie in a relatively short period of time. In the case of Avatar, 35 thousand physical cores were used to produce the movie in a few months. This approach, which is typically based on brute-force, is the most

G. Csurka et al. (Eds.): VISIGRAPP 2011, CCIS 274, pp. 3–16, 2013.

commonly used technique by animation studios, which use to have their own render farms (computer cluster built to render computer-generated imagery).

Nevertheless, there exists another research line that is based on the use of expert knowledge to optimize the configuration parameters of the render engine to obtain good results with unnoticeable quality loss in the generated 2D images. In this work, we are concerned with the use of expert knowledge in order to optimize the rendering process, considering two main alternatives.

On the one hand, the rendering time can be shorten by tuning the configuration parameters of the rendering engine. It is up to the user to choose the optimal settings of these input parameters in terms of time, efficiency, and image quality. Unfortunately, this process requires an advanced knowledge of rendering engines and setting parameters. Usually, this process is addressed through trial and error and, in many cases, the user tends to over optimize the value of the rendering engine parameters so that the final rendering time is considerably increased with unnoticeable improvement in the perceptual quality of the resulting image.

To face this problem, we have taken advantage of the expert knowledge acquired by expert users when setting up the rendering parameters. Thus, this knowledge can be used in order to generate a configuration without directly employing the user-defined parameters. In line with these efforts, we have been studying how to tune the configuration given by the user [11].

On the other hand, we have also explored the use of parallel or distributed computing. So, if a complex 3D scene is divided into a number of smaller problems or *work units*, each one computed by an individual processor, the time spent to render the whole scene can be drastically reduced. Within this context, our proposed solution is based on a multi-agent architecture [22], named MAgArRO, which allows us to distribute the rendering tasks between the agents registered with the system. As we will discuss later, we devise different agents depending on the role played within the architecture.

The rest of the chapter is organized as follows. Section 2 positions our research within the context of relevant related works. In Section 3, we discuss in detail the two previously mentioned approaches for rendering optimization, paying special attention to the use of expert knowledge and describing the multi-agent architecture devised to distribute the rendering of complex scenes. Section 4 gives details about how we evaluate and test our work, distinguishing between automatic scene setting and the use of the multi-agent architecture. Finally, Section 5 concludes and resumes the main ideas of this work and outlines new research lines.

2 Related Work

There are different techniques currently used to speed rendering up. For example, modern graphics processing units can be used as massively parallel streaming processors that run concrete portions of the code of a ray tracer [7]. The use of these GPUs outperforms the standard workstation by a factor of 7 or 8 [4]. Although, these alternatives are very effective to optimize the rendering time, most of them lack of generality and, therefore, have to be specifically adapted for each hardware architecture. Within this context, there are some rendering engines designed to be used with GPU acceleration, such as the Parthenon Renderer [14].

Nowadays, the most common method to distribute the rendering of 3D scenes consists in using a cluster-based approach. In fact, most of animation studies own their render farms to deal with the computational requirements of the rendering process [2]. Thus, when a new scene needs to be rendered, then the user submits the work and the artificial system queues it to be processed later on. There exist more general open-source tools that can be used to distribute rendering in a computer cluster. One of these is OS-CAR [15], a Beowelf [21] type high performance computing cluster. In [5], the authors discussed an example of how to use OSCAR to render geographical information from huge 3D data sets.

Another option to optimize the rendering involves the use of parallel or distributed systems. This solution, which is based on the *divide and conquer* strategy, lies in distributing the rendering of a single frame or a whole animation into multiple computing entities. This approximation guarantees that the rendering time is significantly reduced but depends on an adequate task scheduling strategy in order to not delay the whole process due to excessively complex tasks or work units. Depending on how the 3D scene or animation to be rendered is divided, two main approaches can be distinguished: fine-grained and coarse-grained.

On the one hand, a fined-grained approach refers to a kind of parallel decomposition, widely used for interactive graphics applications, where the processors are connected in parallel to generate one single frame. In realistic image synthesis [16], each frame is divided into separate regions, and each processor renders a specific set of regions. Then, these partial results are combined to obtain the final resulting image.

On the other hand, a coarse grained parallel decomposition strategy renders the successive frames of the animation on separate processors [2]. In this approach, each processing unit computes an entire frame of an animation, commonly sharing the same input configuration of the rendering engine for each scene.

There are few works that apply the multi-agent technology to optimize rendering. Within this context, in the work discussed in [18] the authors proposed the use of a multi-agent system, implemented by using JADE [3], to render complex 3D scenes, paying special attention to the rendering of 3D objects instead of dividing the whole scene into a number of physical areas. In this way, each rendering agent is responsible for rendering an individual object. The partial results are then sent through the network to a 3D visualization process. However, it is not clear the policy adopted to balance the complexity of distributed rendering and there is no mechanism to deal with the most complex objects before the simplest ones.

Another related work, based on a non-realistic rendering method [1], was proposed in [19] and makes use of a multi-agent system for rendering multiple artistic styles. Each one of the rendering agents is responsible for executing its painting function in the environment. These simple agents (named *Render Bots*) execute three actions: simulation, to control the physical behavior of the agent, movement, to translate the agent to another position in the environment, and painting, to generate one stroke in the final image.

Recently, there has been a number of proposals that make use of the grid philosophy [8] to deal with distributed rendering. One of this proposals is discussed in [20], where a volunteer computing project, named *Yafrid*, for intensive rendering was introduced.

This system was aimed to spread the computing requirements of rendering a scene across a large number of computers, as much as possible. In order to achieve this goal, the grid was developed to be multiplatform (in terms of hardware and software). The components of this grid were basically three: i) a server that gets works from a queue and sends them to the providers, ii) the providers of the rendering service, that is, the physical entities that perform the rendering process, and iii) the clients, that is, the external entities which submit rendering works to be carried out by the providers.

This work was later extended and improved by adopting a P2P-based grid architecture that allows users to drastically reduce the global time spent in rendering [13]. In this work, the authors present an evaluation and comparison with a simple rendering cluster to empirically show the advantages and drawbacks of each approach. One of the major contributions of this work is inclusion of a P2P communication mechanism to deal with the distribution of 3D projects that involve significant sizes through the grid.

3   Distributed Rendering Optimization

As previously introduced, the user is responsible for setting up the rendering parameters. Ideally, the configuration of these parameters should allow to get an acceptable quality of the resulting image and minimize the rendering time. This process requires an advanced knowledge in the use of render engines, being necessary to establish particular values for a high number of variables. Usually, this process is addressed through trial and error. In may cases, the user tends to over optimize the value of the rendering engine parameters so that the final rendering time is considerably increased with unnoticeable improvement in the perceptual quality of the resulting image.

The setup time between different users varies depending on the particular experience of each user. In this way, the expert knowledge acquired when setting up the rendering parameters can be used by either generating a configuration without using the user-defined parameters or tuning the configuration given by the user. In the next section, a method to automatically generate a correct configuration will be studied.

3.1   Optimizing the Scene Setting Up

Setting up the scene parameters depends on their nature to a great extent. In other words, setting up an indoor scene differs from setting up an outdoor scene, or applying global illumination is completely different from applying illumination with just three points, and so on.

Figure 1 depicts the architecture of the Yarew approach based on data mining and genetic computing techniques to assist the user when adjusting the rendering parameters [11]. From the user's point of view, this approach works as a black box, since no previous knowledge of the configuration parameters is required. This system is defined by means of two components:

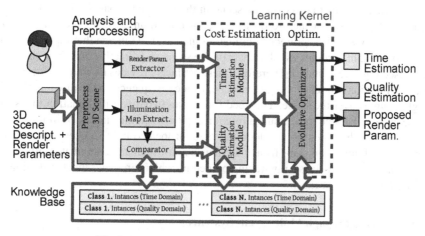

Fig. 1. General architecture of the Yarew approach

- A **knowledge base** containing a collection of known data instances (empirical data) in the same domain that the scene to render.
- A **learning kernel** responsible for providing decision support based on hypothesizes induced from the data in the knowledge base. There are three key components in this level:
  - **The Quality Estimation Module.** Conversely to the rendering time, the image quality is a discrete measure, labeled with categorical values. The learning methods used to estimate the classes are Quinlan's C4.5 and ID3 to induce classification trees and k-nearest neighbors, supporting Euclidean and Manhattan distance measures.
  - **The Time Estimation Module.** Since the rendering time is a continuous measure, the regressors used in the current version are a variation of Quinlan's C4.5 where the splitting measure used to induce the tree is the mean squared error (MSE) and k-nearest neighbors method.
  - **Evolutive Optimizer.** The problem of suggesting adequate rendering values may be seen as a problem of searching the best solution from the space of possible solutions. So, this component uses a genetic algorithm to obtain a good solution for the configuration problem. Furthermore, the evolutive optimizer provides the configuration of the rendering parameters and the time and quality estimation for the best solution.

When the user uploads a new scene to be rendered, it is first analyzed by the components of the *Analysis and Preprocessing* Module, which goal is to extract all the relevant data from the user scene and to make up a data instance of which goal attributes will later be estimated. This first level is also responsible for discovering which scene in the knowledge base is most similar to the user input scene. Once the process has passed through the user scene analysis level, the next level, named *Learning Kernel*, estimates the rendering time and the image quality which are to be achieved by the rendering configuration and the scene provided by the user. Besides, this module also searches for a better rendering configuration.

The approach needs to discover the scene in the knowledge base which is the most similar one to the user scene. To do this, we have used an artifact called *direct illumination map*. We define a direct illumination map as a 2D image that represents the distribution of light particles which impact on the scene and directly come from the light sources (see Figure 3 b and c). Therefore, these artifacts provides us with an estimation of the illumination model of the given scene, as a consequence of the direct action of the light sources over the scene. The need for having two direct illumination maps for every scene is to be able to compute a relationship between the amount of illumination in the scene which comes from indoor and outdoor located light sources. The extraction of direct illumination maps from a scene is a non-trivial and computationally quite complex process. It involves a ray tracing procedure which simulates the distribution of light rays through the scene.

3.2 Optimizing through Multi-agent Systems

The overall architecture of the agent platform that supports the architecture is based on the design principles of the FIPA committee [6]. From the user's point of view, the whole architecture works exactly as local render engines do, but the rendering process is actually performed by different rendering agents that can be spread over the Internet.

Basically, the architecture is composed of five kind of agents that cooperate to carry out the rendering process:

- The **Analyst** agent, which is responsible for dividing the input 3D scene and generating the set of tasks or work units that compose it.
- The **Master** agent, which is responsible for coordinating a number of rendering agents to perform the rendering of the work units and composing the resulting 2D image from the partial results submitted by the rendering agents.
- The **Rendering** agents, which are responsible to render the different work units that compose a 3D scene by applying expert knowledge.
- The **Repository** agent, which is responsible for managing the model repository, which centralizes the storage of the 3D scenes submitted by the user.
- The **Blackboard** agent, which is responsible for managing a blackboard architecture where the agents can read/write data about the works that are being performed.

Figure 2 graphically shows the work flow of the multi-agent architecture proposed to optimize the rendering of complex 3D scenes. Next, this work flow is described so that the reader can understand how the agents interact with one another in order to optimize the rendering of 3D scenes provided by the user.

1. Initially, the user submits the work to MAgArRO. The interface of the system is represented by the Analyst.
2. The Analyst perform the division of the input scene into a number of work units or tasks, depending on the division method chosen by the user. It employs the idea of estimating the complexity of the different tasks in order to achieve a load-balanced partitioning. The output of this process is the named *Importance Map*, a grey scale image where dark zones represent the less complex areas and the white zones the more complex ones (see [12] for a detailed description of this process).

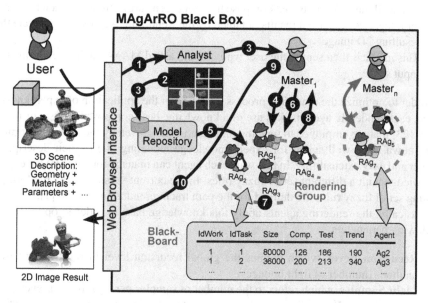

Fig. 2. Multi-agent architecture for distributed rendering

3. Once the Analyst has performed the complexity analysis of the input scene, this agents notifies to one of the Masters of the platform and sends the input scene to the Master and Repository agents.

4. There exists a relation between a Master agent and a set of Rendering Agents. This association configures a *rendering team* and the master coordinates the rendering process while the rendering agents perform the distributed rendering process. The architecture allows different rendering teams to coexist. The relationship between a master and a set of rendering agents is established by means of subscriptions, initially established. Thus, the Master informs its associated rendering team about the existence of a new work.

5. The Rendering Agents download the input scene from the model repository and perform a fast rendering, in parallel, of the different work units in order to get a more accurate estimation of the complexity of each of them. Specifically, the agents perform a low resolution rendering (around 5% of the final number of rays) of each task. As a result of this profiling, the Rendering Agents update the blackboard so that all the agents know the estimated rendering time of all the work units.

6. Once all the work units have been estimated, the Master agent orders the final rendering.

7. Each time a rendering agent completes the rendering of a work unit, it updates the blackboard by interacting with the Blackboard agent.

8. After rendering a work unit, a rendering agent bids for another one to be rendered. The Master coordinates the different auctions that take place and decides which is the most qualified agent for rendering a particular work unit (see [12] for a detailed description of the auction process).

9. When all the work units that compose the input scene are completed, then the Master integrates the partial results obtained by the Rendering Agents and generate the resulting 2D image.
10. This image is then sent to the user who initially asked MAgArRO for rendering the input scene.

In order to optimize the rendering process by means of the application of expert knowledge, each rendering agent makes use of a knowledge base composed of a set of fuzzy rules [23] that are employed to tune the input parameters given by the user. Fuzzy rules are known to be well suited for expert knowledge modeling due to their descriptive power and easy extensibility. In this way, each agent can manage (or capture) the expert knowledge with a different set of fuzzy rules. In the current version of the platform, a testing set of fuzzy rules are defined for the path tracing rendering method [1].

Basically, the rendering agents apply this knowledge base in order to optimize the following parameters:

- **Recursion Level**, which defines the global recursion level in ray tracing-based methods (number of light bounces).
- **Light Samples**, which refers to the number of samples per light in the scene.
- **Interpolation Band Size**, which represents the size in pixels of the interpolation band between adjacent work units. This parameters is used in the final composition of the image, performed by the Master.

These three parameters, whose values are initially set by the user, are tuned by the rendering agents depending on the following parameters, which are the antecedents of the fuzzy rules:

- **Complexity**, which represents the complexity/size ratio of the work unit to be rendered.
- **Neighbor Difference**, which is the complexity difference of the current work unit in relation to its neighbor work units.
- **Size**, which refers to the size in pixels of the work unit.
- **Optimization Level**, which is selected by the user and it determines the optimization level (more or less aggressive depending on the initial parameters customized by the user).

In the case of the path tracing method, the knowledge base is composed of a set of thirty rules. These rules model the knowledge of an expert who has used a path tracer rendering engine for 3 years. The reader is encouraged to refer to [12] for a detailed description of the rules that comprise the knowledge base of the rendering agents.

4   Experimental Validation

In this section, some results obtained with the two approaches will be studied. First, the automatic configuration of the parameters of a scene will be discussed in section 4.1. Next, the use of the multi-agent architecture will be also validated in section 4.2.

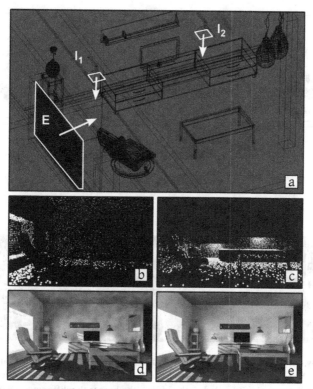

Fig. 3. Results of the case of study: (**a**) Positions of the external light source E and the two internal light sources I_1 and I_2 in the scene. (**b**) Direct illumination map of the external light source. (**c**) Direct illumination map of the internal light source. (**d**) Result with *medium* optimization level. (**e**) Result with *high* optimization level.

4.1   Scene Setting Up

The indoor scene to be rendered, depicted in Figure 3, contains 88482 faces and three light sources. This example illustrates a typical lighting design problem in indoors. In this indoor scene there are three light sources; two internal light sources I_1 and I_2 and one external light source E. In the next stage, the direct illumination is computed using a ray-tracing algorithm over the geometry of the scene. Once this stage is finished, two different list of hit points are obtained: one with those points caused by indoor-located light sources and another with those hit points caused by outdoor-located light sources (see Figure 3 b and c).

These illumination maps are used to select in the knowledge base which is most similar to the current one. Each scene in the knowledge base is stored along with its own direct illumination map. The employed measure is the RMSD (root mean square deviation).

The scene was optimized using three values: *Low*, *Medium* and *High*. This value configures the number of iterations in the evolutive optimization algorithm. Because of the random nature of algorithm, the obtained results with the same input scene might be

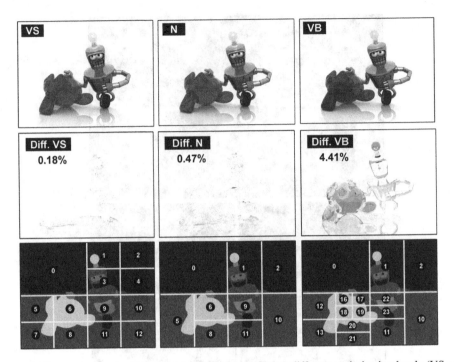

Fig. 4. First row. Results of the robot scene when applying different optimization levels (VS = Very Small, N = Normal, VB = Very Big). **Second row.** Quality differences between the results with and with no optimization (the darker the image, the bigger the difference). **Third row.** The three available partitioning methods by the Analyst agent.

different in different experiments. In Figure 3.d and 3.e, two concrete images with *Medium* and *High* optimization levels are shown. The corresponding configurations obtained for these images are represented in Table 1. When applying different optimization levels, some fragments of the proposed configurations are maintained (such as *EPower* and *GIPower* between Medium and High). This fact is due to the good fitness value of this configuration for this class of scenes.

Table 1. Configurations of render parameters suggested by different optimization levels

OptLevel	RayDepth	OSA	GIQual	Depth	PCount	PRad	PMix	ShQual	Prec	ShRef	EPower
Low	36	8	Low	1	273863	33.7	454	0.31	39	0.56	0.23
Medium	12	5	High	1	100927	1.9	193	0.18	44	0.75	0.58
High	12	8	High	6	498776	1.9	384	0.06	52	0.75	0.58

4.2 Multi-agent Approach

Figure 4 depicts the results obtained after rendering the test scene, applying three different optimization levels. The higher the optimization level is, the bigger the quality difference is (see row 2 of the image). It is important to remark that the most complex

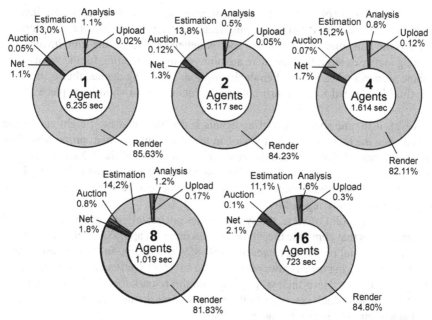

Fig. 5. Time percentages of the different stages of the rendering process performed by proposed system when deploying one, two, four, eight, and sixteen agents, respectively. The optimization level applied was normal.

part of the scene are the monkey head and the robot bulb, for the attached materials involve light reflexion and refraction. In this particular experiment, the use of an aggressive optimization level can generate undesirable effects or quality loss. For instance, the monkey head when applying the VB optimization level shows an internal color which is not realistic if it is compared when applying a normal optimization level. This is due to an aggressive optimization in the recursion level parameter of the rendering engine.

Figure 4 graphically shows the importance maps generated by the Analyst presented in Section 3.2. Each one of these maps is associated to a particular division method of the three provided by this agent. Darker colors represent areas that do not involve significant computing, whereas lighter colors represent the opposite case.

On the other hand, Figure 5 shows the time spent in each one of the steps that comprise the rendering process, that is, i) work upload, ii) initial analysis, iii) rendering time estimation, iv) auctioning, v) rendering, and vi) networking times due to remote procedure calls. Each one of the charts refers to a different experiment with a specific number of rendering agents, which is represented in the center of the chart along with the total time spent in the whole process. Nevertheless, the partitioning method by the Analyst remains constant. In this case study, the third method was applied to conduct all the experiments.

Rendering the test scene with a single rendering agent involved 6,235 seconds, that is, 104 minutes approximately. As the reader can guess, most of the time was spent in the final rendering performed by the agent. However, the estimation also represents a significant part of the process.

As the number of deployed rendering agent grows up, the time is reduced in inverse proportion. For example, if two rendering agents are deployed, then the total time is reduced to the half, that is, 52 minutes approximately. However, the time involved in auctioning increases slightly since there are now two agents bidding for the work units. The same scenario takes place when deploying four rendering agents, that is, the rendering time is reduced to the fourth and represents the most significant piece of the chart.

However, if the number of rendering agents is doubled, that is, if eight agents are deployed, then the total time is not reduced in the same, but a similar, proportion. This can be due to the relation between the number of work units of the 3D scene (21) and the number of rendering agents. Eventually, one of the last work units to be completed can slightly delay the whole rendering process. This fact can be also appreciated when deploying sixteen rendering agents.

From a general point of view, the system scales adequately since the percentage of the different steps that comprise the whole process remains, approximately, the same. In other words, the final rendering represents a 80-85% of the time in the five tests, while the estimated rendering time is always around the 11-15%. These two processes are the most significant ones. Nevertheless, it is important to remark that deploying a number of rendering agents which is similar to the number of work units can introduce a small delay due to the rendering of the last work units.

5   Conclusions and Future Work

In this work we have discussed how the use of expert knowledge at different levels of the rendering process can reduce the time spent in this computationally expensive process. Our approach is based on distributed computing but we think the integration of Artificial Intelligence techniques can play a key role in order to optimize rendering. That is why we propose a multi-agent architecture where there are software agents specialized in different tasks and cooperate to face the challenge of Photorealistic Image Synthesis. Particularly, we have addressed the automatic generation of the rendering engine setting up, the intelligent division of 3D scenes to balance the complexity of the different work units, and the customization of the rendering parameters given by the user before actually performing the rendering process.

The experimental study conducted in this chapter clear shows how our approach can be adopted due to not only the reduction of the rendering time but also the unnoticeable quality loss of the resulting images. This assumption can be justified thanks to the scalability of the system when deploying the rendering agents since the rendering time is in inverse proportion to the number of deployed agents.

Currently, we are assessing the impact of employing multiple rendering methods for a single 3D scene at the same time. In other words, we are studying how a number of agents, being each one of them specialized in a different rendering method, can work together in order to reduce even more the rendering time. For instance, a very fast but inaccurate rendering method can be used to render those parts of the 3D scene that are really far from the camera, that is, parts that are not relevant to generate high-quality images. However, those objects that are close to the camera should ideally be rendered by using an accurate, and therefore complex, method so that the user cannot notice noise or artifacts that affect the quality of the resulting image.

Acknowledgements. This work has been funded by the Regional Government of Castilla-La Mancha (Research Project PII1C09-0137-6488) and by the Ministry of Science and Innovation (Research Project TIN2009-14538-C02-02).

References

1. Akenine-Moller, T., Haines, E., Hoffman, N.: Real-Time Rendering, 3rd edn. AK Peters, Ltd, Natick (2008)
2. Apodaca, A.A., Gritz, L., Barzel, R.: Advanced RenderMan: Creating CGI for motion pictures. Morgan Kaufmann Publishers (2000)
3. Bellifemine, F., Caire, G., Greenwood, D.: Developing multi-agent systems with JADE. Springer, Heidelberg (2007)
4. Buck, I., Foley, T., Horn, D., Sugerman, J., Fatahalian, K., Houston, M., Hanrahan, P.: Brook for GPUs: Stream Computing on Graphics Hardware. In: Proceedings of SIGGRAPH 2004, pp. 777–786 (2004)
5. Coelho, A., Nascimento, M., Bentes, C., de Castro, M.C.S., Farias, R.: Parallel Volume Rendering for Ocean Visualization in a Cluster of PC's. In: Brazilian Symposium on GeoInformatics-GeoInfo, pp. 291–304 (2004)
6. Foundation for Intelligent Physical Agents, FIPA Agent Management Specification (2004), http://www.fipa.org/specs/fipa00023
7. Foley, T., Sugerman, J.: KD-tree acceleration structures for a GPU raytracer. In: Proceedings of the ACM SIGGRAPH/EUROGRAPHICS Conference on Graphics Hardware, pp. 15–22 (2005)
8. Foster, I., Kesselman, C.: The Grid: Blueprint for a New Computing Infrastructure. Morgan Kaufmann (2004)
9. Gonzalez-Morcillo, C., Weiss, G., Jimenez, L., Vallejo, D., Albusac, J.: A MultiAgent System for Physically Based Rendering Optimization. In: Klusch, M., Hindriks, K.V., Papazoglou, M.P., Sterling, L. (eds.) CIA 2007. LNCS (LNAI), vol. 4676, pp. 149–163. Springer, Heidelberg (2007)
10. Gonzalez-Morcillo, C., Weiss, G., Jimenez, L., Vallejo, D.: A Multi-Agent Approach to Distributed Rendering Optimization. In: Innovative Applications of Artificial Intelligence Conference (IAAI 2007), vol. 22(2), pp. 1775–1780 (2007)
11. Gonzalez-Morcillo, C., Lopez-Lopez, L.M., Castro-Schez, J.J., Moser, B.: A Data-Mining Approach to 3D Realistic Render Setup Assistance. In: Innovative Applications of Artificial Intelligence Conference (IAAI 2009), vol. 1, pp. 93–98 (2009)
12. Gonzalez-Morcillo, C., Weiss, G., Vallejo, D., Jimenez-Linares, L., Castro-Schez, J.J.: A MultiAgent Architecture for 3D Rendering Optimization. Applied Artificial Intelligence 24(4), 313–349 (2010)
13. Gonzalez-Morcillo, C., Vallejo, D., Albusac, J., Jimnez, L., Castro-Schez, J.J.: A New Approach to Grid Computing for Distributed Rendering. In: Sixth International Conference on P2P, Parallel, Grid, Cloud and Internet Computing (in press, 2011)
14. Hachisuka, T.: High-quality global illumination rendering using rasterization. In: GPU Gems, vol. 2, pp. 615–633. Addison-Wesley Professional (2005)

15. Haddad, I., Leangsuksun, C., Scott, S.L.: HA-OSCAR: the birth of highly available OSCAR. Linux Journal (115), 1 (2003)
16. Jensen, H.W.: Realistic image synthesis using photon mapping. AK Peters, Ltd., Natick (2001)
17. Kajiya, J.T.: The rendering equation. ACM SIGGRAPH Computer Graphics 20(4), 143–150 (1986)
18. Rangel-Kuoppa, R., Aviles-Cruz, C., Mould, D.: Distributed 3D rendering system in a multi-agent platform. In: Proceedings of the Fourth Mexican International Conference on Computer Science, pp. 168–175 (2003)
19. Schlechtweg, S., Germer, T., Strothotte, T.: RenderBots-Multi-Agent Systems for Direct Image Generation. Computer Graphics Forum 24, 137–148 (2005)
20. Fernandez-Sorribes, J.A., Gonzalez-Morcillo, C., Jimenez-Linares, L.: Grid architecture for distributed rendering. In: Proceedings of Ibero-American Symposium in Computer Graphics 2006 (SIACG 2006), pp. 141–148 (2006)
21. Sterling, T.L.: Beowulf Cluster Computing with Linux. MIT Press (2002)
22. Weiss, G.: Multiagent systems: a modern approach to distributed artificial intelligence. The MIT Press (1999)
23. Zadeh, L.A.: Fuzzy logic = computing with words. IEEE Transactions on Fuzzy Systems 4(2), 103–111 (1996)

Part I
Computer Graphics Theory and Applications

Dual Spherical Spline and Its Application in Tool Path Planing for 5-Axis Flank Milling

Yayun Zhou[1], Jörg Schulze[2], and Stefan Schäffler[3]

[1] Siemens AG, CT T DE TC3 GTF MSO, Otto-Hahn-Ring 6, 81739 Munich, Germany
[2] Universität Stuttgart, Pfaffenwaldring 47, 70569 Stuttgart, Germany
[3] Universität der Bundeswehr München, Werner-Heisenberg-Weg 39, 85577 Neubiberg, Germany

Abstract. Dual spherical spline is a newly proposed spline which is an alternative representation of ruled surfaces. This representation has advantages in the ruled surface manufacture due to its close relation to kinematics. In this paper, a new tool path planning approach is proposed based on the offset theory and the kinematic ruled surface approximation. The novelty of this approach is to denote the drive surface as a dual spherical spline, which provides a convenient conversion to the tool motion. Based on this representation, a novel design and manufacuture process is proposed to derive a flank millable surface. The designed surface is represented as a flank milling tool path with a cylindrical cutter in CNC machining. This approach delivers more accuracy compared with convectional tool position optimization methods. By integrating the manufacture requirements into the design phase, this approach also reduces the developing cycle time and the manufacturing cost.

Keywords. Dual spherical spline, Ruled surface, Flank milling, Blade design, Manufacture.

1 Introduction

Considering the aerodynamics requirements and the manufacturing cost, blade surfaces are usually designed as ruled surfaces, which are a special type of surfaces that can be generated by moving a line in space. In industry, the flank milling method is often used to machine ruled surfaces. Different from the face milling (point milling) method, flank milling (side milling) uses the side of the manufacturing tool instead of the tip of the manufacturing tool to touch the surface and remove the stock in front of the cutter. Since the whole length of the cutter is involved in the cutting process, this method has high material removal rate and high machining efficiency. Besides, no scallops are left behind in single pass flank milling, less surface finishing work is required. Especially for the manufacturing of a turbocharger compressor/impeller, it is necessary to use 5-axis flank milling, because the tunnel between two adjacent blades is too small with respect to the size of blades. Hence, designing a flank millable blade is appealing in many fields.

A common way to derive a flank millable blade surface is to adopt a certain ruled surface approximation algorithm before the surface is delivered to the manufacturer. Theoretically, if the manufacturing tool is considered as a line, a ruled surface can be

G. Csurka et al. (Eds.): VISIGRAPP 2011, CCIS 274, pp. 19–32, 2013.

accurately produced by moving this line. However, the machine tool usually has certain size and shape (i.e., cylindrical cutter or conical cutter), so the ideal position for the cutting tool is to offset the ruling in the direction of a surface normal at a distance equal to the radius of the cutting tool. Because the surface normals rotate along the ruling, at some point the cutting tool will begin to deviate from the desired surface. Generally, the machined surface is not a ruled surface, but a curved surface. At each tool position, the effective contact between the cutting tool and the swept surface is a curve (grazing curve), not a straight line.

Researchers developed a variety of cutter location (CL) data optimization methods to minimize the manufacturing error. The simplest way is to locate a cylindrical cutting tool tangentially to the given surface at one point on the ruling and make the tool axis parallel to the ruling. Alternatively, the tool can also be positioned to touch two points on the ruling. Both ideas belong to the direct tool position method [9]. An improvement of the direct tool position method is to locate the tool step by step [3] [11]. In those approaches, the initial position of the cutting tool is determined by one of the direct tool position methods, afterwards the tool is lifted and twisted in order to reduce the manufacturing error. The computation time of the step by step method is usually long. The third type of tool positioning method combines the techniques used in the two classes above. The tool contacts three points on the given surface (two on the guiding curves and one on the ruling). Those three points are obtained by solving seven transcendental equations based on certain geometrical conditions [15]. Figure 1 shows a conventional flow of flank milling in 5-axis CNC machining.

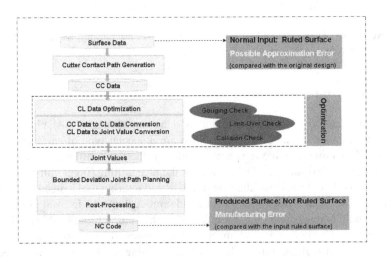

Fig. 1. A conventional flow of flank milling in 5-axis CNC machining

However, those methods all focus on the local error reduction corresponding to each tool location. The kinematic error between successive CL points can still be large. In order to get a global optimal tool path, a new type of approach is developed [8] [4] [16] [22]. The authors propose a global optimization method to generate the tool axis trajectory surface which is also a ruled surface. The cutting tool is positioned so that the maximum deviation between the tool axis trajectory surface and the offset surface is minimized. The trajectory surface of the tool axis (drive surface) is often represented as a tensor product B-spline surface, therefore each tool position is determined.

In this paper, we propose a new strategy to represent the drive surface as a dual spherical spline [23], in which every ruling of the ruled surface is written as a dual vector. It indicates the orientation of the tool axis with respect to a specific point on the workpiece and has the same mathematical representation of screws [6]. Using the dual vector calculation rules, the tool axis position is easily converted to the tool motion. Compared with the conventional tensor product B-spline surface representation, it is more effective to specify a 5-axis CNC machining tool path by relating both the position and orientation to a single parameter. Based on this representation, it is possible to check whether the desired path is within the workspace of the machine tool by applying the kinematics and robotics analysis. Fig. 2 compares this new approach with the conventional design and manufacturing methods. The new approach not only inherits the advantages of global path optimization methods which ensure low manufacturing cost and avoid introducing double errors, but also provides a novel representation which is closely linked to the tool movement.

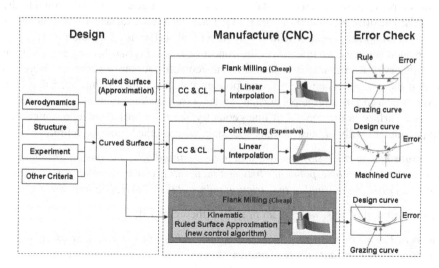

Fig. 2. A comparison of different design and manufacturing diagram

The organization of this paper is as follows. Section 2 lays the theoretical basis of this approach, including the offset theory and ruled surface representations. Then the definition of dual spherical spline is briefly introduced and its advantages in motion conversion are shown in Section 3. In Section 4, the drive surface is derived from the offset surface of original design based on a kinematic ruled surface approximation algorithm. This algorithm can be modified to embrace more manufacture constrains corresponding to difference CNC machines. This approach is tested with some given turbocharger blade surfaces. The simulation results are presented in Section 5. Finally, a conclusion is drawn in Section 6.

2   Theoretical Basis

The approach proposed in this paper mainly contains two key steps: first deriving an offset surface from the original design, then generating a drive surface from the offset data. The drive surface is a ruled surface, which is denoted as a dual spherical spline. In this section, the offset theory and representations of ruled surface are introduced.

2.1   Offset Theory

If $\mathbf{R}(\mathbf{u}) = \mathbf{R}(u_1, u_2)$ represents a surface, its *offset surface* $\mathbf{R}_o(\mathbf{u})$ is defined by the equation [10]:

$$\mathbf{R}_o(\mathbf{u}) = \mathbf{R}(\mathbf{u}) + d \cdot \mathbf{n}(\mathbf{u}), \tag{1}$$

where $\mathbf{n}$ is a normal vector in $\mathbf{R}(\mathbf{u})$ and d is the distance between the surfaces. This is the classical offset surface definition. It is also referred as *parallel offset*. In [12], Pottmann and Lü study the *"circular offset"* of ruled surfaces, which arises when a cylindrical or conical cutter with a circular edge is used in flank milling. The authors proved that the circular offsets of a rational ruled surface are rational in general except the developable surfaces and conoidal ruled surfaces with generators orthogonal to the tool-axis. The offset of a ruled surface is in general not a ruled surface. In fact, the offset curve of a nontorsal generator with respect to a ruled surface is a rational quadric [12].

For ruled surfaces, we often meet the concept *Bertrand offset*. It is a generalization of the theory of *Bertrand curves* based on line geometry. A pair of curves are Bertrand mates if there exists a one-to-one correspondence between their points such that both curves share a common principal normal at their corresponding points [14]. Considering the ruled surface in the context of line geometry, the ruled surface is represented as a one-parameter family of lines. Simply speaking, we have the following definition [14]:

Definition 1. *Two ruled surfaces are said to be Bertrand offsets of one another if there exists a one-to-one correspondence between their rulings such that both surfaces have a common principal normal at the striction points of their corresponding rulings.*

For the Bertrand offsets, we have an important theorem [14]:

Theorem 1. *Two ruled surfaces which are Bertrand offsets of each other as defined in Definition 1 are constant offsets of one another.*

Inspired by this theorem, if the given surface is a ruled surface, the drive surface can be derived by constructing the Bertrand offset of the given surface. Consequently, the given surface is also a Bertrand offset surface of the drive surface. This relationship provides the initial inspiration of our approach. Generally, the original designed surface is not a ruled surface. In our algorithm, we calculate the "circular offset" of the given surface instead.

2.2   Ruled Surface Representations

In Euclidean space $\mathbb{R}^3$, a ruled surface Φ possesses a parametric representation [7]:

$$\mathbf{x}(u, v) = \mathbf{a}(u) + v\mathbf{r}(u), \ u \in I, v \in \mathbb{R}, \tag{2}$$

where $\mathbf{a}(u)$ is called the *directrix curve* and $\mathbf{r}(u)$ is a direction vector of *generator*. Alternatively, a ruled surface Φ can be parameterized by two directrix curves $\mathbf{p}(u)$ and $\mathbf{q}(u)$:

$$\mathbf{x}(u, v) = (1 - v)\mathbf{p}(u) + v\mathbf{q}(u). \tag{3}$$

The straight line denoted as $\mathbf{x}(u_0, v) = (1 - v)\mathbf{p}(u_0) + v\mathbf{q}(u_0)$ is called a *ruling*.

By applying the Klein mapping and the Study mapping, a ruled surface can be written in a more compact way using dual numbers. The dual numbers were first introduced by Clifford [5]. A *dual number* can be written in the form $\hat{a} = a + \epsilon a^\circ$, where $a, a^\circ \in \mathbb{R}$ and ϵ is the dual element with:

$$\begin{aligned} \epsilon &\neq 0, \\ 0\epsilon &= \epsilon 0 = 0, \\ 1\epsilon &= \epsilon 1 = \epsilon, \\ \epsilon^2 &= 0. \end{aligned} \tag{4}$$

Extending the dual numbers to the vector space, the space $\mathbb{D}^3$ is defined as a set of all pairs of vectors:

$$\hat{\mathbf{a}} = \mathbf{a} + \epsilon \mathbf{a}^\circ \text{ where } \mathbf{a}, \mathbf{a}^\circ \in \mathbb{R}^3. \tag{5}$$

In line geometry, a line in Euclidean space can be represented as a unit vector in $\mathbb{D}^3$ [13]. Those unit vectors constitute a sphere called *Dual Unit Sphere* (DUS). In this form, a ruled surface defined by Eq. (2) is written as a curve on the DUS :

$$\hat{L}(u) = \mathbf{l}(u) + \epsilon \mathbf{l}^\circ(u) = \frac{\mathbf{r}(u)}{\|\mathbf{r}(u)\|} + \epsilon \frac{\mathbf{a}(u) \times \mathbf{r}(u)}{\|\mathbf{r}(u)\|}. \tag{6}$$

A dual vector representation of ruled surface can be converted to a point representation:

$$\mathbf{x}(u, v) = \mathbf{l}(u) \times \mathbf{l}(u)^\circ + v\mathbf{l}(u). \tag{7}$$

Now, a mapping between a ruled surface representation in Euclidean space and a curve representation on the DUS is set up. Instead of solving a surface approximation problem in the Euclidean space, we solve a curve approximation problem on the DUS.

3 Definition of Dual Spherical Spline

The dual vector representation of ruled surface links the path and the physical motion of the tool [17] [18]. K. Sprott proposed an algorithm to generate a free-form curve on the DUS [20], but defining a spline strictly lying on the DUS is not trivial. Due to the non-linearity of the space, conventional spline definitions as a linear combination of basis functions are not working on the DUS.

3.1 Dual Spherical Spline

The definition of dual spherical spline is inspired by [1], in which a spline on a real sphere is defined based on a least squares minimization. Based on the transfer principle, which simply states that for any operation defined for a real vector space, there is a dual version with similar interpretation, we can derive a similar definition of a spline on the DUS:

Definition 2. *Let* $\hat{\mathbf{p}}_1, \ldots, \hat{\mathbf{p}}_n$ *be control points on the Dual Unit Sphere* $\hat{S}^2$ *in* $\mathbb{D}^3$: *a spline on the DUS is defined as a result of a least squares minimization. In other words, it contains the points* $\hat{\mathbf{s}}(t)$ *on* $\hat{S}^2$ *which minimizes the value:*

$$\hat{f}(\hat{\mathbf{s}}(t)) = \frac{1}{2} \sum_i \omega_i \cdot dist_S(\hat{\mathbf{s}}(t), \hat{\mathbf{p}}_i)^2, \tag{8}$$

where $dist_S(\hat{\mathbf{s}}(t), \hat{\mathbf{p}}_i)$ *is the dual spherical distance between* $\hat{\mathbf{s}}(t)$ *and* $\hat{\mathbf{p}}_i$. *This spline on the DUS is denoted as a dual spherical spline:*

$$\hat{\mathbf{s}}(t) = \widetilde{\sum_{i=1}^{n}} f_i(t)\hat{\mathbf{p}}_i. \tag{9}$$

The distance between two points on the DUS is defined by a dual angle between two lines. It has the form $\hat{\theta} = \theta + \epsilon d$, where θ is the angle between the lines and d is the minimum distance along the common perpendicular. For two points $\hat{\mathbf{x}}$ and $\hat{\mathbf{y}}$ on the DUS, we have the following equation:

$$\hat{\mathbf{x}} \cdot \hat{\mathbf{y}} = \cos \hat{\theta}. \tag{10}$$

The dual arc cosine function is defined as:

$$\hat{\theta} = \cos^{-1}(x + \epsilon x^\circ) = \cos^{-1}(x) - \epsilon \frac{x^\circ}{\sqrt{1 - x^2}}. \tag{11}$$

The basis functions of a dual spherical spline must always satisfy the property:

$$\sum_{i=1}^{n} f_i(t) = 1, \; f_i(t) \geq 0 \; \forall i, \tag{12}$$

for t in the interval $[a, b]$.

Since Bernstein polynomials and B-spline basis functions both satisfy the requirement Eq. (12), the dual spherical Bézier curve or B-spline curve $\hat{\mathbf{s}}(t)$ can be defined in the form of Eq. (9).

It is proven that there is a neighborhood of $\hat{\mathbf{p}}_1, \ldots, \hat{\mathbf{p}}_n$, in which the $\hat{\mathbf{s}}(t)$ is a C^∞-function of $\hat{\mathbf{p}}_1, \ldots, \hat{\mathbf{p}}_n$. Hence the regularity of the dual spherical spline is determined by the basis functions. The proof of uniqueness and continuity property follows the similar strategy as [1], the details can be found in [21].

3.2   Advantages in Motion Conversion

Now the drive surface, which is a ruled surface, is represented as a continuous, differentiable dual spherical spline $\hat{\mathbf{x}}(u)$. Following this definition, a local coordinate frame can be set up consisting of three concurrent lines – $\{\hat{\mathbf{x}}, \hat{\mathbf{n}}, \hat{\mathbf{t}}\}$. This frame is called *generator trihedron*, where $\hat{\mathbf{x}}$ represents a ruling and the other two lines are defined by the following equations:

$$\hat{\mathbf{t}} = \frac{\frac{d\hat{\mathbf{x}}(u)}{du}}{\|\frac{d\hat{\mathbf{x}}(u)}{du}\|}, \tag{13}$$
$$\hat{\mathbf{n}} = \hat{\mathbf{x}} \times \hat{\mathbf{t}}.$$

The line $\hat{\mathbf{t}}$ is called the *central tangent*, which is tangent to the surface at the striction point. The line $\hat{\mathbf{n}}$ called *central normal* is the normal of the surface at the striction point. It can be proven that these three lines are orthogonal to each other and the intersection point of the three lines is the *striction point* of the ruling $\hat{\mathbf{x}}$. This point is the point of minimum distance between neighboring rulings. The locus of striction points is called the *striction curve* [19]. The generator trihedron can be rewritten as dual vectors:

$$\begin{aligned}
\hat{\mathbf{x}} &= \mathbf{x} + \epsilon(\mathbf{a} \times \mathbf{x}), \\
\hat{\mathbf{n}} &= \mathbf{n} + \epsilon(\mathbf{a} \times \mathbf{n}), \\
\hat{\mathbf{t}} &= \mathbf{t} + \epsilon(\mathbf{a} \times \mathbf{t}),
\end{aligned} \tag{14}$$

where $\mathbf{a}$ is the striction point, $\mathbf{x}$ is a vector directing along the ruling, the vector $\mathbf{t}$ is perpendicular to $\mathbf{x}$ and tangent to the surface at the striction curve, the vector $\mathbf{n}$ is perpendicular to $\mathbf{x}$ and $\mathbf{t}$. Fig. 3 shows this frame on a ruled surface. The center line of the cylindrical cutter (a ruling of the drive surface) undergoes a screw motion about the axis $\hat{\mathbf{t}}$. According to the screw theory, the distance between successive rulings is defined as a dual angle between two screws. The successive rulings are denoted as $\hat{\mathbf{x}}_1 = \hat{\mathbf{x}}(u_1) = \sum_{i=0}^{n} B_{i,p}(u_1)\hat{\mathbf{p}}_i$ and $\hat{\mathbf{x}}_2 = \hat{\mathbf{x}}(u_2) = \sum_{i=0}^{n} B_{i,p}(u_2)\hat{\mathbf{p}}_i$. The dual angle is calculated by the following equations:

$$\hat{\mathbf{x}}_1 \cdot \hat{\mathbf{x}}_2 = \cos\hat{\omega} = x + \epsilon x^{\circ}, \tag{15a}$$

$$\begin{aligned}
\hat{\omega} &= \phi + \epsilon d \\
&= \cos^{-1}(\hat{x}) \\
&= \cos^{-1}(x + \epsilon x^{\circ}) \\
&= \cos^{-1}(x) - \epsilon \frac{x^{\circ}}{\sqrt{1-x^2}}.
\end{aligned} \tag{15b}$$

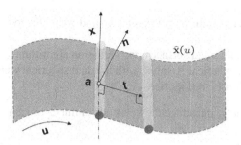

Fig. 3. Generator trihedron on ruled surface

This means the cutter tool translates the distance d and rotates the angle ϕ along the axis $\hat{\mathbf{t}}$ in order to move from position $\hat{\mathbf{x}}_1$ to position $\hat{\mathbf{x}}_2$. The ratio between d and ϕ is called *distribution parameter* [20]:

$$p = \frac{d}{\phi}. \tag{16}$$

The distribution parameter indicates the amount of twisting associated with the ruled surface. A cone or tangent developable surface has a zero valued distribution parameter, while the distribution parameter of parallel rulings remains undefined. Generally, a twisted ruled surface has a non-zero distribution parameter. If adopting time t as the parameter of the dual spherical spline, it is quite easy to convert the tool path to the motion code. The velocity of the line is given by the expression:

$$\frac{d\hat{\mathbf{x}}}{dt} = \dot{\hat{\mathbf{x}}} = \hat{\omega} \times \hat{\mathbf{x}}, \tag{17}$$

where the angular velocity vector $\hat{\omega} = \omega + \epsilon v$ denotes the rotation and translation along the screw axis $\hat{\mathbf{t}}$. In this local coordinate frame, an arbitrary point $\mathbf{P}$ along the ruling is written as $\mathbf{P} = s\mathbf{r}$, where $\mathbf{r} = \frac{\mathbf{x}}{\|\mathbf{x}\|}$ and s is the distance from the striction point $\mathbf{a}$. The velocity of this point will have a term perpendicular to $\mathbf{r}$ due to the rotation about the line $\hat{\mathbf{t}}$ and a term in the direction of $\hat{\mathbf{t}}$ due to the translation along the line. The velocity of the point can be written as [20]:

$$\begin{aligned} \mathbf{v}_p &= \omega\mathbf{t} \times s\mathbf{r} + v\mathbf{t} \\ &= -\omega s\mathbf{n} + v\mathbf{t}. \end{aligned} \tag{18}$$

4   Tool Path Planning Approach

Based on the definition of dual spherical spline, a kinematic approximation algorithm is developed to construct a ruled surface from an offset surface. This ruled surface is the drive surface. In this paper, we propose a tool path planning approach for flank milling with cylindrical tools. The framework of the tool path planning approach contains four parts:

1. Generate an offset surface from the original design surface according to the tool radius;
2. Extract the CL data from the offset surface and write the coordinates as dual vectors;
3. Apply the kinematic ruled surface approximation algorithm;
4. Evaluate the dual spherical B-spline with the dual spherical weighted average algorithm and convert it to tool motion.

In this section, we briefly introduce the key steps of this approach.

4.1   Offset Surface Generation and CL Data Extraction

Initially, the blade surface is designed as a free-form surface. In order to derive the cutter location (CL) data, the original design is taken as an input and the offset surface is derived according to Eq. 1. The distance d between the offset surface and the original design equals to the radius of the cylindrical tool. The cutter locations are determined by a ruling search process. It is to find a discrete system of line segments close to the given surface. In order to fit the manufacture procedure, the search process starts from the leading edge of the blade surface and marches towards the trailing edge. The lines are chosen using the least squares minimization method. The march distance is constrained by the velocity of the milling machine and most importantly, the intersection of the line segments must be avoided. Other constrains of manufacture machines can also influence the search process. In the end of this step, a sequence of line segments $l_0, \ldots, l_N$ are obtained which are close to the given surface. The details of this step can be found in [2].

4.2 Kinematic Ruled Surface Approximation

After the rulings are extracted and represented as dual vectors, a kinematic ruled surface approximation algorithm is applied to approximate the line sequences as a ruled surface. The manufacture machine constrains should be included in the objective functional. Due to the variety of manufacture systems, the main task of this paper is to minimize the difference between the offset surface and drive surface. Its essence is a dual spherical spline interpolation algorithm on the DUS. In this paper, we take the dual cubic B-spline interpolation algorithm as an example. It can be easily extended to higher order B-splines.

The key idea of this algorithm is to use the logarithmic map which maps all points $\hat{\mathbf{p}}_i$ on the DUS to the tangent hyperplane at $\hat{\mathbf{q}}$, then interpolate the points in the hyperplane and maps the result back to the DUS by the exponential map. As long as the given points satisfy the uniqueness condition, the algorithm converges. Fig. 4 shows the flowchart of the dual spherical cubic B-spline interpolation algorithm, in which the logarithmic map $l_{\hat{\mathbf{q}}}(\cdot)$ maps the point $\hat{\mathbf{p}}_i$ to the tangent hyperplane at $\hat{\mathbf{q}}$ and the exponential map $\exp_{\hat{\mathbf{q}}}(\cdot)$ maps the result back to the DUS. α_i, β_i, γ_i denote the non-zero elements in the basis matrix:

$$\begin{pmatrix} 1 & 0 & 0 & \ldots & & 0 & 0 \\ \alpha_2 & \beta_2 & \gamma_2 & 0 & \ldots & & 0 \\ 0 & \alpha_3 & \beta_3 & \gamma_3 & 0 & & \vdots \\ \vdots & \ddots & \ddots & \ddots & & 0 \\ 0 & \ldots & 0 & \alpha_{n-1} & \beta_{n-1} & \gamma_{n-1} \\ 0 & 0 & \ldots & 0 & 0 & 1 \end{pmatrix}. \tag{19}$$

4.3 Dual Spherical Spline Evaluation on the DUS

After the control points are derived, the dual spherical B-spline is evaluated as weighted averages of control points. The weighted average on the DUS is defined similarly:

Definition 3. *Let $\hat{\mathbf{p}}_1, \ldots, \hat{\mathbf{p}}_n$ be points on the Dual Unit Sphere $\hat{S}^2$ in $\mathbb{D}^3$: a weighted average of these n points using real weight values $\omega_1, \ldots, \omega_n$ such that each $\omega_i \geq 0$ and $\sum \omega_i = 1$ is defined as a result of a least squares minimization. In other words, it is the point $\hat{\mathbf{C}}$ on $\hat{S}^2$ which minimizes the value:*

$$\hat{f}(\hat{\mathbf{C}}) = \frac{1}{2} \sum_i \omega_i \cdot dist_S(\hat{\mathbf{C}}, \hat{\mathbf{p}}_i)^2, \tag{20}$$

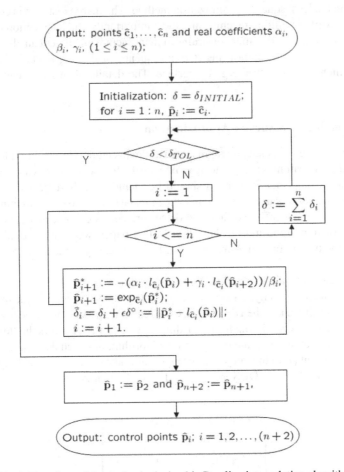

Fig. 4. Flowchart of the dual spherical cubic B-spline interpolation algorithm

where $dist_S(\hat{\mathbf{C}}, \hat{\mathbf{p}}_i)$ *is the dual spherical distance between* $\hat{\mathbf{C}}$ *and* $\hat{\mathbf{p}}_i$. *The weighted average on the DUS is denoted as:*

$$\hat{\mathbf{C}} = \widetilde{\sum_{i=0}^{n}} \omega_i \hat{\mathbf{p}}_i. \tag{21}$$

The flowchart of the algorithm calculating the weighted average on the DUS is shown in Fig. 5.

5   Simulation Result

We test this approach with different blade surfaces and simulate the manufacturing process of a blade with a cylindrical cutter. A blade consists of two sides: pressure

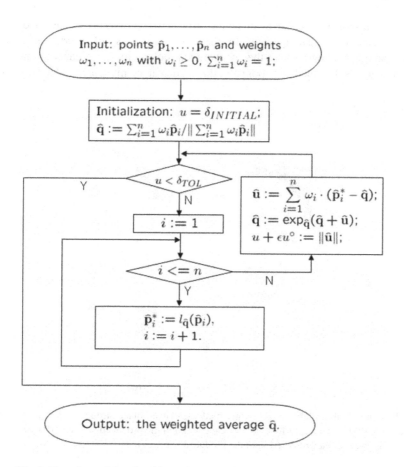

Fig. 5. Flowchart of the algorithm calculating the weighted average on the DUS

surface and suction surface. The tool path planning strategies for both sides are similar. Here, we only take one example to explain the procedure.

To achieve large material removal rate, the radius of the cylinder should be large, but it must be less than the distance between two blades. Therefore, for different blades, the tool sizes are varied. For this test case, the radius of the cylinder is chosen as $R = 2$ mm. The input file is a "blade.ibl" file exported from the software "Bladegen". It contains discrete points on blade surfaces. We first extract the data for the pressure side of the blade. The offset surface is derived based on Eq. (1) and $d = R$.[1]

The simulation results of this approach are shown in Fig. 6. Fig. 6(a) shows the given surface and its offset surface. Fig. 6(b) shows the discrete cutter locations which are extracted from the offset surface. Then the kinematic ruled surface approximation algorithm is applied to the offset surface to get the drive surface as a ruled surface. Fig. 6(c) shows the movement of the cylindrical cutter. Consequently, a surface is produced due to the movement of the cylindrical cutter. Fig. 6(d) compares the produced surface with

---

[1] An affine map is applied to the data due to confidential requirements.

the original design surface. We evaluate the error between two surfaces as the distance along z direction. The average error for these two surface is only $0.0027mm$, which is much smaller compared with the convectional tool position optimization methods. Since the blade is designed as a tool path, this blade can be manufactured accurately.

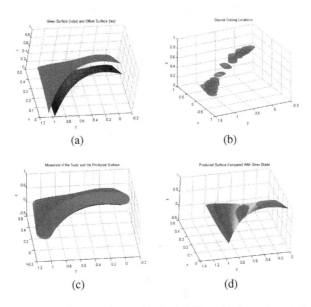

Fig. 6. Design a flank millable turbocharger blade: (a) Given blade surface (colored) and offset surface (red); (b) CL data; (c) Movement of the cutter and the produced surface; (d) Comparison between the given surface (colored) and the produced surface (red)

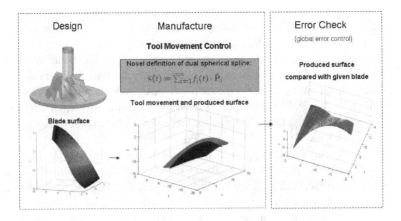

Fig. 7. A novel design and manufacturing procedure for turbocharger blades

Based on the approach described above, we get a flowchart of a turbocharger blade design and manufacture. In Fig. 7, the design and manufacture phases are combined together. This new approach avoids introducing the approximation error twice and reduces the developing time.

6   Conclusions and Future Work

In this paper, we propose a novel way to plan a tool path for the 5-axis flank milling method in CNC machining. It combines the kinematic ruled surface approximation algorithm with the offset theory. Integrating the constrains of different CNC machines, it can be used as a control program to guide the movement of the manufacturing tool in flank milling process. A tool path of a cylindrical cutter is given in the form of a dual spherical spline, which describes the movement of the cylindrical cutter axis. This representation of tool path provides a convenient conversion to the tool motion, which leads naturally to the post-process. Adopting this new approach to design blade surfaces embraces the manufacturing requirements, which ensures low manufacture cost in the design phase. This approach can also be adapted to generate tool path for face milling, because the movement of the tool axis constitutes a ruled surface. For that application, the objective is to generate a tool path that is related to the normals of the surface. Besides, the manufacturing tool is not only limited to a cylinder. It can be a cone or other general shapes. Considering the different geometry of the manufacturing tools, this algorithm has many other applications. There is still a lot of work that can be accomplished in this area.

References

1. Buss, S.R., Fillmore, J.P.: Spherical averages and applications to spherical splines and interpolation. ACM Transactions on Graphics 20(2), 95–126 (2001),
   citeseer.ist.psu.edu/buss01spherical.html
2. Chen, H., Pottmann, H.: Approximation by ruled surfaces. J. Comput. Appl. Math. 102(1), 143–156 (1999)
3. Choi, B.K., Park, J.W., Jun, C.S.: Cutter-location data optimization in 5-axis surface machining. Computer Aided Design 25(6), 377–386 (1993)
4. Chu, C.H., Chen, J.T.: Tool path planning for five-axis flank milling with developable surface approximation. The International Journal of Advanced Manufacturing Technology 29(7-8), 707–713 (2006)
5. Clifford, W.K.: Preliminary sketch of biquaternions. In: Tucker, R. (ed.) Mathematical Papers. Macmillan (1873)
6. Dimentberg, F.M.: The screw calculus and its application in mechanics. In: Clearinghouse for Federal Scientific and Technical Information. Springfield, Virginia (1965); english Translation: AD680993
7. Edge, W.: Thoery of ruled surface. Cambridge Univ. Press (1931)
8. Gong, H., Cao, L.X., Liu, J.: Improved positioning of cylindrical cutter for flank milling ruled surfaces. Computer Aided Design 37, 1205–1213 (2005)
9. Liu, X.: Five-axis NC cylindrical milling of sculptured surfaces. Computer Aided Design 27(12), 887–894 (1995)

10. Marciniak, K.: Geometric modeling for numerically controlled machining. Oxford University Press, New York (1991)
11. Menzel, C., Bedi, S., Mann, S.: Triple tangent flank milling of ruled surface. Computer Aided Design 36(3), 289–296 (2004)
12. Pottmann, H., Lü, W., Ravani, B.: Rational ruled surface and their offsets. Graphical Models and Image Processing 58, 544–552 (1996)
13. Pottmann, H., Wallner, J.: Computational line geometry. Mathematics and Visualization. Springer, Berlin (2001)
14. Ravani, B., Ku, T.S.: Bertrand offsets of ruled and developable surfaces. Computer Aided Design 23(2), 145–152 (1991)
15. Redonnet, J.M., Rubio, W., Dessein, G.: Side milling of ruled surfaces: optimum positioning of the milling cutter and calculation of interference. Advanced Manufacturing Technology 14, 459–463 (1998)
16. Senatore, J., Monies, F., Landon, Y., Rubio, W.: Optimising positioning of the axis of a milling cutter on an offset surface by geometric error minimization. The International Journal of Advanced Manufacturing Technology 37(9-10), 861–871 (2008)
17. Sprott, K., Ravani, B.: Ruled surfaces, Lie groups and mesh generation. In: 1997 ASME Design Engineering Technical Conferences, Sacramento, California, USA (1997)
18. Sprott, K., Ravani, B.: Kinematic generation of ruled surface. Advances in Computational Mathematics 17, 115–133 (2001)
19. Sprott, K., Ravani, B.: Cylindrical milling of ruled surface. The International Journal of Advanced Manufacturing 38(7-82), 649–656 (2007)
20. Sprott, K.S.: Kinematically generated ruled surfaces with applications in NC maching. Ph.D. thesis, University of California, Davis (2000)
21. Zhou, Y.: Optimization with Ruled Surface. Ph.D. thesis, Universität der Bundeswehr München (2010)
22. Zhou, Y., Schulze, J., Schäffler, S.: Flank millable blade design for centrifugal compressor. In: Proceedings of the Mediterranean Conference on Control and Automation, pp. 646–650. IEEE Computer Society, Los Alamitos (2009)
23. Zhou, Y., Schulze, J., Schäffler, S.: Blade geometry design with kinematic ruled surface approximation. In: SAC 2010: Proceedings of the 2010 ACM Symposium on Applied Computing, pp. 1266–1267. ACM, New York (2010)

Estimating Outdoor Illumination Conditions Based on Detection of Dynamic Shadows

Claus B. Madsen and Brajesh B. Lal

Aalborg University, Department of Architecture, Design and Media Technology
Niels Jernes Vej 14, DK-9220 Aalborg East, Denmark
{cbm,brajesh}@create.aau.dk
www.create.aau.dk/cbm

Abstract. The paper proposes a technique for estimating outdoor illumination conditions in terms of sun and sky radiances directly from pixel values of dynamic shadows detected in video sequences produced by a commercial stereo camera. The technique is applied to the rendering of virtual objects into the image stream to achieve realistic Augmented Reality where the shading and shadowing of virtual objects is consistent with the real scene. Other techniques require the presence of a known object, a light probe, in the scene for estimating illumination. The technique proposed here works in general scenes and does not require High Dynamic Range imagery. Experiments demonstrate that sun and sky radiances are estimated to within 7% of ground truth values.

Keywords: Stereo, Shadow, Illumination, Augmented reality, HDR, Photo-realism.

1 Introduction

For photo-realistic Augmented Reality (AR) the goal is to render virtual objects into real images to create the visual illusion that the virtual objects are real. A crucial element in achieving this illusion is to have a sufficiently correct model of the illumination conditions in the scene to be able to render the virtual objects with scene consistent shading and to render correct shadow interaction between real and virtual geometry.

This paper presents an adaptive illumination estimation technique for outdoor daylight scenes. The technique uses color image sequences, combined with live stereo data, to estimate the radiance of a sky dome (hemi-sphere) and the radiance of the sun. Both radiances are estimated in three color channels. The position of the sun is computed procedurally from GPS and date/time information. Together, this illumination environment (sky dome and sun) can be used to render virtual objects into the scene. As an additional benefit the stereo information provides 3D scene information to cast shadows on and to handle occlusion between real and virtual objects. Figure 1 shows an example result.

The main contribution in this work lie in the fact that the illumination is estimated directly from the image sequence with no need for special purpose objects in the scene, and no need for acquiring omni-directional High Dynamic Range environment maps (light probes) prior to augmentation.

The paper is organized as follows. Section 2 describes related work, and Section 3 describes the assumptions behind the presented work. Section 4 presents the theoretical

G. Csurka et al. (Eds.): VISIGRAPP 2011, CCIS 274, pp. 33–52, 2013.

Fig. 1. Two different augmentations intro frame 139 of a 200 frame sequence. The statue, the diffuse grey box and the three glossy spheres are rendered into the scene with illumination estimated from the shadow cast by the walking person.

framework for our approach, both in terms of detecting shadows and in terms of estimating scene illumination from detected shadows. Sections 5 and 6 present the dynamic shadow detection and the illumination estimation, respectively. Experimental results are presented in Section 7, followed by discussions and ideas for future research in Section 8. Finally, Section 9 presents concluding remarks.

2   Related Work

A survey of real scene illumination modelling for Augmented Reality is given in [17]. The survey indicates that there is no one preferred or most popular family of approaches. No technology has matured to the point of outperforming other types of approaches. In fact, any approach offers a set of possibilities at the price of a set of assumptions or limitations, leaving the application scenario to define which approach to choose.

There are three main categories of approaches: 1) omni-directional environment maps, 2) placing known objects/probes in the scene, and 3) manually or semi-manually model the entire scene, including the light sources, and perform inverse rendering.

The most widely used approach is to capture the scene illumination in a High Dynamic Range (HDR), [9], omni-directional environment map, also called a light probe. The technique was pioneered by Debevec in [7] and used in various forms by much research since then, e.g., [1,8,12,21]. The technique gives excellent results if the dominant illumination in the scene can be considered infinitely distant relative to the size of the augmented objects. The drawbacks are that it is time-consuming and impractical to acquire the environment map whenever something has changed in the scene, for example the illumination. Illumination adaptive techniques based on the environment map idea have been demonstrated in [14,18] but require a prototype omni-directional HDR camera, or a reflective sphere placed in the scene, respectively.

The other popular family of approaches is based on requiring the presence of a known object in the scene. Sato et al. analyze the shadows cast by a known object, [30,31] onto a homogeneous Lambertian surface, or require images of the scene with and without the shadow casting probe object. Hara et al., [13] analyze the shading of a geometrically known object with homogeneous (uniform albedo) Lambertian object, or require multiple images with different polarizations, to estimate the illumination direction of a single point light source. Multiple light sources can be estimated from the shading of a known object with homogeneous Lambertian reflectance using the technique described in [32].

The last family of approaches do not estimate illumination per se as they rely on modelling the entire scene in full detail, including modelling the geometry and the radiances of the light sources. The modelling process is labor intensive. Given the full description of the scene and images of it (in HDR if needed) inverse rendering can be performed to estimate the parameters of applicable reflectance functions of scene surfaces. Subsequently virtual objects can be rendered into the scene with full global illumination since all required information is known. Examples include [3,4,20,34].

A final piece of related work does not fall into the above categories, as it is the only representative of this type of approach. Using manually identified essential points (top and bottom point of two vertical structures and their cast shadow in outdoor sunlight scenes) the light source direction (the direction vector to the sun) can be determined, [5].

In summary existing methods either require pre-recorded full HDR environment maps, require homogeneous Lambertian objects to be present in the scene, require total modelling of the scene including the illumination, or require manual identification of essential object and shadow points. None of the mentioned techniques offer a practical solution to automatically adapt to the drastically changing illumination conditions of outdoor scenes.

The approach proposed in this paper addresses all of these assumption and/or constraints: it does not require HDR environment maps, nor HDR image data, it does not require objects with homogeneous reflectance (entire objects with uniform reflectance), it does not require manual modelling of the illumination (in fact the illumination is estimated directly) and there is no manual identification of essential points.

3   Assumptions behind Approach

Our approach rests on a few assumptions that are listed here for easy overview. It is assumed that we have registered color and depth data on a per pixel level. High Dynamic Range color imagery is not required; standard 8 bit per color channel images suffice if all relevant surfaces in the scene are reasonably exposed. In this paper the image data is acquired using a commercially available stereo camera, namely the Bumblebee XB3 from Point Grey, [26]. It is also assumed that the response curve of the color camera is approximately linear. The Bumblebee XB3 camera is by no means a high quality color imaging camera but has performed well enough. It is also assumed that the scene is dominated by approximately diffuse surfaces, such as asphalt, concrete, or brick, see Figure 1 for an example. There is no homogeneity assumption, and in Section 8 we will briefly describe ongoing/future work to relax the diffuse surface constraint.

To be able to procedurally compute the direction vector to the sun we need to know the Earth location in latitude/longitude (acquired from GPS), the date and time of the image acquisition, and we assume that the camera is calibrated (extrinsic parameters for position and orientation) to a scene coordinate system with xy-plane parallel to a horizontal ground plane (z-axis parallel to the direction of gravity), and x-axis pointing North. The checkerboard in Figure 1 is used for camera calibration.

4   Illumination Model

The purpose of this section is to establish the theoretical foundation for both the shadow detection and the illumination estimation. All expressions in this paper relating to pixel values, radiometric concepts, and surface reflectance et cetera are color channel dependent expressions and are to be evaluated separately for each color channels.

If the response curve of the camera is linear the pixel value in an image is proportional to the outgoing radiance from the scene surface point imaged to that pixel, [10]. The constant of proportionality depends on things such as lens geometry, shutter time, aperture, camera ISO setting, white balancing settings, etc. If the unknown constant of proportionality is termed c the value P of a pixel corresponding to a point on a diffuse surface can be formulated as:

$$P = c \cdot \rho \cdot E_i \cdot \frac{1}{\pi} \qquad (1)$$

where ρ is the diffuse albedo of the surface point, and E_i is the incident irradiance on the point. ρ times E_i yields the radiosity from the point, division by π gives the radiance, and c is the camera constant mapping radiance to pixel value. For a point in sunlight the incident irradiance, E_i, is the sum of irradiance received from the sun and from the sky, provided that we can disregard indirect Global Illumination from other surfaces in the scene, (for a discussion on this please refer to Section 8).

The irradiance received from the sun can be formulated as:

$$E_{\text{sun}} = \boldsymbol{n} \cdot \boldsymbol{s} \cdot E_s^\perp \qquad (2)$$

where $\boldsymbol{n}$ is the unit surface normal at the point, $\boldsymbol{s}$ is the unit direction vector to the sun (both relative to the scene coordinate system) and $E_s^\perp$ is the irradiance produced by the sun on a point with a normal pointing straight into the sun. The direction vector to the sun is computed procedurally from the GPS and date/time information using the approach described in [2].

The irradiance from the sky can be formulated as:

$$E_{\text{sky}} = V_a \cdot E_a^\perp \qquad (3)$$

where V_a is the fraction of the sky dome which is visible from the surface point, and $E_a^\perp$ (subscipt a for "atmosphere" or "ambient") is the irradiance produced by the sky dome on surface point with normal pointing straight into the sky dome and receiving light from the entire dome. In our experiments the visibility fraction V_a is computed on a per point basis using the scene geometry provided by the stereo camera, see Section 6.

The illumination model in this work consists of a hemi-spherical sky dome of uniform radiance, and a sun disk. The diameter of the sun disk as viewed from earth is 0.53 degrees, [10]. The technique for estimating the irradiances (and hence the radiances) of the sky and the sun directly from image measurements represents the main contribution of this paper. Our approach is in two steps: 1) detection of dynamic shadows (cast by moving objects), and 2) using chromatic information from the detected shadows to compute the radiance of the sky dome and the sun, respectively.

Fig. 2. Textured 3D scene mesh generated from stereo disparity information from the image shown in Figure 1. Notice how well the main surfaces in the scene are reconstructed

5   Shadow Detection

Existing work on single image shadow detection does not really handle soft shadows, or requires manual training. Example work includes [24,11,29]. Existing work on dynamic shadow detection from image sequences either rely on a simplistic illumination model (the grey world assumption which is definitely not valid in outdoor scenes), or require a high quality trained background model. Example work includes [16,15,19,6], and a survey can be found in [27].

For this work we have developed a dynamic shadow detection technique which does not rely on a trained background model and utilizes the available depth information. Figure 2 shows an example of the 3D data provided by the Bumblebee camera (and the accompanying API). In this section we briefly describe the approach. For more detail and additional experimental results, please refer to [22].

The shadow detection technique is based on image differencing. A delayed frame (from time $t - \Delta t$) is substracted from the current frame (from time t) both for color images and for stereo disparity images. If, for a given pixel, the color image difference is negative in all three color channels (less light emitted from the point at time t than at time $t - \Delta t$), *and* the disparity difference is zero (no change in depth), the pixel is classified as a *shadow candidate*. If there is a change in depth it is not a potential shadow candidate but rather a pixel belonging to a moving object.

Choosing the length of the frame delay Δt is not critical. If set high (long delay) we achieve better ability to detect the whole shadow since the shadows cast in the two frames are less likely to overlap. On the other hand a long frame delay makes the system less responsive to changes in the illumination conditions. In the experiments reported here we have used a frame delay of 0.5 seconds (the Bumblebee camera delivers color and disparity images at a frame rate of 10 fps in 640x480 pixel resolution).

Figure 3 shows the detected shadow candidates corresponding to the image in Figure 1. Here we have used a Δt of 10 seconds to give a better visual impression of detected shadows. Water poured onto surfaces by the test person (to simulate rain) are also initially classified as shadow candidates.

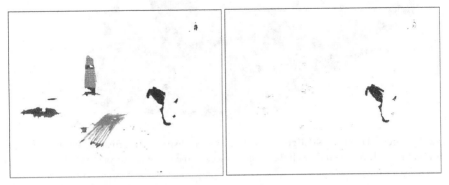

Fig. 3. Top: shadow candidate pixels in frame 139 (compare with Figure 1 and Figure 2). Bottom: verified shadow pixels after chromaticity analysis. Notice that water splashes are not classified as shadow pixels demonstrating robustness to rain.

Further analysis of the shadow candidates is performed in log chromaticity space, where the red and blue channels are normalized with respect to the green channel. In log chromaticity space, combining with the general pixel value expression from Eq. (1), we get two chromaticity values per pixel, r and b (using superscripts $r/g/b$ to indicate RGB color channel specific value):

$$
\begin{aligned}
r &= \log(P^r/P^g) \\
&= \log(P^r) - \log(P^g) \\
&= \log(c^r) - \log(c^g) + \log(\rho^r) - \log(\rho^g) + \log(E_i^r) - \log(E_i^g) \quad (4) \\
b &= \log(P^b/P^g) \\
&= \log(c^b) - \log(c^g) + \log(\rho^b) - \log(\rho^g) + \log(E_i^b) - \log(E_i^g) \quad (5)
\end{aligned}
$$

If a pixel has been marked as shadow candidate it means we have two versions of the same pixel, one from time t and one from time $t - \Delta t$. The color channel values have changed for that pixel, which in turn means that the pixel's location in log chromaticity space has moved. Basically two things can have caused this: 1) sunlight at the surface point corresponding to the pixel was blocked (shadow), or 2) the surface changed albedo, e.g., became wet. Studying the *displacements* in chromaticity space forms the basis for the final classification of shadow pixels. This approach is inspired by [23].

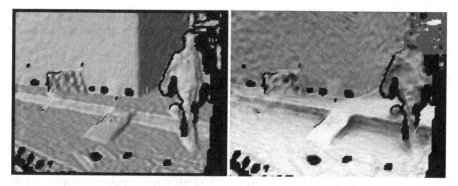

Fig. 4. Left: per pixel normal map encoded as RGB values for the image in Figure 1. Right: per pixel sky dome visibility in the range 0 to 1.

We assume that the camera constants $c^{r/g/b}$ did not change during Δt. If we hypothesize that the surface albedos $\rho^{r/g/b}$ did not change:

$$\Delta r = r(t) - r(t - \Delta t)$$

$$= log\left(\frac{E_i^r(t)}{E_i^r(t - \Delta t)}\right) - log\left(\frac{E_i^g(t)}{E_i^g(t - \Delta t)}\right) \tag{6}$$

$$\Delta b = log\left(\frac{E_i^b(t)}{E_i^b(t - \Delta t)}\right) - log\left(\frac{E_i^g(t)}{E_i^g(t - \Delta t)}\right) \tag{7}$$

Thus, log chromaticity displacements of shadow candidate pixels depend only on the change in incident irradiances, namely the various E_i values (which are of course unknown). This means that all shadow pixels should exhibit displacements that are parallel in log chromaticity space. If a pixel does *not* displace in the same direction it *must* be because the albedo changed (the constant albedo hypothesis is false and eqs. 6 and 7 do not hold), e.g., the surface point became wet, or it otherwise changed color. This is utilized by selecting only the pixels whose displacement orientation (computed as $\theta = \arctan(\Delta b/\Delta r)$) is within a certain threshold of +90 degrees (a displacement towards blue). We have used a threshold of 20 degrees. A shift towards blue is what is expected from a surface point transitioning from being illuminated by both the sun and sky, to only being illuminated by the (blueish) sky. Figure 3 shows the shadow pixels after the chromaticity analysis.

The described methods work well on outdoor imagery, but we do not need perfect shadow detection. We just need robust, fast detection of a population of high confidence shadow pixels to support the illumination estimation.

6   Illumination Estimation

As described in Section 4 the illumination model in this work consists of a hemispherical sky dome of uniform radiance, and a sun disk of uniform radiance. The direction vector, s, is computed procedurally using the method described in [2].

Every detected shadow pixel provides some information about the sun and sky irradiance in the scene. At time $t - \Delta t$ the pixel was not in shadow, and at time t it is. At time $t - \Delta t$, by combining eqs. (1) through (3):

$$
\begin{aligned}
P(t - \Delta t) &= c \cdot \rho \cdot E_i(t - \Delta t) \cdot \frac{1}{\pi} \\
&= c \cdot \rho \cdot \frac{1}{\pi} \cdot \left(E_{\text{sun}}(t - \Delta t) + E_{\text{sky}}(t - \Delta t) \right) \\
&= c \cdot \rho \cdot \frac{1}{\pi} \cdot \left(\boldsymbol{n} \cdot \boldsymbol{s} \cdot E_s^{\perp}(t - \Delta t) + V_a(t - \Delta t) \cdot E_a^{\perp}(t - \Delta t) \right) \quad (8)
\end{aligned}
$$

Here, sky dome visibility fraction, V_a, is time dependent since moving geometry in the scene may change the fraction, especially for points in near proximity of the shadow casting object. At time t the pixel is in shadow and only the sky contributes to the irradiance:

$$
P(t) = c \cdot \rho \cdot \frac{1}{\pi} \cdot V_a(t) \cdot E_a^{\perp}(t) \quad (9)
$$

Eqs. (8) and (9) are per color channel. If we introduce a quantity C which is the ratio of pixel value in shadow to pixel value in sunlight, and assume Δt to be small enough that the sky and sun irradiances at time $t - \Delta t$ equal those at time t:

$$
\begin{aligned}
C &= \frac{P(t)}{P(t - \Delta t)} \\
&= \frac{V_a(t) \cdot E_a^{\perp}(t)}{\boldsymbol{n} \cdot \boldsymbol{s} \cdot E_s^{\perp}(t) + V_a(t - \Delta t) \cdot E_a^{\perp}(t)} \quad (10)
\end{aligned}
$$

Equation (10) is crucial. On the left hand side the ratio C is based only on image measurements (pixel values from the two frames), so this quantity is known. On the right hand side $\boldsymbol{n}$ is the surface point normal, known from the stereo data; $\boldsymbol{s}$ is the sun direction vector, known from the GPS and the date and time information; V_a at time t and at time $t - \Delta t$ is the sky dome visibility fraction, which can be computed from the scene geometry data, see Section 7 and Figure 4. The only unknowns are the sun and sky irradiances. Re-arranging Eq. (10) yields:

$$
E_s^{\perp}(t) = E_a^{\perp}(t) \frac{V_a(t) - C \cdot V_a(t - \Delta t)}{\boldsymbol{n} \cdot \boldsymbol{s} \cdot C} \quad (11)
$$

Now the sun's head-on irradiance is expressed in terms of the sky irradiance times quantities from the images and from scene geometry. Next we introduce a constraint based on the white-balancing of the camera. We assume that the camera is white-balanced. This means that there must be some point in the scene where the combined irradiances of the sun and sky is color balanced, that is, the combined irradiance has the same value, k, in all three color channels. Let $\boldsymbol{n}'$ be the normal of such a point and let V_a' be its sky dome visibility fraction. In our experiments we have used $n' = [0\ 0\ 1]$ (so horizontal surfaces have white-balanced illumination), and set V_a' to the average value of V_a for all horizontal surface points in the scene. This white-balancing constraint says that the sun and sky combined irradiance must sum to the same number k in all color channels, expressible as:

$$k = n' \cdot s \cdot E_s^{\perp}(t) + V_a'(t) \cdot E_a^{\perp}(t) \tag{12}$$

Combining eqs. (11) and (12) yields:

$$E_a^{\perp} = \frac{k}{V_a'(t) + (n' \cdot s/n \cdot s)(V_a(t)/C - V_a(t - \Delta t))} \tag{13}$$

To sum up, we could now, given the pixel values at time t and time $t - \Delta t$ of only one shadow pixel, compute the irradiance ratios $C^{r/g/b}$ in the three color channel using Eq. (10), insert into Eq. (13) to get the sky irradiance in three channels (up to a scale factor of k), then insert into Eq. (11) to get the sun irradiance in three channels (up to a scale factor of k). To solve this overall scale problem we have chosen the following approach. The input image is actually measurements of scene radiances scaled by the camera radiance-to-pixel-value proportionality constants $c^{r/g/b}$ (see Eq. (1)). We wish to scale the estimated irradiances such that the reflected radiance of virtual surface in the augmented scene is on the same brightness level as the input image. k is the irradiance on a horizontal surface in the scene. A suitable average albedo for general surfaces is 0.3 (earth's average albedo), so the reflected radiance from such a surface would be $L_{avg} = \rho_{avg} \cdot k \cdot 1/\pi$. Let P_{avg}^g be the average pixel value in the green channel of the input image. We want the reflected radiance to equal the average image intensity which means that we should set k to:

$$k = \pi P_{avg}^g / \rho \tag{14}$$

By computing the scale factor this way the augmented object changes brightness according to changes to camera illumination sensitivity, e.g., if the camera aperture is changed the luminance level of the image changes, and the luminance level of the augment object changes with the same amount. This allows us to enable the Automatic Gain Control (AGC) of the camera so the method can be applied to very long sequences with large variations in illumination.

This completes the theoretical background for the illumination estimation from shadows. For rendering puporses we need the *radiances* of the sun and the sky, not the irradiances. The radiance of the sky is computed as $L_a(t) = E_a^{\perp}(t)/\pi$ and the radiance of the sun disk is computed as $L_s(t) = E_s^{\perp}(t)/(2\pi \cdot (1 - cos(d/2)))$, where $d = 0.53$ degrees. The denominator is the solid angle subtended by a sun disk of 0.53 degree radius.

In the subsequent Section we describe how the illumination is estimated robustly from a whole population of detected shadow pixels, not just from a single one.

Fig. 5. Dynamic shadow detection based on image differencing (frames 180, 520, and 1741). These are the raw detected shadow pixels. The spurious shadow pixels in the top right of the images are removed with morphological operations.

7   Experimental Results

We have Matlab and C++ versions of the shadow detection, and we have a Matlab implementation of the illumination estimation.

In the C++ version shadow detection is running at approx. 8 Hz on an Intel Core Duo 2 2.3 GHz machine running Windows XP SP2, equipped with 2 GByte RAM. This framerate includes the stereo disparity computations, and the construction of the

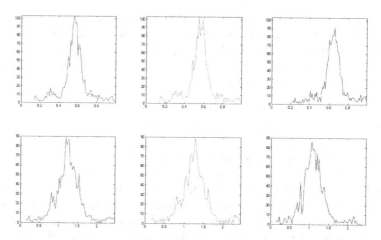

Fig. 6. Top row: sky irradiance histograms for R, G, and B color channels. Bottom row: similar for sun irradiance. For each histogram the horizontal axis shows the irradiance value with a scale factor k of 1, and the vertical axis is number of pixels voting for that irradiance value. The histogram corresponds to the scene in Figure 1.

geometry mesh from the depth data. Figure 5 illustrates the shadow detection on some random frames from a long image sequence with rapidly changing illumination conditions (partly overcast and very windy).

The expressions for estimating the illumination conditions involve quantities relating to the geometry of the scene, namely the sky dome visibility fraction V_a and the surface normals. We construct triangle meshes of the scene from the live disparity data (an example mesh is shown in Figure 2). The disparity data is in 640×480 pixel resolution, which is mean filtered with a kernel size of 5×5. A 160×120 regular vertex grid is imposed on the disparity map and the xyz position of each vertex is found by converting the corresponding disparity value to depth and multiplying the pixel's unit ray direction vector with that depth. Two triangles are formed for every group of 4 vertices, resulting in $2 \times 160 \times 120$ triangles, from which triangles with normals almost perpendicular to the viewing direction are discarded (typically triangles that correspond to depth discontinuities). We get per pixel normals by rendering the scene mesh using a normal shader. For all renderings in this paper we have used the RADIANCE rendering package, [33]. Per pixel sky dome visibility is computed by rendering irradiance values of the mesh (with mesh albedo set to zero to avoid global illumination inter-reflections) when illuminated with a sky dome of radiance $1/\pi$. Using this approach a normal pointing straight into the sky and having un-occluded view of the sky will receive an irradiance of 1, so the V_a values will be in the range of 0 to 1 as desired. Figure 4 shows examples.

With per pixel geometry quantities, and with irradiance ratios C computed per detected shadow pixels using Eq. (10) we have a whole population of pixels voting for the irradiances of the sky and the sun. Each pixel, through Eq. (13), contributes three channel values for the sky irradiance, and through Eq. (11) for the sun irradiance. This is computed for all shadow pixels and histograms are formed of sky and sun irradiances for each color channel, see Figure 6.

From each of these histograms the most voted for irradiance value is selected (histogram peak). Future work includes either fitting a Gaussian distribution, employ a mean shift algorithm, or to use Random Sample Consencus (RANSAC), to find the mean more robustly than just taking peak value. In the example in Figure 6 the elected and finally scaled radiance values are:

$$\text{Sky radiance} = \begin{bmatrix} 0.6548 & 0.6662 & 0.7446 \end{bmatrix}$$
$$\text{Sun radiance} = \begin{bmatrix} 60197 & 57295 & 51740 \end{bmatrix}$$

These numbers indicate primarily that the radiance of the sun is 5 orders of magnitude higher than that of the sky, which is consistent with the fact that the sun's subtended solid angle is 5 orders of magnitude smaller than a hemi-spherical sky dome, but as a rule of thumb provides roughly the same irradiance as the sky dome. Futhermore it can be noticed that the sky's color balance clearly is much more blue than that of the sun. Figure 7 show more examples of objects rendered into scenes with illumination estimated using the technique proposed in this paper.

Fig. 7. Two examples of scenes with augmentations using the proposed technique for estimating illumination from automatically detected shadows

Qualitatively, judging from Figures 1 and 7 the generated results are encouraging and the estimated illumination conditions visually match the real scene conditions sufficiently well to be convincing. Subsequently we present some more controlled experiments.

Synthetic Geometry, Synthetic Illumination. To test the technique's performance on a scene for which ground truth is available for the illumination a synthetic scene has been rendered at two time instances with a shadow casting pole moving from one frame to another, see Figure 8.

The ground truth sky radiance used for rendering the scene in Figure 8 is $[0.0700 \ 0.1230 \ 0.1740]$ and the sun radiance is $[72693 \ 57178 \ 42247]$. The estimated sky radiance is $[0.0740 \ 0.1297 \ 0.1804]$ and the estimated sun radiance is $[71687 \ 55488 \ 40622]$, i.e., estimations are within 5% of ground truth. A large proportion of the deviation between ground truth and estimation result is believed to be due to influence from indirect illumination (light reflecting from one surface on to others),

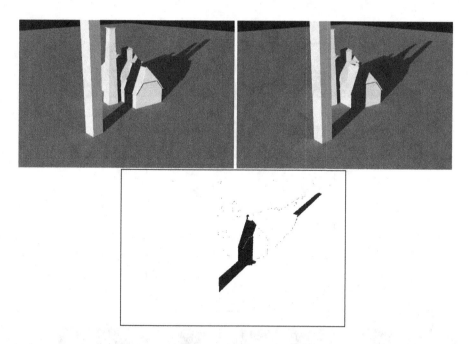

Fig. 8. Top: Two frames of a synthetic scene. Bottom: detected dynamic shadow pixel population to be used for illumination estimation.

a phenomenon which is not taken intro account by the applied two part illumination model (sun and sky are assumed to be the only illuminants in the scene).

Real Geometry, Synthetic Illumination. To test the performance under more realistic conditions a pair of images were produced where the dynamic objects are synthetic, but they are casting shadow on real mesh geometry obtained from the stereo camera. Figure 9 illustrates how these images were generated.

The two frame image sequence thus generated shows synthetically generated dynamic shadows on real stereo geometry, using real camera images as scene albedo, and yet we still have perfect ground truth for the illumination, since the shadows are rendered into the image.

The ground truth sky radiance used for rendering the scene in Figure 9 is $[1.0109\ 1.1644\ 1.2085]$ and the sun radiance is $[83082\ 81599\ 73854]$. The estimated sky radiance is $[1.0658\ 1.2212\ 1.2614]$ and the estimated sun radiance is $[88299\ 82764\ 79772]$, i.e., estimations are within roughly 5% of ground truth, except for the red channel of the sun, which shows an error of around 8%. Figure 10 shows an augmentation into this semi-synthetic scene with the estimated illumination.

As in the previous all synthetic data example the discrepancy is believed to be due to not explicitly taking indirect illumination into account. For example the sun's red channel is somewhat over-estimated, since in the shadow a lot of red-toned illumination from the brick-walled building in the background of Figure 9 vanishes, and the

Fig. 9. First row: frames 25 and 30 from real stereo image sequence. Second row: detected shadow pixels from trees moving in the wind. Third row: frame 30 augmented with moving synthethic objects, using the illumination estimated from the shadow pixels in row two. Notice the reflection of the sky in the artificial chrome ball to the left.

assumed simplified illumination model can only "explain" this by estimating the sun's red channel higher than it actually is.

Fig. 10. Augmentation into the scene were the illumination was estimated from the shadows of moving augmentations, which in turn were rendered into the original scene with illumination estimated from the shadows of trees moving in the wind

Real Geometry, Real Illumination. As a final example of the performance of the presented technique we return to the scene from Figure 1, this time to another frame in the same sequence, approximately 6 seconds earlier, see Figure 11.

In Figure 1 the sky radiance is estimated to $[0.6548\ 0.6662\ 0.7446]$ and the sun radiance to $[60197\ 57295\ 51740]$. From the frame in Figure 11 the same values are estimated at $[0.6106\ 0.5874\ 0.6746]$ and $[68927\ 69784\ 62741]$, respectively.

A significant change in the estimated illumination is noted on the quantitative level, although visually the augmentation in the two cases is equally convincing. The relatively large quantitative differences are, in addition to the fact that this scene in particular involves substantial indirect illumination contributions, due to a lot of the pixels for the sunlit brick wall are saturated in the red channel, i.e., exceed 255 in pixel value. Naturally, such imperfect image exposure makes it difficult for the technique to estimate proper results.

Real Geometry, Real Illumination, High Quality Color Information. The color images produced by the Bumblebee stereo camera are not of high quality, and it is questionable to what extent the camera actually has a linear response curve. Linearity is something that still has to be tested. To demonstrate the proposed technique on color image material of much higher quality we have photographed a scene with a Canon 400D SLR camera set to acquire in raw format, which results in a very linear response.

Fig. 11. Even with the shadow falling on completely different materials and with completely different geometric properties the estimation illumination is comparable to that of Figure 1

The scene was images with the Bumblebee camera for acquiring the geometry, and simultaneously with the Canon camera for acquiring color. The two cameras were calibrated to the same coordinate system, and thus the geometry information (the 3D scene mesh) could be used alongside with the color information from the Canon camera. Figure 12 shows the result of estimating the illumination and rendering a few virtual objects into the image.

8   Discussions and Future Work

The work described here is intended for sequences of limited length (up to minutes). Futhermore it requires the presence of dynamic objects to cast shadows. We are developing additional techniques which will be bootstrapped by the technique presented here, but afterwards will be able to handle illumination estimation also in the absence of dynamic shadows, and over very long image sequences.

The described technique is based on an assumptions that surfaces in the scene are predominantly diffuse. While this is a fair assumption for much outdoor material it is far from satisfactory to have this constraint. We are presently pursuing analysis of very long time sequences (full day, several days) and are developing techniques to classify pixels that do not agree with the majority on how the illumination in the scene changes. Those pixels are either glossy/specular, a leaf has fallen on the surface, or even snow. Our ambition is to develop techniques that are robust enough to handle seasonal changes.

Fig. 12. Scene captured with high quality Canon SLR camera and used for the proposed illumination estimation technique. The 3D scene information was provided by the Bumblebee camera as in the other experiments. The reflection of the sky in the virtual chrome ball is in good correspondence with the directly captured part of the sky in the top right part of the image.

In the illumination estimation approach presented in Section 6 the illumination model does not take into account the indirect global illumination contribution from other surfaces in the scene. We are presently rephrasing this work into a framework that does take this into account. Moreover, we are investigating how to employ a more realistic sky model than the uniform radiance sky dome used here. A more realistic, non-uniform sky dome could be the Perez model, [25], or the Preetham model, [28].

The shadow detection is presently running at 8 Hz including the stereo disparity computation. The illumination estimation process itself poses no real computational load, but the required ambient occlusion map is not straight forward to obtain as this requires some form of ray casting. Real-time global illumination methods are beginning to appear in the litterature, and for the use in conjunction with the work in this paper we only need ambient occlusion factors for the detected shadow pixels, not for the entire image.

9   Conclusions

We have presented a technique for adaptively estimating outdoor daylight conditions directly from video imagery, and the technique has a potential for real-time operation. The main scientific contribution is a theoretically well-founded technique for estimation of the radiances of sky and sun for a full outdoor illumination model directly from Low

Dynamic Range image sequences. The main contribution from a systems point of view is a demonstration that automatic detection of dynamic shadows can feed information to the illumination estimation.

The presented work an be used for rendering virtual objects in Augmented Reality, but we conjecture that illumination estimation can also make many classical computer vision techniques more robust to illumination changes.

Acknowledgements. This work is funded by CoSPE project (project number 26-04-0171) and the BigBrother project (project number 274-07-0264) under the Danish Research Agency. This funding is gratefully acknowledged.

References

1. Barsi, L., Szimary-Kalos, L., Szecsi, L.: Image-based illumination on the gpu. Machine Graphics and Graphics 14(2), 159–169 (2005)
2. Blanco-Muriel, M., Alarcón-Padilla, D.C., López-Moratalla, T., Lara-Coira, M.: Computing the solar vector. Solar Energy 70(5), 431–441 (2001)
3. Boivin, S., Gagalowicz, A.: Image-based rendering of diffuse, specular and glossy surfaces from a single image. In: Proceedings: ACM SIGGRAPH 2001, pp. 107–116 (August 2001), http://www.dgp.toronto.edu/~boivin/
4. Boivin, S., Gagalowicz, A.: Inverse rendering from a single image. In: Proceedings: First European Conference on Color in Graphics, Images and Vision, Poitiers, France, pp. 268–277 (April 2002), http://www.dgp.toronto.edu/~boivin/
5. Cao, X., Shen, Y., Shah, M., Foroosh, H.: Single view compositing with shadows. The Visual Computer, 639–648 (September 2005)
6. Chalidabhongse, T., Kim, K., Harwood, D., Davis, L.: A Perturbation Method for Evaluating Background Subtraction Algorithms. In: Joint IEEE International Workshop on Visual Surveillance and Performance Evaluation of Tracking and Surveillance, Nice, France, October 11-12 (2003)
7. Debevec, P.: Rendering synthetic objects into real scenes: Bridging traditional and image-based graphics with global illumination and high dynamic range photography. In: Proceedings: SIGGRAPH 1998, Orlando, Florida, USA (July 1998)
8. Debevec, P.: Tutorial: Image-based lighting. IEEE Computer Graphics and Applications, 26–34 (March/April 2002)
9. Debevec, P., Malik, J.: Recovering high dynamic range radiance maps from photographs. In: Proceedings: SIGGRAPH 1997, Los Angeles, CA, USA (August 1997)
10. Dutré, P., Bekaert, P., Bala, K.: Advanced Global Illumination. A. K. Peters (2003)
11. Finlayson, G.D., Hordley, S.D., Drew, M.S.: Removing Shadows from Images. In: Heyden, A., Sparr, G., Nielsen, M., Johansen, P. (eds.) ECCV 2002. LNCS, vol. 2353, pp. 823–836. Springer, Heidelberg (2002)
12. Gibson, S., Cook, J., Howard, T., Hubbold, R.: Rapic shadow generation in real-world lighting environments. In: Proceedings: EuroGraphics Symposium on Rendering, Leuwen, Belgium (June 2003)
13. Hara, K., Nishino, K., Ikeuchi, K.: Light source position and reflectance estimation from a single view without the distant illumination assumption. IEEE Trans. Pattern Anal. Mach. Intell. 27(4), 493–505 (2005)

14. Havran, V., Smyk, M., Krawczyk, G., Myszkowski, K., Seidel, H.P.: Importance Sampling for Video Environment Maps. In: Eurographics Symposium on Rendering 2005, Konstanz, Germany, pp. 31–42, 311 (2005)
15. Horprasert, T., Harwood, D., Davis, L.S.: A statistical approach for real-time robust background subtraction and shadow detection. In: Proceedings: IEEE ICCV 1999 FRAME-RATE Workshop, Kerkyra, Greece (September 1999)
16. Huerta, I., Holte, M., Moeslund, T., Gonzàlez, J.: Detection and removal of chromatic moving shadows in surveillance scenarios. In: Proceedings: IEEE ICCV 2009, Kyoto, Japan (September 2009)
17. Jacobs, K., Loscos, C.: State of the art report on classification of illumination methods for mixed reality. In: EUROGRAPHICS, Grenoble, France (September 2004), http://www.cs.ucl.ac.uk/staff/k.jacobs/research.html
18. Kanbara, M., Yokoya, N.: Real-time estimation of light source environment for photorealistic augmented reality. In: Proceedings of the 17th ICPR, Cambridge, United Kingdom, pp. 911–914 (August 2004)
19. Kim, K., Chalidabhongse, T., Harwood, D., Davis, L.: Real-time Foreground-Background Segmentation using Codebook Model. Real-time Imaging 11(3), 167–256 (2005)
20. Loscos, C., Drettakis, G., Robert, L.: Interative virtual relighting of real scenes. IEEE Transactions on Visualization and Computer Graphics 6(4), 289–305 (2000)
21. Madsen, C.B., Laursen, R.: A scalable gpu-based approach to shading and shadowing for photorealistic real-time augmented reality. In: Proceedings: International Conference on Graphics Theory and Applications, Barcelona, Spain, pp. 252–261 (March 2007)
22. Madsen, C.B., Moeslund, T.B., Pal, A., Balasubramanian, S.: Shadow detection in dynamic scenes using dense stereo information and an outdoor illumination model. In: Koch, R., Kolb, A. (eds.) Proceedings: 3rd Workshop on Dynamic 3D Imaging, in conjunction with Symposium of the German Association for Pattern Recognition, Jena, Germany, pp. 100–125 (September 2009)
23. Marchand, J.A., Onyango, C.M.: Shadow-invariant classification for scenes illuminated by daylight. Journal of the Optical Society of America 17(11), 1952–1961 (2000)
24. Nielsen, M., Madsen, C.B.: Graph Cut Based Segmentation of Soft Shadows for Seemless Removal and Augmentation. In: Ersbøll, B.K., Pedersen, K.S. (eds.) SCIA 2007. LNCS, vol. 4522, pp. 918–927. Springer, Heidelberg (2007)
25. Perez, R., Seals, R., Michalsky, J.: All-weather model for sky luminance distribution-preliminary configuration and validation. Solar Energy 50(3), 235–245 (1993), http://www.sciencedirect.com/science/article/B6V50-497T8FV-99/2/69a6d079526288e5f4bb5708e3fed05d
26. PointGrey: Bumblebee XB3 stereo camera, Point Grey Research, Inc. (2009), http://www.ptgrey.com/products/bumblebee/index.html
27. Prati, A., Mikic, I., Trivedi, M., Cucchiara, R.: Detecting Moving Shadows: Algorithms and Evaluation. IEEE Transactions on Pattern Analysis and Machine Intelligence 25, 918–923 (2003)
28. Preetham, A.J., Shirley, P., Smits, B.: A practical analytic model for daylight. In: Proceedings of the 26th Annual Conference on Computer Graphics and Interactive Techniques, SIGGRAPH 1999, pp. 91–100. ACM Press/Addison-Wesley Publishing Co., New York (1999), http://dx.doi.org/10.1145/311535.311545
29. Salvador, E., Cavalarro, A., Ebrahimi, T.: Shadow identification and classification using invariant color models. Computer Vision and Image Understanding 95, 238–259 (2004)
30. Sato, I., Sato, Y., Ikeuchi, K.: Acquiring a radiance distribution to superimpose virtual objects onto a real scene. IEEE Transactions on Visualization and Computer Graphics 5(1), 1–12 (1999)

31. Sato, I., Sato, Y., Ikeuchi, K.: Illumination distribution from brightness in shadows: adaptive estimation of illumination distribution with unknown reflectance properties in shadow regions. In: Proceedings: International Conference on Computer Vision, pp. 875–882 (September 1999)
32. Wang, Y., Samaras, D.: Estimation of multiple directional illuminants from a single image. Image Vision Computing 26(9), 1179–1195 (2008)
33. Ward, G.: Radiance - Synthetic Imaging System (2009),
    http://radsite.lbl.gov/radiance/
34. Yu, Y., Debevec, P., Malik, J., Hawkins, T.: Inverse global illumination: Recovering reflectance models of real scenes from photographs. In: Proceedings: SIGGRAPH 1999, Los Angeles, California, USA, pp. 215–224 (August 1999)

Feature-First Hole Filling Strategy for 3D Meshes

Hanh T.-M. Ngo and Won-Sook Lee

School of Information Technology and Engineeing, University of Ottawa, Ontario, Canada
{tngo087,wslee}@uottawa.ca

Abstract. In this paper we introduce an efficient hole-filling strategy for 3D
meshes and at the same time aesthetically recover the sharp features of the
original 3D model at the hole areas. Commonly, hole filling techniques try to
fill up the hole first then smooth it. Very few have tried to recover the fine
features of the original model at the holes. Our hole filling technique is different
from other existing techniques as features are taken as the first subject to
reconstruct, which eventually drive the feature-definite surface filling process.
Feature curves in the missing part are reconstructed by extending salient
features of the existing parts. The hole is partitioned into several smaller and
more planar sub-holes by the feature curves and then the hole-filling steps are
done on those sub-holes. User intervention is allowed to design features to be in
desired shape. This indeed guides feature curve reconstruction wherever
ambiguity exists or results are unsatisfactory. It is also very efficient as a user
is interfering only with sharp features and the actual hole-filling step is dealing
with only simple holes.

Keywords: Hole filling, Surface reconstruction, 3D modelling, Real time user
interaction.

1 Introduction

3D computer models of real life objects can be obtained by several ways such as 3D
scanning devices, or computer-aided design software (Autodesk Maya, 3DS Max,
etc.). A common scenario, especially when dealing with 3D shapes obtained from 3D
scanning, is to have incomplete surfaces. These appear in areas where the object
geometry occludes the scanning device, notable examples when scanning human
bodies include the area under the chin, armpits or between the fingers, hence limiting
the information obtained. Because of these issues, many post processing techniques
are needed to be applied onto the raw models before being able to use them as the
input of design or animation applications. The repair of incomplete polygon meshes is
a fundamental problem in the reconstruction of 3D models in the field of computer
graphics.

One of key aspects of reconstruction of 3D models is hole-filling. This is to
complete the shape of the 3D object where surface information is missing. This is
essential for a wide range of applications such as computer animation, pattern
recognition, or character design. Hole-filling techniques aim to keep the filled surface
continuously and smoothly fitted at the boundary of the hole to conform to the shape

G. Csurka et al. (Eds.): VISIGRAPP 2011, CCIS 274, pp. 53–68, 2013.
© Springer-Verlag Berlin Heidelberg 2013

of the original model. Although there is a large body of research on hole filling, very little attention has been devoted to the problem of recovering fine features of the 3D object, for instance the sharpness of the edge geometry. Most research focuses on automatic methods that require performing complex optimization processes [1] [4] [7] [10] [12] [14] [18]. In many cases, although the models obtained are hole-free, interpolation algorithms fail to preserve fine details, ignoring sharp edges and corner shapes.

Due to the complexity of the regions where holes are generated, automatic model modification methods may not give satisfactory results in dealing with holes. Complex optimization frameworks are computationally expensive. In addition, processing large and complicated models is a time consuming task. Despite of the great computational overhead, fine features in models are not recovered. Since there are potentially several possible results for the surface recovery process, the user should have the ability to influence the quality of the output surface. Furthermore, although there are ways to set the constraints for automatic methods to resolve ambiguous topology problem, there will always be the cases that require high-level knowledge to disambiguate or have multiple answers, where the selection depends on user's preference. We believe a program interface that allows user intervention efficiently helps to reduce the implementation effort, to give better visually plausible results and to enhance the versatility of the system since the user would have the ability to choose the desired feature-topology and the shape of the filled mesh.

We are motivated by the need of a hole filling system that is able to plausibly recover the fine geometry features of the 3D models, especially the sharp features, with some possible simple guidance by users at the hole locations using a real time Graphics User Interface (GUI). Our goal is to develop a system that can repair the holes of the 3D models and, at the same time, aesthetically preserve the sharpness of the model at the hole locations with the aid from user intervention.

Our main contributions are two-fold: (i) salient features of the mesh geometry are taken as the first subject to reconstruct, which eventually drive the feature-definite surface filling process; (ii) the user is allowed to influence the hole filling process at feature designing level while the rest is taken care by the automatic functions. Our results show missing hole features are recovered with high quality while supporting flexibility.

2   Related Works

Many researches on hole filling topic have been done up to now. However, there are only few hole-filling approaches attempting to preserve and to recover the sharp features of the 3D model. In this section we focus our discussion on feature sensitive recovering methods for 3D meshes as they are of our special interest.

Barequet and Kumar [2] proposed a method that allows users to inspect the automatic results of the first iteration and also to mark the areas to be corrected. The second iteration produces the final results. The approach can produce "intuitively-correct" filling of the holes with the aid of the user.

In the paper by Ohtake et al. [13], to preserve the shape of sharp edges and corners at the hole locations, a multilevel piecewise surface fitting method is employed to represent a mesh model that has fine structures. Local approximation for fitting edges and corners are based on the piecewise quadric surface fitting method. It consists of a number of tests (edge tests and corner tests) in order to determine the type of approximation surface or shape function that should be used. Edges and corners are automatically recognized by clustering the normals of the mesh vertices.

In Sharf et al. [15], a context-based completion method is proposed to recover the missing fine details in a repaired hole. The method employs the idea of texture synthesis, by replicating portions of regions from adequate examples. Based on this idea, the fine structure of the 3D model is recovered by finding a piece in the original model or in the template models that is similar in shape to replace the initial repaired hole. Hence, this method is particularly efficient for repairing holes in textured mesh model.

Attene et al. [1] proposed a method to recover the sharp features of 3D mesh model which are lost by reverse engineering or by remeshing processes that use a non-adaptive sampling of the original surface. The algorithm starts by identifying the smooth edges in the mesh model then applying the filters to get the chamfer edges. Each chamfer edge and its incident triangles are subdivided by inserting new vertices. These vertices are calculated so that they lie on intersections of planes that locally approximate the smooth surfaces that meet at the sharp features.

In Chen et al. [5], holes are filled and sharpness is recovered by applying a sharpness-dependent filter. The filter operates based on the distribution of the sharpness values of triangle faces in the vicinity of a hole boundary. In this context, the vicinity of a hole boundary is defined as its two-ring neighborhood. For any triangle face, its sharpness value is computed as the variance of the angles between its normal and each of the normals of the neighboring faces.

In He and Chen [9], both automatic and interactive methods are employed for hole-filling. A novel hole-filling system that makes use of a haptic device is proposed. After the hole identification phase, the hole boundaries are smoothed in the interpolation step. This step is to correct boundary topologies and to adjust the boundary edge lengths in order to avoid the uneven distribution of points at the hole boundary. Then the user can decompose those complex holes into simpler ones in stitching process. Sub-holes are then automatically triangulated using regular triangulation methods. The user can repeat the intervention process until obtaining satisfactory results. The authors proposed an interesting idea about using haptic for 3D user intervention. However, the limitation of this method is the lack of an automatic method to detect the fine features of the mesh to serve as the guidance for the user.

In Zhap et al. [19], holes are detected then triangulated using the modified minimum-weight triangulation technique. Sharp features are recovered by crest line fairing. The system makes use of the crest line detection technique in paper [17] to detect the feature lines in the original mesh. Crest lines are the salient surface features defined via the first- and the second-order curvature derivatives. Detected crest lines are then used in region growing and fairing processes to recover the sharp features at the hole areas. The users are also able to connect some crest lines before the region growing step.

Chen and Cheng [4] presented a sharpness-based method for filling holes. The whole algorithm performs in two steps: an interpolation step for filling the hole which produces the first approximation of the final model, and a post-processing step which modifies the approximation model to match the original. The patch for the hole is interpolated using the radial basis function to create a smooth implicit surface to fill the holes. The implicit surface is triangulated using a regularized matching tetrahedral algorithm. Then the triangulated surface patch is stitched to the hole boundary to obtain the repaired model. In the post-processing step, a sharpness-dependent filter is applied to the repaired model to recover its sharp features. In this paper, the sharpness-dependent filter is an improvement of the one presented in paper by Chen et al. [5]. Although the algorithm works quite effectively in repairing the models, the system is difficult to implement.

Although an automatic system is always desirable, dealing with fine features at the hole areas is a challenging task. In spite of a complicated hole-filling optimization engine to get the results automatically as in paper by Zhat et al. [18], the fine features are not adequately recovered in many cases. Most of the systems require user intervention to obtain the best guess of fine features at the hole areas and to correct the automatic results [2] [19].

Our hole-filling system provides both fully automatic and semi-automatic capabilities where semi-automatic allows user to be comfortable dealing with only several feature elements. If there is no ambiguity in pairing the feature points and no inaccurate crest lines detected at the hole vicinities, our system can fully automatically produce aesthetical results. Furthermore, while most hole filling algorithms provide only automatic function and manual hole filling takes a lot of user's time and effort as it is at surface mesh level with numerous points to touch and requires expert knowledge about the objects and about how to manipulate on the 3D mesh, our hole filling method, in the more complex cases, need a very limited user intervention at the feature level to support the hole filling procedure.

3   User-Guided Feature Sensitive Hole Filling

Our hole filling algorithm can completely fill the holes of a model and aesthetically recover the sharpness of the model at the hole areas, if any. It includes the solution for efficient preservation of sharpness properties of 3D mesh models during the hole filling procedure; the solution for implementation of a user-friendly interface to support user intervention in real-time.

3.1   Algorithm Overview

Fig. 1 shows a high level view of our user-guided feature sensitive hole filling system. The input model information is loaded into our designed data structure for further usage in two modules: Crest Line Detection and Hole Identification. Crest line information helps to find feature points in the holes and their vicinities, which are used later for sharp feature interpolation. Here, the user can interfere the crest point positions and design the shape of the patch mesh. Using this corrected information, our system performs a feature line interpolation procedure over the holes. This process defines the expected fine features of the hole geometries and also divides large complex holes into smaller and more planar ones. For each of these simpler holes, patch is generated by projecting the hole on its projection plane, performing triangulation and then mapping the triangulated topology back to 3D space. The 3D patch is then stitched into the 3D model, and it is regularized to make the patch consistent with the original mesh, in order to produce the final repaired mesh model.

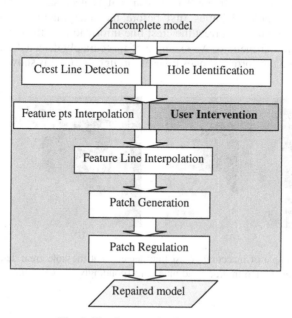

Fig. 1. The framework of our system

3.2   Crest Line Detection

Defined in paper by Yoshizawa et al. [16], the crest lines are the salient surface features defined via the first- and the second-order curvature derivatives. Crest line detection has a significant role in our system since it guides the user to pair the feature points on the hole boundaries and to correctly interpolate the feature lines over the holes. In our implementation, we employed the crest line detection approach proposed in paper [16].

Consider an oriented surface S and denote k_{max} and k_{min} its maximal and minimal principal curvatures. Denote by t_{max} and t_{min} the corresponding principal directions. Denote c_{max} and c_{min} the derivatives of the principal curvatures along their corresponding curvature directions. The *convex crest lines,* also called *ridges,* are given by

$$c_{max} = 0, \quad \delta c_{max}/\delta t_{max} < 0, \quad k_{max} > |k_{min}| \tag{1}$$

while the *concave crest lines,* also called *ravines,* are characterized by

$$c_{min} = 0, \quad \delta c_{min}/\delta t_{min} > 0, \quad k_{min} < -|k_{min}| \tag{2}$$

It also turns out that in our cases, the mesh models are usually with holes, the crest lines that suppose to pass over the holes areas are missing after the crest line detection phase and need to be recovered by some way. Furthermore, since there is no surface information at the hole areas the detected crest lines in the hole vicinity are usually go incorrectly comparing to the case when the mesh model is complete. In our algorithm, the detected crest line information is used to interpolate the missing parts. Hence, in order to have the accurate interpolation results it is necessary to correct the crest information at the hole vicinities first before the interpolation is proceeded. We believe user intervention to correct the crest line information is the most efficient way and it is chosen in our method. An example of inaccurately detected crest lines at the hole's vicinity and the corrected ones by user through our GUI is showed in Fig. 2.

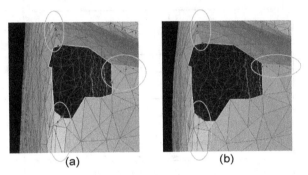

(a)   (b)

Fig. 2. (a) An example of inaccurate crest line detection at the hole area: detected crest lines and crest points are colored in green and blue correspondingly; (b) Crest lines are corrected by user intervention

3.3   Hole Identification

In the loading phase, all of the 1-ring neighbourhood and connected component information of vertices, edges and triangles of the input mesh model are calculated and stored in our designed data structures to facilitate further processing. Hence, at this step, all boundary edges can be easily identified by checking the numbers of their adjacent triangles, i.e. for an edge, if the number of its adjacent triangles is equal to one then that edge is a boundary edge. Its two end vertices are the boundary vertices and its adjacent triangle is the boundary triangle. Once the boundary edge is detected, its two end vertices are used as seeds to trace along the connected boundary edges and vertices. If all identified points form a closed loop they make up a hole.

3.4   Feature Line Interpolation

At this step, before doing the filling work, we attempt to recover the sharp features, i.e. the feature lines that suppose to pass over the hole areas. After the feature lines are interpolated, the holes are also subdivided by these feature lines into the smaller and more planar ones. This indeed facilitates the later hole filling procedure.

3.4.1 Basic Concepts
In our system convention, *feature points* are defined as the crest points, either *detected* or *interpolated*, that lie on the feature line segment passing over a hole.

Detected feature point is defined as the intersection point between the crest line, either ridge or ravine, with the hole boundary (see Fig. 3). Intersection point are the detected crest point, either ridge- or ravine- point, that lies on hole edge, also called boundary edge. *Interpolated feature point* is the feature point obtained during the feature line interpolation process. Figure 3 provides illustration of these concepts.

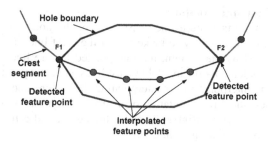

Fig. 3. An example of interpolating the feature lines over a hole using spline interpolation: the interpolated feature line is colored in blue, the interpolated feature points are colored in green

In the same way with Jun [10], we consider two types of holes: *simple hole* and *complex hole*. Simple holes are those that can be filled with planar triangulations, which is the case when all boundary edges can be projected into a plane, without self-intersection (as illustrated in Fig. 4(a)). It is not adequate to fill the complex hole with planar triangulations since there are usually self-intersections when projecting the complex hole boundaries into a plane (Fig. 4(b)). Thus, in our perspective, we attempt to properly subdivide the complex holes into simple ones in order to fill the holes by planar triangulation (see Section 3.4.4).

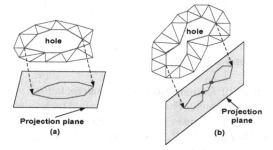

Fig. 4. Example of projecting holes onto planes: (a) Simple hole makes no self-intersections; (b) Complex hole creates self-intersections (colored in red) on the projection plane

3.4.2   User Intervention
Once feature points are detected in the previous step, some limited user intervention at feature level is needed

- to pair the detected feature points to avoid ambiguity for the case there are multiple feature lines passing over the hole;

- to adjust the inaccurately detected crest points to enhance the accuracy and the quality of the final result; and to specify the hole at the corner of the object model by specifying the triple of detected feature points lying on the hole boundary at the corner area.

3.4.3   Feature Line Interpolation

To interpolate the missing feature lines passing over the holes, the following issue should be addressed: since we try to make use of the crest line information which is automatically detected by the system, the interpolated feature lines passing over the hole should be interpolated by the available crest lines and crest points.

We choose spline interpolation for interpolating the feature lines at the hole areas. A spline is a mathematical representation of a curve. It consists of a series of points, called control points, at certain intervals along the curve, and a function that allows defining additional points within an interval.

Two requirements for the spline interpolation in our case are

1. The curve should pass through all the control points, as they define feature line, and its segments act as the edges in the polygonal mesh model;
2. It is necessary to be able to calculate the exact positions of missing control points of the spline based on the available ones.

There are various functions available for approximating a curve and Catmull-Rom spline is the one that satisfy the above requirements.

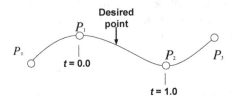

Fig. 5. The Catmull-Rom spline passes through all of its control points

Recall the properties of Catmull-Rom spline interpolation, a new point can be found between two control points. This point is specified by a value t that represents a proportion of the distance from one control point to the next one, as shown in Fig. 5. Given the control points P_0, P_1, P_2, P_3 and parameter t, $0 \le t \le 1.0$, we can compute the new point location q using the following equation:

$$q(t) = 0.5 * (1.0, t, t^2, t^3) * \begin{pmatrix} 0 & 2 & 0 & 0 \\ -1 & 0 & 1 & 0 \\ 2 & -5 & 4 & -1 \\ -1 & 3 & -3 & 1 \end{pmatrix} * \begin{pmatrix} P_0 \\ P_1 \\ P_2 \\ P_3 \end{pmatrix} \tag{3}$$

Figure 3 illustrates our method to interpolate a feature line passing over a hole using the detected crest line information. In our implementation, to interpolate a feature line passing over a hole, the pair of feature points on the hole boundary and their adjacent crest points make four initial control points for the Catmull-Rom interpolation equation (3). Since we attempt to interpolate a feature line that has the point density as consistent as possible to the original mesh, the value t that appears in equation (3) is approximated in our implementation as follow:

Given a hole that has n edges on its boundary. Denote $length(e_i)$ the length of boundary edge e_i; denote a the average edge length of the hole boundary. We have:

$$a = \frac{\sum_{i=1}^{n} length\ (e_i)}{n} \qquad (4)$$

Denote d the Euclidean distance between the feature points F_1 and F_2 then we have

$$t = \frac{d}{a} \qquad (5)$$

3.4.4   Hole Partitioning

Once all the feature lines at the holes are interpolated, a hole tracing procedure is executed. For each hole, the procedure starts with a vertex on the hole boundary, then it does the tracing along the connected boundary edges and its corresponding feature lines. If all identified points form a closed loop they make up a hole. By involving feature lines in the hole identification process at this step, the original complex holes are indeed subdivided into smaller, more planar and simpler sub-holes right at the feature line locations.

In [10], the author discusses the self-intersection problem when projecting a complex hole onto a plane. This means some edges on the hole boundary may overlap each other in the projection plane. In our system, since the holes are split at the salient feature curves, the sub-holes obtained are already quite planar. In addition, by using of the tangent plane of the hole boundary as its projection plane our approach avoids efficiently the self-intersection of the hole boundary.

3.5   Hole Filling

After all the polygonal holes in the original mesh model are identified, for each hole its boundary edges are then projected onto a projection plane for further triangulation.

3.5.1 Projection Plane Calculation

For each hole or sub-hole identified in the input mesh, we need to calculate the plane to project its boundary onto. The requirement for such a plane is that the projection of the boundary edges of a polygonal hole on it is a bounded domain and it should limit the possibility of creating the problem of self-intersecting of the projected boundary as much as possible.

We use the method to calculate the projection plane that is based on the maximum area vector method. The direction of the plane is derived from the normalized sum of the normals of the boundary triangles. The illustration of a hole and the direction of its projection plane are shown in Fig. 6. The formula for computing the normal N of the projection plane P for a hole is as follow:

$$N = \sum_{i=1}^{v} n_i \qquad (6)$$

where v is the number of the boundary triangles of the hole, n_i is the normal of the ith boundary triangle of the hole.

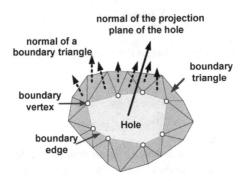

Fig. 6. An example of a hole and the direction of its projection plane

3.5.2 Filling Holes through Planar Triangulation

In our system, for each hole, once its boundary in the original mesh model are projected onto its corresponding projection plane, the projected boundary vertices are used as the input for the constrained Delaunay triangulation to get the patch mesh for the hole in 2D. The procedure of mapping back to 3D space of the patch mesh is done by applying the topological structure of the constructed 2D triangulation to the original 3D boundary.

4   Results and Validation

The visualization system Hole3D was developed as the implementation to demonstrate our user-guided feature sensitive hole filling system presented in this paper. The visualization and user interface were implemented in MS Visual Studio 2005 Development Environment with Coin3D (a high-level 3D graphics toolkit for developing cross-platform real-time 3D visualization and visual simulation software), VTK (the Visualization Toolkit) and MFC (Microsoft® Foundation Classes). The programming language used is C++.

We demonstrate how the proposed algorithm can be used to reconstruct hole regions. Basically, the test cases are processed in two mesh models, the moai model and the stripped fandisk model. Many possible cases of hole are created and filled by our system to verify its effectiveness.

Fig. 7 shows the input moai model with two holes and concave sharp edges at the neck area. The sharp features are recovered properly using our method. The patches stitched to the hole areas are marked with the yellow boundary. Although we do not implement mesh refinement and fairing techniques in our system, the patch is adequate to complete the model in expected way. Fig. 12 shows the result of filling a fandisk model with a concave corner hole (Fig. 12(a)). The final mesh model after applying our feature sensitive hole filling algorithm are displayed in Fig. 12(b)(c).

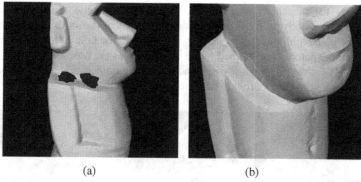

(a)   (b)

Fig. 7. Applied our algorithm: (a) The input moai model with two holes and concave sharp edges; (b) Hole filling result obtained in our system with user intervention to pair the feature points

As shown in Fig. 9, with the hole at the convex sharp edge, our system can achieve the proper results. Fig. 9(b) shows the hole filling result obtained automatically by our system without a user correcting the detected crest lines. Better result can be obtained with user interaction to correct the detected crest lines before interpolating feature lines passing over the hole as shown in Fig. 9(c).

We demonstrate the robustness of our system by comparing our experiment results with the results presented in papers [5] [19]. As shown in Fig. 10, there are three holes in fandisk mesh model, which has one, two and three ridges passed through them (Figure 10(a)). As presented in [19], the method in [12] can only close the holes (Fig. 10(b)), the method in [19] produces better result but the geometry at the corner hole is not recovered properly (Fig. 10(c)). Fig. 11 demonstrates the hole filling results for convex and concave corner holes obtained after applying the *sharpness dependent filter* hole filling method in [5].

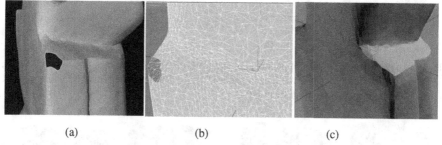

(a)   (b)   (c)

Fig. 8. Applied our algorithm: (a) The input moai model with a convex corner hole; (b) Our final hole filling result with polygonal presentation, the hole patch is colored in red; (c) Flat shaded render of the final result

To have a visual comparison with the aforementioned algorithms, as shown in Fig. 13, we applied our hole filling method to the fandisk model with holes at the same locations as in the input mesh model in Fig. 10 that reproduced from paper [19]. Indeed, the modified mesh model shows three typical kinds of holes that have sharp features need to be recovered: one hole with one feature line passing over, one hole with two feature lines passing over and one hole at the corner. The results of our hole filling technique are shown in Fig. 13: the sharp edges are recovered aesthetically; the corner shape is reconstructed consistently with the original shape. Fig. 13(b) shows the final hole filling result with the hole highlighted in green. Fig. 13(c) shows the hole filling result obtained by our system, the patches are stitched to the input mesh as the hole areas to get the final mesh model. The sharp features at the concave corner hole in Fig. 12 are recovered nicely using our method comparing to the result shown in Fig. 11(b).

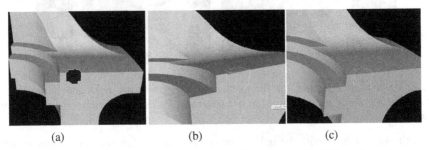

(a)   (b)   (c)

Fig. 9. Applied our algorithm: (a) The input stripped fan disk model with a hole on the convex sharp edge; (b) Our hole filling result without the user intervention to correct the detected crest points at the hole area; (c) Our hole filling result where the detected crest points are corrected at the hole area

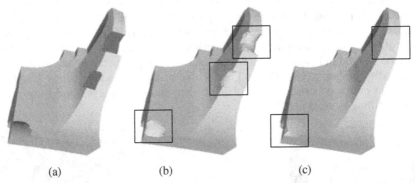

(a)   (b)   (c)

Fig. 10. Applied the algorithms in papers [12] and [19]: (a) The input mesh model with 3 holes; (b) The result obtained by using method in paper [12]; (c) The result obtained by using method in paper [19] (reproduced from paper [19]))

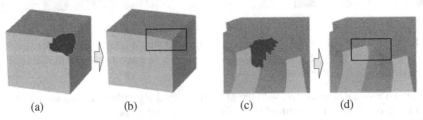

(a)   (b)   (c)   (d)

Fig. 11. Applied the hole filling algorithm in paper [5] to the holes at the corners: (a) A original mesh model with a convex corner hole; (b) The result after filling the hole in the model in (a); (c) A original mesh model with a concave corner hole; (d) The result after filling the hole in the model in (c) (reproduced from paper [5])

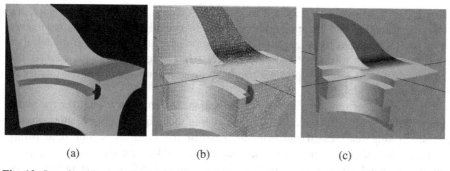

(a)   (b)   (c)

Fig. 12. Our algorithm results: (a) The input stripped fandisk model with a concave corner hole; (b) Our final hole filling result with polygonal presentation, the hole patch is colored in green; (d) Flat shaded render of the final result model

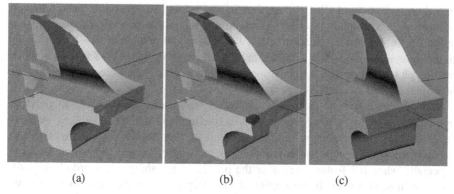

(a)   (b)   (c)

Fig. 13. Applied our algorithm to a fandisk model with 3 types of holes: (a) The original mesh model with 3 kinds of holes; (b) The final result obtained by our system with the highlighted patches; (c) Flat shaded render of the final mesh result

The experiments show that our method can produce excellent results for filling the holes at the corners. The mesh quality of the patches could be improved to make them more consistent with the original mesh quality by applying mesh refinement techniques.

5 Discussion

Certainly, fully automated methods for hole filling have several advantages over a method that requires user intervention. However, from the point of view of the complexity of the hole, a fully automated method may not work correctly for holes with complex geometries. Our research aims to combine manual and automatic methods to improve current hole-filling methods, making this process more versatile, robust and effective.

Most of the feature sensitive hole-filling methods rely significantly on the normals of the vertices around the hole areas to decide whether or not there exist fine features.

This makes those methods sensitive to the mesh quality, e.g. the point density, the shapes of triangles and the point distribution. In our algorithm, since the feature curves are interpolated from the salient information detected in the mesh model, user intervention allows to correct the detected crest line information. This enables the whole algorithm to produce the final results quite independently from the quality of the input mesh model.

The core idea of our algorithm using the salient information to recover the sharp feature is simple but effective. Among the existing techniques that have attempted to reconstruct fine features of the original mesh at the hole areas, our hole filling techniques is different since the fine features are taken as the first subjects to reconstruct, which eventually drive the feature-definite surface filling process. Our results show the effectiveness of our method in filling the hole and preserving aesthetically the sharp edges.

The accuracy of our method depends to a great extent on the accuracy of the crest line detection method. We expect that improvements in crest line detection will produce a higher quality results from a fully automatic procedure based on our approach. In our implementation, all of the salient and polygonal-based information of the input mesh model are extracted and stored in our designed data structures in the loading phase then further computation is limited to areas near holes. This makes the algorithm efficient to run on large models.

Our system improves the visual quality of the results with respect to previous approaches and provides real-time user interaction. On the other hand, it strongly relies on crest line detection, and therefore it is very sensitive to changes in this geometrical feature. Our system is able to recover efficiently the sharp features, especially when the feature curves or the profile of the sharp edges are close to the cubic splines. However, if the profile of the sharp edges in the input mesh is more complex than cubic splines, the results may not be necessarily accurate and may even be far from the real geometry.

Further mesh refinement and fairing methods may be used to improve the quality of the generated patch meshes. By doing this, the point density and triangle shape in the patch mesh will be more consistent with the input mesh.

Our feature-first strategy can be easily applied to edge-area inpainting. As an example in many movies, actors/actresses use wire techniques to perform certain actions (e.g. flying, jumping) and the wire needs to remove as a post-processing. After deleting pixels corresponding to wire in the image, a conventional method is to fill the gap with surrounding pixel by smoothing. However this does not guarantee the sharp edges to be revived. Our feature-first strategy can be applied here, first by detecting sharp features and then do the filling process by smoothing and then overlaying the features on top of it.

6   Conclusions

We have presented a novel technique for filling holes in 3D triangulated mesh models which is able to recover efficiently the sharp features of the original geometry, producing plausible results which are consistent with the geometry of the original mesh models. For each input mesh, our system identifies its holes and crest line information. Then it uses this information to interpolate the feature curves at the hole areas. These curves then geometrically segment complex holes into simple approximately planar holes, called sub-holes. The patch meshes that are used to fill those sub-holes are generated by using planar triangulation algorithm for the point set at the hole boundaries. Then these patch meshes are mapped back to the 3D space and stitched to the original model at the hole areas to achieve the final result. The user is able to interact with our system through correcting the crest lines, adjusting the feature points defined by the crest lines and the hole boundaries, pairing the feature points or specifying the corner hole locations. The adjustment of the location of the crest lines by users results in modification in the shape of the patch mesh which is later stitched to the original model, as holes are filled using different geometric information. To validate our approach, we have tested our technique on different mesh models with many possible cases, and the results show that our methods effectively reconstruct the sharp features. Most approaches for hole filling in literature do not reconstruct these fine details due to the interpolation schemes used. We overcome this limitation by including additional information on the object shape in areas of high curvature and by some limited user intervention.

References

1. Attene, M., Falcidieno, B., Rossignac, J., Spagnuolo, M.: Edge-Sharpener: Recovering Sharp Features in Triangulations of Non-adaptively Re-meshed Surfaces. In: Proceedings of the First Eurographics Symposium Geometry Processing (SGP 2003), pp. 63–72. Eurographics Association, Aire-la-Ville (2003)
2. Barequet, G., Kumar, S.: Repairing CAD Models. In: Proceedings of the 8th Conference on Visualization 1997, pp. 363–371. IEEE Computer Society Press, Los Alamitos (1997)
3. Barequet, G., Dickerson, M., Eppstein, D.: On triangulating three-dimensional polygons. Journal Computational Geometry: Theory and Applications 10(3), 155–170 (1998)
4. Chen, C.-Y., Cheng, K.-Y.: A sharpness-dependent filter for recovering sharp features in repaired 3D mesh models. IEEE Transactions on Visualization and Computer Graphics 14(1), 200–212 (2008)
5. Chen, C.-Y., Cheng, K.-Y., Liao, H.Y.M.: A Sharpness Dependent Approach to 3D Polygon Mesh Hole Filling. In: Proceedings of Annual Conference European Association on Computer Graphics (Eurographics 2005), Short Presentations, pp. 13–16 (2005)
6. Chew, P.L.: Guaranteed-Quality Triangular Meshes. Technical report 89-983, Department of Computer Science. Cornell University, Ithaca, NY (1989)
7. Chui, C.K., Lai, M.-J.: Filling Polygonal Holes Using C^1 Cubic Triangular Spline Patches. Journal of Computer Aided Geometric Design 17(4), 297–307 (2000)
8. Dunlop, R.: Introduction to Catmull-Rom Splines. Technical articles, Microsoft DirectX MVP (2005), http://www.mvps.org/directx/articles/catmull/
9. He, X.J., Chen, Y.H.: A Haptics-guided Hole-filling System Based on Triangular Mesh. Computer Aided Design and Application 3(6), 711–718 (2006)
10. Jun, Y.: A Piecewise Hole Filling Algorithm in Reverse Engineering. Computer-Aided Design 37(2), 263–270 (2005)

11. Kobbelt, L.P., Botsch, M., Schwanecke, U., Seidel, H.-P.: Feature Sensitive Surface Extraction from Volume Data. In: Proceedings of the 28th Annual Conference on Computer Graphics and Interative Techniques (SIGGRAPH 2001), pp. 57–66. ACM, New York (2001)
12. Liepa, P.: Filling holes in Meshes. In: Proceedings of the 2003 Eurographics/ACM SIGGRAPH Symposium on Geometry Processing, pp. 200–205. Eurographics Association, Aire-la-Ville (2003)
13. Ohtake, Y., Belyaev, A., Alexa, M., Turk, G., Seidel, H.-P.: Multi-level Partition of Unity Implicits. Journal of ACM Transaction on Graphics (TOG) - Proceedings of ACM SIGGRAPH 2003 22(3), 463–470 (2003)
14. Podolak, P., Rusinkiewicz, S.: Atomic Volumes for Mesh Completion. In: Proceedings of the 3rd Eurographics Symposium on Geometry Processing, Eurographics Association Aire-la-Ville, Switzeland (2005)
15. Sharf, A., Alexa, M., Cohen-Or, D.: Context-based Surface Completion. Journal of ACM Transactions on Graphics – Proceedings of ACM SIGGRAPH 2004 23(3) (2004)
16. Yoshizawa, S., Belyaev, A.G., Seidel, H.-P.: Fast and Robust Detection of Crest Lines on Meshes. In: Proceedings of the 2005 ACM Symposium on Solid and Physical Modeling, pp. 227–232. ACM, New York (2005)
17. Yoshizawa, S., Belyaev, A., Yokota, H., Seidel, H.-P.: Fast and Faithful Geometric Algorithm for Detecting Crest Lines on Meshes. In: Proceedings of the 15th Pacific Conference on Graphics Applications, pp. 231–237. Computer Society, Washington, DC (2007)
18. Zhao, W., Gao, S., Lin, H.: A Robust Hole-Filling Algorithm for Triangular Mesh. Journal of the Visual Computer: International Journal of Computer Graphics 23(12), 987–997 (2007)
19. Zhao, M., Ma, L., Mao, Z., Li, Z.: Feature Sensitive Hole Filling with Crest Lines. In: Jiao, L., Wang, L., Gao, X.-b., Liu, J., Wu, F. (eds.) ICNC 2006. LNCS, vol. 4222, pp. 660–663. Springer, Heidelberg (2006)

Inhomogeneous Axial Deformation for Orthopedic Surgery Planning

Sergei Azernikov

Siemens Corporate Research, 755 College Road East, Princeton NJ 08540, U.S.A.
sergaz@gmail.com

Abstract. Intuitive global deformation of complex geometries is very important for many applications. In particular, in the biomedical domain, where interactive manipulation of 3D organic shapes is becoming an increasingly common task. Axial deformation is natural and powerful approach for modeling of tubular structures, like bones. With this approach, the embedding space is associated with deformable curve, the handle axis, which guides deformation of the embedded model. As a result, the produced deformation is homogeneous and independent of the model representation and shape. However, in many situations it is beneficial to incorporate geometric and physical properties of the model into the deformation formulation. This leads to *inhomogeneous* axial deformation which allows to achieve more intuitive results with less user interaction. In this work, the inhomogeneous axial deformation is achieved through *deformation distribution function (DDF)* induced on the guiding axis by the embedded model. Since with the proposed formulation the DDF can be pre-computed, run-time computational complexity of the method is similar to the original axial deformation approach.

Keywords. Feature preserving spatial deformation, Weighted arc-length curve parametrization, Orthopedic surgery planning.

1 Introduction

Growing amount of available high definition 3D data opens broad opportunities in many different areas. In particular in biomedical domain, increasing number of procedures are planned and executed in computer-aided environment using 3D models of patient's anatomy. Manipulation of these anatomical models, however, often requires new tools and methods, which are not provided in the traditional geometric modeling systems (see for example [1]).

One of the earliest yet powerful and intuitive methods for shape manipulation is spatial deformation pioneered by Barr [2]. Later, Sederberg and Parry [3] extended the spectrum of possible deformations by introducing the free-form deformation (FFD) approach. Due to its attractive properties and conceptual simplicity this approach was extensively used in geometric modeling and computer animation [4]. The basic idea of the FFD approach is to parameterize the embedding space as a tri-variate tensor product volume. The shape of this volume can be manipulated by grid of control points. Once control points are repositioned, the volume is warped and the embedded objects

G. Csurka et al. (Eds.): VISIGRAPP 2011, CCIS 274, pp. 69–85, 2013.

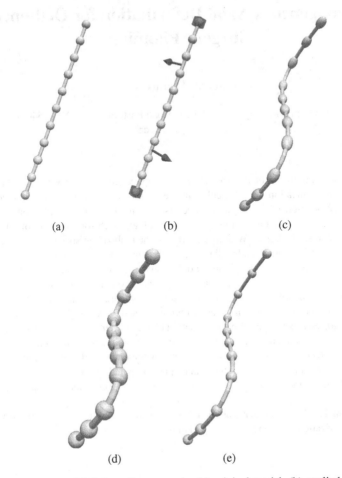

Fig. 1. Inhomogeneous axial deformation example: (a) original model, (b) applied deformation and constraints cause stretching, (c) homogeneous axial deformation produces distortion of the spheres, (d) scaling can prevent distortion but modifies size of the spheres, and(e) proposed inhomogeneous axial deformation preserves shape and size of the spheres, while transferring the deformation to cylindrical regions invulnerable to stretching

are deformed accordingly. The drawback of the grid-based FFD is that because of the high number of control points that should be moved, it may require significant user interaction even for simple deformations. In order to reduce the amount of required user interaction, lower dimensional variations of the original trivariate FFD method were introduced: surface deformation [5] and axial deformation (AxDf) [6]. With the AxDf approach, the ambient space deformation is guided by axial curve, which can be represented as a straight segment chain [6] or parametric curve [7]. The major drawback of spatial deformation is that it is global, and as such, does not preserve shape of the local features.

Recently, mesh-based deformation techniques gained popularity in the computer graphics community [8, 9]. These techniques are formulated directly on the polygonal mesh and explicitly designed to preserve local surface features. From the user perspective, with these techniques the deformable object behaves like elastic *homogeneous* material.

Popa et al. [10] applied material-aware scheme for mesh deformation assigning stiffness property to various regions of the mesh. As a result, the deformation is non-uniformly distributed. Kraevoy et al. [11] proposed a method for feature-sensitive scaling of 3D shapes. With this approach, the embedding volume is voxelized and scaling function is evaluated in each voxel based on the embedded shape variation. When scaling is applied, the deformation is distributed in a non-uniform manner according to the assigned scaling function values. These methods attempt to mimic behavior of elastic *inhomogeneous* material. The work described in this paper is inspired by this idea and introduces inhomogeneous axial deformation framework.

2 Inhomogeneous Axial Deformation

When the handle axis length is modified during the modeling session, the aspect ratio of the deformed object is naturally modified as well. Since the deformation is global, the stretching is distributed equally along the axis. Although this behavior is often perfectly desired, it may cause distortion of local features as shown in Figure 1(c). One way to deal with this problem is to scale the model to compensate for the length change. This, however, may lead to non-intuitive results, as can be seen in Figure 1(d). In order to overcome this issue, the *inhomogeneous* axial deformation formulation is proposed in this paper. The basic idea is to redistribute the deformation along the axis such that most of the distortion is applied on invulnerable portions of the model. This behavior attempts to mimic the physical behavior of an inhomogeneous bar under axial load [12], which is briefly described in Section 2.1. Based on this analogy, deformation distribution function (DDF) is introduced in Section 2.3. In order to prevent distortion of the model features, the axial curve is re-parameterized according to the DDF, as described in Section 2.2. Section 2.5 describes embedding of the model into the axial parametric space. When the axial curve is deformed, its deformation is transferred to the embedded model following the established embedding. The flow chart of the proposed deformation method is shown in Figure 2.

2.1 Inhomogeneous Bar Deformation under Axial Load

Let B be a bar with variable cross section $A(t), , t \in [0,1]$ and length L, as shown in Figure 3. The local deformation δs of B under axial load P can be computed as [12]:

$$\delta s(t) = \int_0^t \frac{P}{E(t)A(t)} dt, \tag{1}$$

where $E(t)$ is the Young modulus of the bar [12]. Introducing stiffness notion $k(t) = A(t)E(t)$ and assuming constant force $P = const$,

$$\delta s(t) = P \int_0^t k^{-1}(t) dt. \tag{2}$$

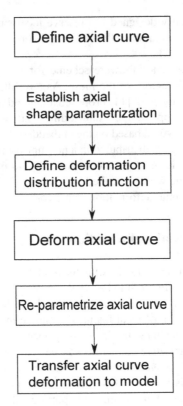

Fig. 2. Flow chart of the proposed deformation method

Then, the total deformation of the bar is

$$\delta L = P \int_0^1 k^{-1}(t)dt. \tag{3}$$

In the inverse problem, total deformation δL of the bar is given, when local deformation and stress should be found. Then, the local deformation $\delta s(t)$ can be rewritten in terms of the given total deformation and bar's properties,

$$\delta s(t) = \delta L \frac{\int_0^t k^{-1}(t)dt}{\int_0^1 k^{-1}(t)dt}. \tag{4}$$

Let $w(t) \in [0,1]$ be the *deformation distribution function (DDF)* along the bar such that,

$$w(t) = \frac{\int_0^t k^{-1}(t)dt}{\int_0^1 k^{-1}(t)dt}. \tag{5}$$

Then Eq. (4) can be rewritten in a more compact form,

$$\delta s(t) = \delta L w(t). \tag{6}$$

For the uniform case when $k(t) = const$,

$$w(t) = \frac{\int_0^t dt}{\int_0^1 dt} = t. \tag{7}$$

The local deformation $\delta s(t)$ is then reduces to the uniform scaling,

$$\delta s(t) = \delta L t, t \in [0,1]. \tag{8}$$

Similar results can be obtained for inhomogeneous bar under torsion [12]. By replacing the local stretching $\delta s(t)$ with local rotation angle $\delta \theta(t)$ and total length change with total rotation angle $\delta \Theta$, Eq. (6) can be rewritten as,

$$\delta \theta(t) = \delta \Theta w(t). \tag{9}$$

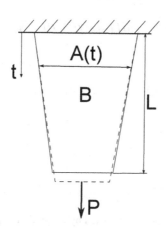

Fig. 3. Bar with variable cross section under axial load

2.2 Deformation Distribution Function

Function $w(t)$ controls deformation distribution along the handle axis. With the proposed approach, $w(t)$ is designed to avoid distortion of the important features of the model while obeying the boundary conditions imposed by the user. Kraevoy et al. [11] estimate local *vulnerability* of the model to non-uniform scaling as a combination of slippage measure [13] and normal curvature in the direction of deformation. Since in our case the deformation of the model M is guided by the axial curve $C(t)$, the proposed vulnerability measure is based on shape variation of M along $C(t)$. Assuming that length preserving bending does not introduce distortion as long as $C(t)$ remains smooth, axial deformation can produce two types of distortion:

1. **Stretching:** by modifying the total length of $C(t)$.
2. **Torsion:** by imposing twist around the $C(t)$.

Stretching will not introduce any distortion in regions where the cross section of the model $\chi_M(t)$ is constant along $C(t)$. Therefore, for regions with constant cross section the vulnerability to stretching $v_{\delta L}(t)$ should be close to zero, and where cross section is rapidly changing, $v_{\delta L}(t)$ should be high. In other words, $v_{\delta L}(t)$ is proportional to the gradient of $\chi_M(t)$ along $C(t)$,

$$v_{\delta L}(t) \sim \|\nabla \chi_M(t)\| \tag{10}$$

In order to compute the vulnerability to stretching, difference between two subsequent cross sections χ_1 and χ_2 is defined as integral of point-to-point distances, when χ_1 and χ_2 are projected on the same plane (see Figure 4):

$$diff_{axial}(\chi_1,\chi_2) \triangleq \int_\theta dist(\theta)d\theta. \tag{11}$$

Using this definition, $v_{\delta L}(t)$ is computed as,

$$v_{\delta L}(t) = diff_{axial}(\chi(t),\chi(t+\delta t)). \tag{12}$$

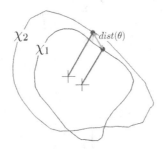

Fig. 4. Cross section difference is computed by integration of point-to-point distances

On the other hand, torsion should be allowed where the shape contour is close to circular and prevented elsewhere to avoid distortion. So, the vulnerability to torsion $v_{\delta\Theta}(t)$ can be estimated integrating the magnitude of radius gradient across the shape profile $\chi(t)$,

$$v_{\delta\Theta}(t) \sim \int_{\chi(t)} \|\nabla r_{\chi(t)}\|, \tag{13}$$

where $r_{\chi(t)}$ is the local radius of the shape contour $\chi(t)$ as shown in Figure 5. In the current implementation, the vulnerability to torsion $v_{\delta\Theta}(t)$ at the contour χ is computed as,

$$v(\chi)_{\delta\Theta} \triangleq \int_\theta (r_{\theta+\delta\theta} - r_\theta)^2 d\theta \tag{14}$$

Replacing stiffness $k(t)$ in Eq. (5) with the above vulnerability measures, deformation distribution functions (DDFs) $w_{\delta L}(t)$ and $w_{\delta\Theta}(t)$ can be can be formulated as,

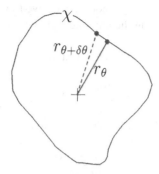

Fig. 5. Cross section radius change

$$w_{\delta L}(t) = \frac{\int_0^t v_{\delta L}^{-1}(t)dt}{\int_0^1 v_{\delta L}^{-1}(t)dt},$$ (15)

$$w_{\delta\Theta}(t) = \frac{\int_0^t v_{\delta\Theta}^{-1}(t)dt}{\int_0^1 v_{\delta\Theta}^{-1}(t)dt}.$$ (16)

The resulted DDF for stretching is presented on Figure 6.

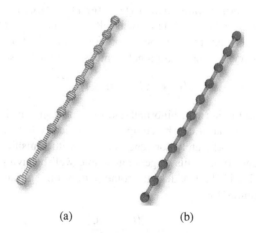

(a)   (b)

Fig. 6. Deformation Distribution Function (DDF) on the cylinders model: (a) extracted cross sections, (b) DDF color mapping

These functions are used to define weighted arc-length parametrization of the axial curve $C(t)$ and to establish weighted rotation minimizing frame along $C(t)$.

2.3   Weighted Arc-Length Parametrization

Arc-length preserving axial deformation produces natural results and therefore very useful in animation [7]. However, when the length of the model is modified in purpose, arc-length of the axial curve $C(t)$ cannot be preserved everywhere. However, it can be preserved *locally* by weighting the arc-length change with deformation distribution function (DDF) $w_{\delta L}(t)$.

The curve $C(t)$ is initially parameterized w.r.t. its arc-length $s(t)$ such that [14],

$$t = \frac{s(t)}{L}, t \in [0, 1], \tag{17}$$

where L is the total length of the curve. When L is modified by δL, the new parametrization $\tilde{t}$ is computed as follows:

$$\tilde{t} = \frac{s(t) + \delta s(t)}{L + \delta L}, \tag{18}$$

where $\delta s(t)$ is the weighted local deformation,

$$\delta s(t) = w_{\delta L}(t)\delta L. \tag{19}$$

This new parametrization is used to transfer the deformation of the axial curve $C(t)$ to the model M, as will be explained in Section 2.5. As a result, the deformation δL is redistributed according to the DDF $w_{\delta L}(t)$.

2.4   Weighted Rotation Minimizing Frame

Establishing an appropriate frame field $F(t) = (e_1(t), e_2(t), e_3(t))$ is a basic task in curve design and analysis [15]. While e_3 is usually associated with the tangent vector of the curve, another axis has to be defined in order to set up the frame field completely. In differential geometry, the classical Frenet frame is commonly used,

$$(e_1, e_2, e_3) \triangleq (n, b, t), \tag{20}$$

where n, b and t are the normal, binormal and tangent respectively [16]. The advantage of Frenet frame is that it can be computed analytically for any point on a twice differentiable curve. Unfortunately, for general curves with vanishing second derivative or high torsion, Frenet frame fails to generate stable well-behaving frame field. As a better alternative, Klok [17] introduced the rotation minimizing frame (RMF), which is formulated in differential form,

$$e_1' = -\frac{(C'' \cdot e_1)C'}{\|C'\|^2}, \tag{21}$$

with initial condition $e_1(0) = e_1^0$. Although no analytic solution is available in that case, there is a simple and effective method to approximate RMF by discretizing the curve and propagating the first frame defined by the initial condition e_1^0 along the curve [17].

With additional boundary constraint $e_1(1) = e_1^1$, twist has to be introduced into the RMF (see Figure 7). The twisting angle $\delta\Theta$ is then propagated along the axis according to the parameter $t \in [0, 1]$,

$$\delta\theta(t) = \delta\Theta t. \tag{22}$$

The resulted frame field is shown in Figure 7(b).

As was already mentioned, imposing twist may distort certain features of the model. This effect is demonstrated in Figure 7(a). Using the proposed inhomogeneous approach, the twist $\delta\theta(t)$ distribution will be adapted to the DDF $w_{\delta\theta}(t)$,

$$\delta\theta(t) = \delta\Theta w_{\delta\theta}(t). \tag{23}$$

With this weighted torsion distribution, shown in Figure 7(d), the distortion of the features is avoided and applied in the invulnerable regions, as can be seen in Figure 7(c).

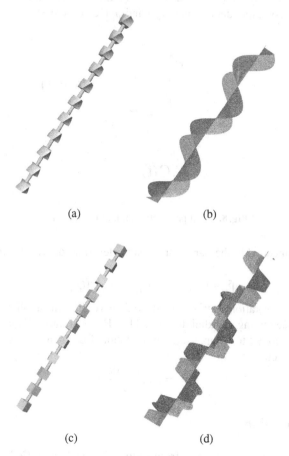

(a)   (b)

(c)   (d)

Fig. 7. Comparison of Klok's RMF with the proposed weighted RMF: (a),(b) RMF creates distortion of the cubes, (c),(d) the proposed weighted RMF preserves the cubes while obeying the twist angle

2.5   Model Embedding and Deformation Transfer

One of the important advantages of spatial deformation in general, and axial deformation in particular, is its independence of the deformed model M representation [2]. M's shape is assumed to be completely defined by position of finite set of control points $P = \{\mathbf{p}_i(x, y, z), i = 0..n)\}$. For polygonal meshes, P is the list of the vertices, while for parametric surfaces, P will represent the control points.

The axial deformation consists of two mapping $\mathbb{R}^3 \mapsto \mathbb{R}^3$ [6]:

1. Embedding of the model M in parametric space of the axial curve $C(t)$.
2. Transfer of the deformation from $C(t)$ to M.

To embed the model M in the parametric space, each control point $\mathbf{p}_i \in M$ is equipped with triple $(t_{\mathbf{p}_i}, \theta(t_{\mathbf{p}_i}), r(t_{\mathbf{p}_i}))$, where $t_{\mathbf{p}_i}$ is parameter of the handle axis $C(t)$, $\theta(t_{\mathbf{p}_i})$ is the rotation angle relative to the moving frame defined in Section 2.4, and $r(t_{\mathbf{p}_i})$ is the distance between correspondent point $C(t_{\mathbf{p}_i})$ and $\mathbf{p}_i$ (see Figure 8).

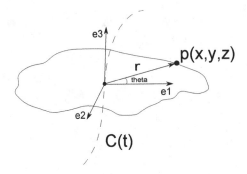

Fig. 8. Axial parametrization of the model

Once M is embedded in the parametric space, deformation transfer from $C(t)$ to M is straight forward,

$$\tilde{\mathbf{p}}_i = C(t_{\mathbf{p}_i}) + R(\theta_{t_{\mathbf{p}_i}}) \mathbf{e}_1(t_{\mathbf{p}_i}) r(t_{\mathbf{p}_i}), \tag{24}$$

where $R(\theta_{t_{\mathbf{p}_i}})$ is the rotation matrix around axial curve. In some applications, it may be useful to introduce scaling in radial direction [18]. For example in Figure 1(d), uniform radial scaling is applied to compensate for stretching δL. Then, $r(t)$ is multiplied by a constant scaling factor,

$$\tilde{r}(t) = r(t) \frac{L + \delta L}{L}. \tag{25}$$

3   Implementation

The axial deformation session starts from setting the axial curve $C(t)$ and associating control points $P = \{\mathbf{p}_i, i = 1..n\}$ of the model M with this curve. First, M is oriented such that z axis is aligned with its maximal principal component. Afterwards, $C(t)$ is initialized to the center line of M's bounding box, as shown in Figure 10(a). Thus, parameter t_{p_i} of the control point $\mathbf{p}_i$ can be directly computed from z_{p_i},

$$t_{p_i} = \frac{z_{p_i}}{z_{max} - z_{min}}. \tag{26}$$

These values are associated with each control point and stored. In addition, initial curve length $L = z_{max} - z_{min}$ is stored.

Afterwards, the model M is sliced with m planes perpendicular to the center line and the shape profiles are stored (see Figure 10(b). Based on these profiles, vulnerability measures $v_{\delta L}$ and $v_{\delta \Theta}$ are estimated for each profile using Eqs. (10) (13). And DDFs $w_{\delta L}$ and $w_{\delta \Theta}$ are computed using Eq. (15) and stored.

When the axial curve $C(t)$ is modified to $\tilde{C}(t)$, it is re-parameterized according to the new arc-length and the stored $w_{\delta L}$ DDF using Eq. (18). If twist deformation is introduced, it is distributed according to the pre-computed $w_{\delta \Theta}$ function.

For initially curved models it may be more intuitive to initialize $C(t)$ to follow the shape of the model [6]. One simple approach is to extract shape profiles parallel to some pre-defined plane and to fit $C(t)$ to the centers of these profiles (see Figure 9). In that case, several practical questions arise. First, for each control point **p** closest

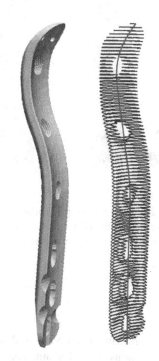

Fig. 9. Axis computation for initially curved plate

point on $C(t)$ has to be found, which may take significant computational effort for big models [18]. Second, models with complex topology (see for example model shown in Figure 12) may require special treatment in order to compute stable axial curve. Moreover, this simple approach may fail completely for certain models. In that case, a complete skeletonization should be applied [19] and the resulting skeleton curve may be used as the deformation axis.

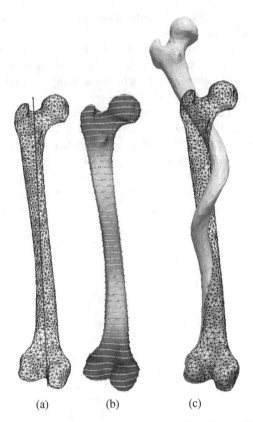

       (a)   (b)   (c)

Fig. 10. Femur model embedding and deformation: (a) handle axis initialized to the center line, (b) mesh vertices are parameterized along the center line and model profiles are extracted, (c) deformation transfer from the axis to the model; notice the shape preservation of the femoral head and the knee joint

4 Applications

The major motivation for this work came from bone modeling for orthopedic surgery planning. Currently, most interventions are still planned based on the pre-operative 2D X-ray images. Although significant amount of research work was dedicated to 3D orthopedic surgery planning [20], it is assumed that pre-operative 3D image of the patient's anatomy is available. Unfortunately, this is not always the case. One way to overcome this issue is to recover 3D geometry from the available 2D data. This can be done by overlaying a template bone model on the image and deforming the model to approximate patient's pathology [21]. Figure 11 shows tibia deformity that is going to be treated with Ilizarov spatial frame [22]. In order to simulate this procedure, 3D tibia model is deformed to match the available 2D image using the proposed inhomogeneous AxDf approach. With this approach, tibia features can be automatically preserved during the deformation, without explicit user specified constraints, as can be seen in Figure 11.

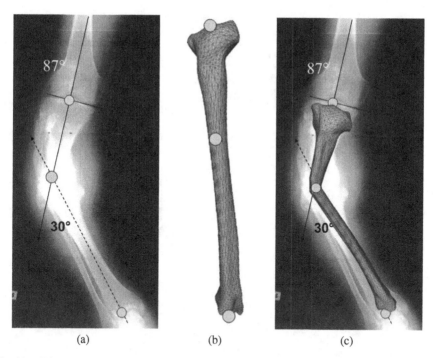

(a)   (b)   (c)

Fig. 11. Tibia deformity modeling: (a) X-ray image of the tibia pathology, (b) template tibia model, and (c) overlay of the deformed 3D tibia on the 2D image

Due to its feature preserving property, the proposed approach is also used for implant modeling for pre-operative planning of fracture reduction and fixation. Figure 12 shows how shape of the implant holes is preserved under axial load with the proposed inhomogeneous axial deformation method. This is important since distortion of the holes will make it difficult or impossible insertion of the fixation screws. Fracture care systems that are currently in clinical use perform planning in 2D and require manual reduction of the fracture and fitting of the implant to the bone. With the proposed semi-automatic implant placement, the surgeon just needs to mark region on the bone where the implant should be placed. Then, the system will automatically adapt the implant's shape and size to the bone, as shown in Figure 13. This is achieved by computing implant path on the bone from the provided guiding points using the shortest-path algorithm [23]. From the computed path, plate length is estimated and the appropriate plate is chosen automatically from the implant library. Finally, the chosen plate is deformed preserving shape of the holes, while the path is used as the deformation axis.

Generality of the axial deformation scheme allows to utilize the proposed approach with various shape representations. Most existing CAD systems use NURBS for freeform geometry modeling and representation. Figure 14 shows adaptation of a complex femoral plate in the *native* NURBS representation. In the future, this feature will allow direct CNC machining of patient-specific plates for osteosynthesis procedures, which will significantly reduce the burden from the operating surgeon.

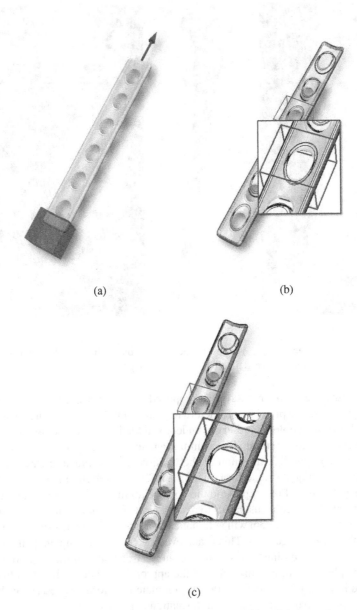

(a)   (b)

(c)

Fig. 12. Plate deformation (original model is shown as solid and deformed as wire frame): (a) plate with shown boundary conditions, (b) after simple scaling holes are distorted, (c) with inhomogeneous deformation shape of the holes is preserved; notice the precise matching of the hole after deformation

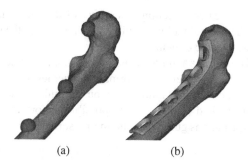

(a)   (b)

Fig. 13. Semi-automatic implant placement on the femoral bone: (a) guiding points placed by the user, (b) appropriate plate is automatically picked from the implant database and deformed to fit the bone

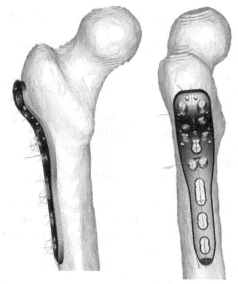

Fig. 14. NURBS model of a complex plate adapted to the femoral bone

5 Conclusions and Future Work

In this paper, inhomogeneous axial deformation was introduced and demonstrated on a number of important applications in orthopedic surgery planning. The proposed method inherits all the attractive properties of the classical axial deformation and introduces shape sensitivity to the original formulation. This allows to preserve shape and size of the features while reducing required user interaction. Moreover, due to the generality of axial deformation, the proposed method can be employed with various shape representations. In this work, polygonal meshes and NURBS were utilized.

Currently, only shape of the model is used for the DDF formulation. However, physical material properties can be easily incorporated into the proposed framework.

Another promising research direction is learning of deformation modes from provided examples [10]. This would allow intelligent adaptation of the deformation distribution functions to the specific domain.

By definition, AxDf supports a limited class of deformations. The proposed approach can be extended to handle more general deformation schemes. In particular, it would be interesting to combine the proposed inhomogeneous formulation with the sweep-based freeform deformation method [18]. It is also possible to formulate two-dimensional DDFs to consider deformations guided by parametric surfaces [5].

References

1. Azernikov, S.: Sweeping solids on manifolds. In: Haines, E., McGuire, M. (eds.) Proceedings of the 2008 ACM Symposium on Solid and Physical Modeling, June 2-4, pp. 249–255. ACM, Stony Brook (2008)
2. Barr, A.H.: Global and local deformations of solid primitives. In: ACM Computer Graphics SIGGRAPH 1984, pp. 21–30 (1984)
3. Sederberg, T.W., Parry, S.R.: Free-form deformation of solid geometric models. In: Evans, D.C., Athay, R.J. (eds.) Computer Graphics (SIGGRAPH 1986 Proceedings), Dallas, Texas, vol. 20, pp. 151–160 (1986)
4. Gain, J.E., Bechmann, D.: A survey of spatial deformation from a user-centered perspective. ACM Trans. Graph. 27 (2008)
5. Feng, J., Ma, L., Peng, Q.: A new free-form deformation through the control of parametric surfaces. Computers & Graphics 20, 531–539 (1996)
6. Lazarus, F., Coquillart, S., Jancène, P.: Axial deformations: an intuitive deformation technique. Computer-Aided Design 26, 607–613 (1994)
7. Peng, Q., Jin, X., Feng, J.: Arc-length-based axial deformation and length preserved animation. IEEE Computer Society (1997)
8. Sorkine, O.: Laplacian mesh processing. In: Chrysanthou, Y., Magnor, M. (eds.) STAR Proceedings of Eurographics 2005, pp. 53–70. Eurographics Association, Dublin (2005)
9. Lipman, Y., Sorkine, O., Levin, D., Cohen-Or, D.: Linear rotation-invariant coordinates for meshes. ACM Transactions on Graphics 24, 479–487 (2005)
10. Popa, T., Julius, D., Sheffer, A.: Material-aware mesh deformations. In: Shape Modeling International. IEEE Computer Society (2006)
11. Kraevoy, V., Sheffer, A., Shamir, A., Cohen-Or, D.: Non-homogeneous resizing of complex models. ACM Trans. Graph. 27, 111 (2008)
12. Timoshenko, S.: Theory of Elasticity. McGraw Hill (1970)
13. Gelfand, N., Guibas, L.J.: Shape segmentation using local slippage analysis. In: Fellner, D., Spencer, S. (eds.) Proceedings of the 2004 Eurographics/ACM SIGGRAPH Symposium on Geometry Processing (SGP-2004), pp. 219–228. Eurographics Association, Aire-la-Ville (2004)
14. do Carmo, M.P.: Differential Geometry of Curves and Surfaces. Prentice-Hall, Inc. (1976)
15. Farin, G.: Curves and Surfaces for Computer-Aided Geometric Design - A Practical Guide. Academic Press (1997)
16. Koenderink, J.J.: Solid Shape. MIT Press (1990)
17. Klok, F.: Two moving coordinate frames for sweeping along a 3D, trajectory. Computer Aided Geometric Design 3, 217–229 (1986)

18. Yoon, S.-H., Kim, M.-S.: Sweep-based freeform deformations. Computer Graphics Forum 25, 487–496 (2006)
19. Au, O.K.-C., Tai, C.-L., Chu, H.-K., Cohen-Or, D., Lee, T.-Y.: Skeleton extraction by mesh contraction. ACM Trans. Graph. 27, 1–10 (2008)
20. Hazan, E., Joskowicz, L.: Computer-assisted image-guided intramedullary nailing of femoral shaft fractures. Techniques in Orthopedics 18 (2003)
21. Messmer, P., Long, G., Suhm, N., Regazzoni, P., Jacob, A.L.: Volumetric model determination of the tibia based on radiographs using 2d/3d database. Computer Aided Surgery 6, 183–194 (2001)
22. Rozbruch, S.R., Fragomen, A.T., Ilizarov, S.: Correction of tibial deformity with use of the ilizarov-taylor spatial frame. Journal of Bone and Joint Surgery 88, 156–174 (2006)
23. Surazhsky, V., Surazhsky, T., Kirsanov, D., Gortler, S.J., Hoppe, H.: Fast exact and approximate geodesics on meshes. ACM Trans. Graph. 24, 553–560 (2005)

Modelling of 3D Objects Using Unconstrained and Uncalibrated Images Taken with a Handheld Camera

Minh Hoang Nguyen[1], Burkhard Wünsche[1], Patrice Delmas[2], and Christof Lutteroth[1]

[1] University of Auckland, Dept. of Computer Science, Graphics Group
Private Bag 92019, Auckland, New Zealand
hngu039@aucklanduni.ac.nz, {burkhard,lutteroth}@cs.auckland.ac.nz
[2] University of Auckland, Dept. of Computer Science, Intelligent Vision Group
Private Bag 92019, Auckland, New Zealand
p.delmas@auckland.ac.nz

Abstract. 3D models are an essential part of computer graphics applications such as games, movie special effects, urban and landscape design, architecture, virtual heritage, visual impact studies, and virtual environments such as *Second Life*. We have developed a novel technique which allows the construction of 3D models using image sequences acquired by a handheld low-cost digital camera. In contrast to alternative technologies, such as laser scanners, structured lighting, and sets of calibrated cameras, our approach can be used by everyone having access to a consumer-level camera. The user only has to create a set of images from different view directions, input them into our algorithm, and a 3D model is returned. We use a novel combination of advanced computer vision algorithms for feature detection, feature matching, and projection matrix estimation in order to reconstruct a 3D point cloud representing the location of geometric features estimated from input images. In a second step a full 3D model is reconstructed using the projection matrix and a triangulation process. We tested our algorithm using a variety of data sets of objects of different scales acquired under different weather and lighting conditions. The results show that our algorithm is stable and enables inexperienced users to easily create complex 3D content using a simple consumer level camera.

1 Introduction

The design of digital 3D scenes is an essential task for many applications in diverse fields such as architecture, engineering, education and arts. Traditional modelling systems such as Maya, 3D Max or Blender enable graphic designers to construct complicated 3D models via 3D meshes. However, the capability for inexperience users to create 3D models has not kept pace. Even for trained graphic designers with in-depth knowledge of computer graphics, constructing a 3D model using traditional modelling systems can still be a challenging task [1]. Hence, there is a critical need for a better and more intuitive approach for reconstructing 3D scenes and models.

The past decade has seen significant progress toward this goal. There are three common approaches: laser scanners, structured lighting, and image-based modelling approach. Laser scanners are very robust and highly accurate. However, they are very

G. Csurka et al. (Eds.): VISIGRAPP 2011, CCIS 274, pp. 86–101, 2013.
© Springer-Verlag Berlin Heidelberg 2013

costly and have restrictions on the size and the surface properties of objects in the scene (Hu et al., 2008). Structured lighting is cheaper and works for a wide variety of materials, but is less accurate and restricts the size and distance of imaged objects.

In contrast, an image-based modelling approach reconstructs the geometry of a complex 3D scene from a sequence of images. The technique is usually less accurate, but offers a very intuitive and low-cost method for reconstructing 3D scenes and models.

We aim to create a low-cost system that allows users to obtain 3D reconstruction of a scene using an off-the-shelf handheld camera. Users acquire images by freely moving the camera around the scene. The system will then perform 3D reconstruction using the following steps:

1. Image Acquisition and Feature Extraction
2. Feature Matching
3. Fundamental Matrix and Projection Matrix Estimation
4. Bundle Adjustment and Refinement
5. Point Cloud Generation
6. Surface Reconstruction

The remainder of this paper is structured as follows. Section 2 discusses relevant literature in the field. Section 3 presents our approach for reconstructing 3D scenes. Section 4 discusses our results. Section 5 concludes and summarises the paper and section 6 gives a brief outlook on directions for future research.

2   Related Work

2.1   Image-Based Modelling

The reconstruction of 3D models from 2D images of objects has long been a major research field in Computer Vision. If the object geometry is relatively smooth and the material homogeneous, then surface geometry can be estimated from illumination gradients. This class of algorithm is called "shape from shading" [2]. However, the technique has too many constraints with respect to the object geometry and the environment in order to be useful in general applications.

A different approach is to only consider the silhouette of an object from different view points. This "shape from silhouette" class of algorithms is very fast and stable with regard to object colour, texture and material, but is very limited in the object geometries it can handle [3,4].

A more stable and general approach with respect to object geometry is "structured lighting", which projects a stable pattern of light onto a surface and reconstructs geometry from its deformation [5]. When combined with a camera both object geometry and texture can be recovered. This approach is used by the popular *Kinect* controller [6]. However, the device is not as portable as a camera, and the type of objects which can be reconstructed is constrained, since structured lighting only works within a limit range of distances and object sizes.

More general shape reconstruction algorithms can be developed by analysing features in camera images and video data. This class of techniques has usually less limitations, since cameras are designed to work for objects of vastly different scale, within a large range of distances, and for both indoor and outdoor environments. Furthermore, the technique can be used by a wide number of users, since cameras are readily available, very portable, and exist already in a large number of consumer devices such as mobile phones.

Brown and Lowe [7] presented an image-based modelling system which aims to recover camera parameters, pose estimates and sparse 3D scene geometry from a sequence of images. Snavely et al. [8] presented the *Photo Tourism* (*Photosynth*) system which is based on the work of Brown and Lowe, with some significant modifications to improve scalability and robustness. Schaffalitzky and Zisserman [9,10] proposed another related technique for calibrating unordered image sets, concentrating on efficiently matching points of interest between images. Although these approaches address the same SFM concepts as we do, their aim is not to reconstruct and visualise 3D scenes and models from images, but only to allow easy navigation between images in three dimension.

Debevec et al. [11] introduced the Facade system for modelling and rendering simple architectural scenes by combining geometry-based and image-based techniques. The system requires only a few images and some known geometric parameters. It was used to reconstruct compelling fly-throughs of the Berkeley campus and it was employed for the MIT City Scanning Project, which captured thousands of calibrated images from an instrumented rig to compute a 3D model of the MIT campus. While the resulting 3D models are often impressive, the system requires input images taken from calibrated cameras.

The work by Martinec and Pajdla [12] is closest to our research in the sense that the authors use arbitrary unconstrained input images. The solution is optimised to deal with cases where information is sparse, e.g., where some features occur on only two images. The given reconstruction results, especially for buildings, seem to be inferior to our method, but a comparison is difficult without using the same input data sets.

Hua et al. [13] tried to reconstruct a 3D surface model from a single uncalibrated image. The 3D information is acquired through geometric attributes such as coplanarity, orthogonality and parallelism. This method only needs one image, but this approach often poses severe restrictions on the image content.

Criminisi et al. [14] proposed an approach that computes a 3D affine scene from a single perspective view of a scene. Information about geometry, such as the vanishing lines of reference planes, and vanishing points for directions not parallel to the plane, are determined. Without any prior knowledge of the intrinsic and extrinsic parameters of the cameras, the affine scene structure is estimated. This method requires only one image, but manual input is necessary.

2.2   Surface Reconstruction

Image-based reconstruction methods match features in images and estimate their 3D position. The reconstruction of surfaces from such "point clouds" has been studied extensively in computer graphics in the past decade. A Delaunay-based algorithm

---

Algorithm for 3D Object Reconstruction

Input: n unordered and unconstrained images

1. Extract features from all input images using a SIFT operator
2. Find t nearest neightbours for each feature
3. For each image:
   a. Select k candidate matching images (those which have the highest number of features matched to this image)
   b. Find geometrically consistent feature matches using RANSAC to solve for the fundamental matrix between pairs of images.
4. Compute the 3D camera pose and the scene geometry using Bundle Adjustment.
5. Reconstruct a surface for the obtained point clouds.
6. (Future work) Apply hole-filling alogorithms for the resulting model.

Output: 3D model of the object

Fig. 1. Overview of our algorithm for reconstructing 3D models from a set of unconstrained and uncalibrated images

proposed by Cazals and Giesen [15] typically generates meshes which interpolate the input points. However, the resulting models often contain rough geometry when the input points are noisy. These methods often provide good results under prescribed sampling criteria [16].

Edelsbrunner et al. presented the well-known α-shape approach [17]. It performs a parameterised construction that associates a polyhedral shape with an unorganized set of points. A drawback of α-shapes is that it becomes difficult and sometimes impossible to choose α for non-uniform sampling so as to balance hole-filling against loss of detail [18].

Amenta et al. proposed the power crust algorithm [18], which constructs a surface mesh by first approximating the medial axis transform (MAT) of the object. The surface mesh is then produced by using an inverse transform from the MAT.

Approximating surface reconstruction methods often use an implicit surface representations followed by iso-surfacing. Hoppe et al. [19] presented a clean abstraction of the reconstruction problem. Their approach approximated the signed distance function induced by the surface F and constructed the output surface as a polygonal approximation of the zero-set of this function. Kazhdan et al. presented a method which is based on an implicit function framework. Their solution computes a 3D indicator function which is defined as 1 for points inside the model and as 0 for points outside the model. The surface is then reconstructed by extracting an appropriate isosurface [20].

3 Design

The main steps of our solution are summarised in figure 1. Each step is explained in more detail in the subsequent subsections.

Fig. 2. Extracted features displayed with red arrows indicating scale, orientation and location

3.1 Feature Matching

The input for our reconstruction algorithm is a sequence of images of the same object taken from different views. The first step is to find feature points in each image. The accuracy of matched feature points affects the accuracy of the fundamental matrix and the computation of 3D points significantly. Many sophisticated algorithms have been proposed such as the Harris feature extractor [21,22] and the SUSAN feature extractor [23]. We use the SIFT (Scale Invariant Feature Transform) operator to detect, extract and describe local feature descriptors [24]. Feature points extracted by SIFT are distinctive and invariant to different transformations, changes in illumination and have high information content [13,7].

The SIFT operator works by first locating potential keypoints of interest at maxima and minima of the result of the Difference of Gaussian (DoG) function in scale-space. The location and scale of each keypoint is then determined and keypoints are selected based on measures of stability. Unstable extremum points with low contrast and edge response features along an edge are discarded in order to accurately localise the keypoints. Each found keypoint is then assigned one or more orientations based on local image gradients. Finally, using local image gradient information, a descriptor is produced for each keypoint [24]. Figure 2 shows an example.

Once features have been detected and extracted from all the images, they are matched. Since multiple images may view the same point in the world, each feature is matched to the nearest neighbours. During this process, image pairs whose number of corresponding features is below a certain threshold are removed. In our experiment, the threshold value of 20 seems to produce the best results.

The matching of features between two images can be achieved by comparing the spatial relationship between keypoints. The Euclidean distance

$$D(A,B) = ||A - B||_2 = \sqrt{\sum_{i=1}^{dim}(A_i - B_i)^2}$$

is used to measure the similarity between two keypoints A and B. A small distance indicates that the two keypoints are close and thus of high similarity [25]. However, a small Euclidean distance does not necessarily mean that the points represent the same feature. In order to accurately match a keypoint in the candidate image, we identify the closest and second closet keypoints in the reference image using a nearest neighbour search strategy. If the ratio of them is below a given threshold, the keypoint and the closest matched keypoint are accepted as correspondences, otherwise that match is rejected [25].

An example demonstrating detected matching features is given in figure 3. Note that for some regions neighbouring features are matched to completely different features in the second input image, whereas for other regions matched features have a consistent spatial relationship.

3.2   Image Matching

The next stage of our algorithm attempts to find all matching images. Matching images are those which contain a common subset of 3D points. From the feature matching stage, we have identified images with a large number of corresponding features. As each image could potentially match every other image, the problem may seem at first to be quadratic in the number of images. However, it has been shown [7] that it is only necessary to match each image to k neighbouring images in order to obtain a good solution for the image geometry. In our system, we use $k = 6$.

3.3   Feature Space Outlier Rejection

We employ a feature space outlier rejection strategy that uses information from all of the images in the n-image matching context to remove incorrect matches. It has been shown that comparing the distance of a potential match to the distance of the best incorrect match is an effective strategy for outlier rejection [7].

Fig. 3. Matching features between two images indicated by red lines. Note that in the initial matching step the majority of matches are spurious and often refer to completely different objects, such as the top of the statue and the tip of a streetlight in the above pictures.

The outlier rejection method works as follows: Assuming that there are n images which contain the same point in the world. Matches from these images are placed in an ordered list of nearest-neighbour matches. We assume that the first $n-1$ elements in the list are potentially correct, but the element n is incorrect. The distance of the nth element is denoted as outlier distance. We then verify the match by comparing the match distance of the potential correct match to the outlier distance. A match is only accepted if the match distance is less than 80% of the outlier distance, otherwise it is rejected. In general, the feature space outlier rejection test is very effective and reliable. For instance, a substantial number of the false matches (up to 80%) can be simply eliminated for a loss of less than 10% of correct matches. This allows for a significant reduction in the number of RANSAC iterations required in subsequent steps [7].

3.4 Fundamental Matrix Estimation

At this stage, we have a set of putative matching image pairs, each of which shares a set of individual correspondences. Since our matching procedure is only based on the similarity of keypoints, it inevitably produces spurious matches. We eliminate many of these spurious matches by using a geometric consistency test, which is based on the epipolar geometry of a given image pair expressed using the fundamental matrix $\mathbf{F}$.

For each pair of matching images, we use their corresponding features to estimate the fundamental matrix. This geometric relationship of a given image pair can be expressed as

$$\mathbf{u}^T \mathbf{F} \mathbf{v} = 0 \tag{1}$$

for any pair of matching features $\mathbf{u} \leftrightarrow \mathbf{v}$ in the two images. The coefficients of the equation 1 can be written in terms of the known coordinates $\mathbf{u} = (x', v', 1)$ and $\mathbf{v} = (x, y, 1)$:

$$x'xf_{11} + x'yf_{12} + x'f_{13} + y'xf_{21} + y'yf_{22} + y'f_{23} + xf_{31} + yf_{32} + f_{33} = 0$$
$$\Leftrightarrow (x'x, x'y, x', y'x, y'y, y', x, y, 1)\mathbf{f} = 0$$

where

$$\mathbf{f} = (f_{11}, f_{12}, f_{13}, f_{21}, f_{22}, f_{23}, f_{31}, f_{32}, f_{33})^T$$

From a set of n correspondent points, we can obtain a set of linear equations of the form

$$\mathbf{Af} = \begin{pmatrix} x'_i x_i & x'_i y_i & x'_i & y'_i x_i & y'_i y_i & y'_i & x_i & y_i & 1 \\ \vdots & \vdots & \vdots & \vdots & \vdots & \vdots & \vdots & \vdots & \vdots \\ x'_n x_n & x'_n y_n & x'_n & y'_n x_n & y'_n y_n & y'_n & x_n & y_n & 1 \end{pmatrix} \mathbf{f} = 0$$

Thus a unique solution of $\mathbf{F}$ (up to scale) can be determined if we are given 8 correspondences [26]. Usually considerable more than 8 correspondences are used because of inaccuracies in the feature estimates. The resulting overdetermined system can be solved resulting in a solution optimal in a least squares sense, which is then used to compute the fundamental matrix.

Many solutions have been proposed to estimate the fundamental matrix. In our system, we use RANSAC [26] to robustly estimate F. Inside each iteration of RANSAC, the 8-point algorithm, followed by anon-linear estimation step, is used to compute a fundamental matrix [26]. The computed epipolar geometry is then used to refine the matching process.

3.5 Bundle Adjustment

Next, given a set of geometrically consistent matches between images, we need to compute a 3D camera pose and scene geometry. This step is critical for the accuracy of the reconstruction, as concentration of pairwise homographies would accumulate errors and disregard constrains between images. The recovered geometry parameters should be consistent. That is, the reprojection error, which is defined by the distance between the projections of each keypoint and its observations, is minimised [7].

This error minimization problem can be solved using *Bundle Adjustment*, which is a well-known method of refining a visual reconstruction to produce jointly optimal 3D structure and viewing parameter estimates. It attempts to minimise the reprojection error e between observed image points $\tilde{\mathbf{p}} = (\tilde{x}_{ij}, \tilde{y}_{ij})$ and predicted image points $\mathbf{p} = (x_{ij}, y_{ij})$. This error is expressed [7]:

$$e = \sqrt{\frac{1}{NM} \sum_{i=1}^{N} \sum_{j=1}^{M} [(\tilde{x}_{ij} - x_{ij})^2 + (\tilde{y}_{ij} - y_{ij})^2]} \tag{2}$$

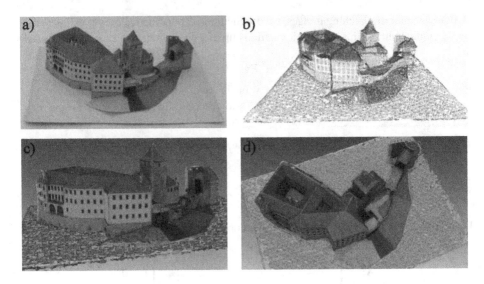

Fig. 4. An example of the surface reconstruction process: (a) The original object, a paper model of the Daliborka tower at Prague castle [28]; (b) The point cloud resulting from matching features in images and estimating their 3D position using bundle adjustment; and (c,d) the 3D model obtained by reconstructing the surface represented by the point cloud

The minimization can be formulated as a non-linear least squares problem and solved with algorithms such as Levenberg-Marquardt (LM). Such algorithms are particularly prone to bad local minima, so it is important to provide a good initial estimate of the parameters [8].

The bundle adjustment algorithm starts by selecting an initial image pair, which has a large number of matches and a large baseline. This is to ensure that the location of the 3D observed point is well-conditioned. The bundle adjustment algorithm will then estimate geometry parameters for the given pair. Subsequent images are added to the bundle adjuster one at a time, with the best matching image (maximum number of matching features) being added at each step. Each image is initialised with the same rotation and focal length as the image to which it best matches. This has proved to work very well even though images have different rotation and scale [27,8,7]. Figure 4 (a) shows one image of a set of images of a paper model of the Daliborka tower at Prague castle [28]. Part (b) of the figure shows the point cloud resulting from matching features in images and estimating their 3D position using bundle adjustment.

3.6   Surface Reconstruction

The final step is to reconstruct surfaces from the obtained point clouds. Our objective is to find a piecewise linear surface that closely approximates the underlying 3D models from which the point clouds was sampled [20]. Many sophisticated surface reconstructions have been proposed and extensively studied. In our system, we employ the Power Crust algorithm [18] for remeshing the surface.

Fig. 5. An image of the statue of Queen Victoria in Mt Albert Park, Auckland (left) and the 3D model reconstructed from 37 images of the statue with resolution 2592x1944 (right). The computation time was about 4 hours.

The Power Crust algorithm reconstructs surfaces by first attempting to approximate the medial axis transform of the object. The surface representation of the point clouds is then produced by the inverse transform. The algorithm is composed of 4 simple steps:

1. A 3D Voronoi diagram is computed from the sample points.
2. For each point s, select the furthest vertex v_1 of its Voronoi cell, and the furthest vertex v_2 such that the angle v_1sv_2 is greater than 90 degree.
3. Compute the Voronoi diagram of the sample point and the Voronoi vertices selected from the second stage.
4. Create a Delaunay triangulation from the Voronoi diagram in the previous stage.

Figure 4 (c) and (d) show the result of applying the Power Crust algorithm to the point cloud in part (b) of the figure.

4   Results

We have tested our system with a number of different datasets, including indoor and outdoor scenes and objects of different scale. In all of our test cases, the system produces good results for rough, non-uniform and feature-rich datasets. Datasets with smooth and uniform surfaces often result in inadequate number of 3D points generated, since the feature detector (SIFT) has trouble detecting and extracting features from these images. The size of our test datasets varies from as few as 6 images to hundreds of images, which are all taken with a simple handheld camera. Note that instead of many individual images the user can also create a short video sequence.

4.1   Dataset 1 - Statue of Queen Victoria

The first test data set consists of 37 images of the statue of Queen Victoria in Mt Albert Park, Auckland. The images were taken from arbitrary view directions on ground

Fig. 6. Two images of the Saint Benedict Church in Auckland, New Zealand (top) and the 3D model reconstructed from 55 images of the church with resolution 2592x1944 (bottom). The computation time was about 6 1/2 hours.

level using a normal consumer-level SONY DSC-W180 camera. The reconstructed 3D model, shown in figure 5 on the right, has 19568 faces and is of moderate quality. The original object can be easily identified. Some holes exist near concave regions and near sharp corners. This is caused by large variations in the point cloud density, which the surface reconstruction algorithm was unable to deal with.

4.2   Dataset 2 - Saint Benedict Church

The second test data set comprises 55 images of Saint Benedict Church in Auckland, New Zealand. The photos were taken at ground level from only two sides of the church. The other two sides were not accessible. The images were taken with the same camera as in the previous example and under slightly rainy conditions. The reconstruction results are satisfactory as illustrated in the image on the bottom of figure 6. The resulting 3D model is composed of 37854 faces has a high resemblance with the original object and even the inaccessible sides look plausible. A few details, such as inaccurately reconstructed windows, are causing holes in the model.

Fig. 7. Image of the Saint George Church (left) and the 3D model reconstructed from 63 images of the church with resolution 2048x3072 (right). The computation time was about 9 hours.

4.3   Dataset 3 - Saint George Church

The third test data set consisted of 63 images of Saint George church. All images were taken from ground level. Since the roof of that building is quite flat, few images show the roof area. Consequently a large part of the area is not covered by any images, and for the remaining parts of the roof feature matching becomes very difficult. Figure 7 illustrates that this results in large gaps in the roof region. In future work we intend to overcome this type of problems with a sketch-based interface, which allows the users to add missing geometric details. The reconstructed model contains 28846 faces.

4.4   Dataset 4 - Paper Model of the Daliborka Tower at Prague Castle

The fourth test data set comprises 65 images taken from many different views of a paper model of the Daliborka tower at Prague castle [28]. Figure 4 shows that the reconstruction is of very good quality and the final model has a high resemblance with the original object. Small details such as windows are also properly reconstructed. The improved reconstruction is due to more pronounced and less complex features, a smaller number of features, and a more even illumination compared to outdoor scenes. The resulting model is composed of 29768 polygons. The computation time of this data set is over 9 hours.

Fig. 8. Three images of a small bunny model (left) and the resulting reconstruction (bottom) using 46 input images with a resolution of 2592 x 1944 pixels

4.5   Dataset 5 - Small Bunny Model

The last test data set consists of 46 images of a small bunny model with a resolution of 2592 x 1944 pixels. The images were taken with a consumer-level SONY DSC-W180 camera, and covered all view directions. The original model has a very bumpy surface, which is extremely difficult to reconstruct. Figure 8 shows that the reconstruction is of good quality and has a high resemblance to the original object. One visible artifact is the difference in texture compared to the original model. This is due to the large brightness differences between pixels representing the same surface point in different images.

4.6   Comparison

Table 1 shows a comparison of the results of our algorithm for different input data sets. All computations were performed on an Intel Quad Core i7 with 6GB RAM. The computation time for the presented data sets varies from 4 hours to more than 9 hours. It is largely dependent on the number and size of images, but also the complexity and material properties of the objects in the scene, which influence the number of features detected in each image. Reconstruction quality depends on the ability of the algorithm to correctly match corresponding features in different images and an adequate coverage of all areas of an object in the input data set. A common practical limitation is the top of large objects such as buildings.

Table 1. Comparison of reconstruction results for different input data sets

Data set	Statue of Queen Victoria	Saint Benedict Church	Saint George Church	Daliborka Tower Tower	Bunny Figure
Number of Images	37	55	63	65	64
Image Resolution	2592 × 1944	3648x2056	2048x3072	4064x2704	2592 x 1944
Computation time	4.1 hours	6.4 hours	9.0 hours	>9.0 hours	4 hours
Number of polygons	19568	37854	28846	29768	33858
Artifacts	Lack of surface details, holes	Roof texture not smooth, Small details missing	Roof missing, holes	Ground plane poorly represented	Surface texture inaccurate

5 Conclusions

We have discussed a novel approach for reconstructing realistic 3D models from a sequence of unconstrained and uncalibrated images. Geometry parameters such as cameras' pose are estimated automatically using a bundle adjustment method. 3D point clouds are then obtained by triangulation using the estimated projection matrix. We reconstruct surfaces for the point clouds to recover the original model.

In contrast to previous approaches, we acquired the input images in just a few minutes with a simple hand-held consumer level camera. Our results demonstrate that our algorithm enables inexperienced users to easily create complex 3D content using a simple consumer level camera. This significantly simplifies the content creation process when constructing virtual environments. Advantages of our approach are scalability (permitted size and distance of objects), high stability with regard to different environment conditions, and ease-of-use and affordability (a consumer level camera is sufficient).

Problems, such as holes, still exist with the resulting 3D models. This is caused by large variation in the point cloud's density. The algorithm also has problems for large areas without features (e.g. flat uni-coloured surfaces) and regions with rough surface geometry. Another disadvantage is that the computation is quite expensive (the system takes over 4 hours to process 37 images, and about 9 hours for 63 images on a Intel Quad Core i7 with 6GB RAM), but this is only an issue in applications where the user needs the content immediately. A common problem with this application is that not all views of a model are obtainable. Especially the roof is often not fully or not at all visible. Similarly in some cases the backside of a building or object might not be accessible.

6 Future Work

We propose to use sketch input and symmetry information to "complete" regions not properly reconstructed in the 3D model due to lack of coverage on the input images. Additional future work will concentrate on improved hole filling algorithms and on speeding up the algorithm by using an GPU implementation.

References

1. Yang, R., Wünsche, B.C.: Life-sketch: a framework for sketch-based modelling and animation of 3d objects. In: Proceedings of the Eleventh Australasian Conference on User Interface, AUIC 2010, vol. 106, pp. 61–70. Australian Computer Society, Inc. (2010), http://www.cs.auckland.ac.nz/ burkhard/Publications/ AUIC2010_YangWuensche.pdf

2. Zhang, R., Tsai, P.S., Cryer, J.E., Shah, M.: Shape from shading: A survey. IEEE Trans. Pattern Anal. Mach. Intell. 21, 690–706 (1999)

3. Matusik, W., Buehler, C., Raskar, R., Gortler, S.J., McMillan, L.: Image-based visual hulls. In: Proceedings of the 27th Annual Conference on Computer Graphics and Interactive Techniques, SIGGRAPH 2000, pp. 369–374. ACM Press/Addison-Wesley Publishing Co., New York (2000)

4. Franco, J.S., Lapierre, M., Boyer, E.: Visual shapes of silhouette sets. In: International Symposium on 3D Data Processing Visualization and Transmission, pp. 397–404 (2006)

5. David Fofi, T.S., Voisin, Y.: A comparative survey on invisible structured light. In: Proceedings of SPIE, vol. 5303, pp. 90–98 (2004)

6. Zollhöfer, M., Martinek, M., Greiner, G., Stamminger, M., Süßmuth, J.: Automatic reconstruction of personalized avatars from 3d face scans. Comput. Animat. Virtual Worlds 22, 195–202 (2011)

7. Brown, M., Lowe, D.G.: Unsupervised 3d object recognition and reconstruction in unordered datasets. In: Proceedings of the Fifth International Conference on 3-D Digital Imaging and Modeling, pp. 56–63. IEEE Computer Society, Washington, DC (2005)

8. Snavely, N., Seitz, S.M., Szeliski, R.: Photo tourism: exploring photo collections in 3d. ACM Trans. Graph. 25, 835–846 (2006)

9. Schaffalitzky, F., Zisserman, A.: Multi-View Matching for Unordered Image Sets, or How Do I Organize My Holiday Snaps? In: Heyden, A., Sparr, G., Nielsen, M., Johansen, P. (eds.) ECCV 2002. LNCS, vol. 2350, pp. 414–431. Springer, Heidelberg (2002)

10. Schaffalitzky, F., Zisserman, A.: Automated location matching in movies. Comput. Vis. Image Underst. 92, 236–264 (2003)

11. Debevec, P.E., Taylor, C.J., Malik, J.: Modeling and rendering architecture from photographs: a hybrid geometry- and image-based approach. In: Proceedings of the 23rd Annual Conference on Computer Graphics and Interactive Techniques, SIGGRAPH 1996, pp. 11–20. ACM, New York (1996)

12. Martinec, D., Pajdla, T.: 3d reconstruction by gluing pair-wise euclidean reconstructions, or "how to achieve a good reconstruction from bad images". In: Proceedings of the Third International Symposium on 3D Data Processing, Visualization, and Transmission (3DPVT 2006), 3DPVT 2006, pp. 25–32. IEEE Computer Society, Washington, DC (2006), http://cmp.felk.cvut.cz/~martid1/articles/Martinec-3DPVT2006.pdf

13. Hua, S., Liu, T.: Realistic 3d reconstruction from two uncalibrated views. International Journal of Computer Science and Network Security 7, 178–183 (2007)

14. Criminisi, A., Reid, I., Zisserman, A.: Single view metrology. International Journal of Computer Vision 40, 123–148 (2000)

15. Cazals, F., Giesen, J.: Delaunay triangulation based surface reconstruction: Ideas and algorithms. In: Effective Computational Geometry for Curves and Surfaces, pp. 231–273. Springer, Heidelberg (2006)

16. Amenta, N., Bern, M.: Surface reconstruction by voronoi filtering. In: Proceedings of the Fourteenth Annual Symposium on Computational Geometry, SCG 1998, pp. 39–48. ACM, New York (1998)

17. Edelsbrunner, H., Mücke, E.P.: Three-dimensional alpha shapes. ACM Trans. Graphics 13, 43–72 (1994)
18. Amenta, N., Choi, S., Kolluri, R.K.: The power crust. In: Proceedings of the Sixth ACM Symposium on Solid Modeling and Applications, SMA 2001, pp. 249–266. ACM, New York (2001)
19. Hoppe, H., DeRose, T., Duchamp, T., McDonald, J., Stuetzle, W.: Surface reconstruction from unorganized points. SIGGRAPH Comput. Graph. 26, 71–78 (1992)
20. Kazhdan, M., Bolitho, M., Hoppe, H.: Poisson surface reconstruction. In: Proceedings of the Fourth Eurographics Symposium on Geometry Processing, SGP 2006, pp. 61–70. Eurographics Association, Aire-la-Ville (2006)
21. Harris, C., Stephens, M.: A combined corner and edge detector. In: Proceedings of the 4th Alvey Vision Conference, pp. 147–151 (1988)
22. Derpanis, K.G.: The harris corner detector (2004),
    http://www.cse.yorku.ca/~kosta/CompVis_Notes/harris_detector.pdf
23. Muyun, W., Mingyi, H.: Image feature detection and matching based on susan method. In: Proceedings of the First International Conference on Innovative Computing, Information and Control, ICICIC 2006, vol. 1, pp. 322–325. IEEE Computer Society, Washington, DC (2006)
24. Lowe, D.G.: Object recognition from local scale-invariant features. In: Proceedings of the International Conference on Computer Vision, ICCV 1999, vol. 2, p. 1150. IEEE Computer Society, Washington, DC (1999)
25. Hu, S., Qiao, J., Zhang, A., Huang, Q.: 3d reconstruction from image sequence taken with a handheld camera. In: International Society for Photogrammetry and Remote Sensing, Congress Beijing 2008, Proceedings of Commission IV, pp. 559–562 (2008),
    http://www.isprs.org/proceedings/XXXVII/congress/4_pdf/99.pdf
26. Hartley, R., Zisserman, A.: Multiple View Geometry in Computer Vision, 2nd edn. Cambridge University Press (2004)
27. Zhang, J., Boutin, M., Aliaga, D.G.: Robust bundle adjustment for structure from motion. In: Proceedings of IEEE International Conference on Image Processing, pp. 2185–2188 (2006)
28. Betexa, Z.S. s.r.o.: The prague castle, paper model of the biggest castle complex in the world. Scale 1:450 (2006)

Part II
Imaging Theory and Applications

Blind Image Deconvolution of Linear Motion Blur

Florian Brusius, Ulrich Schwanecke, and Peter Barth

RheinMain University of Applied Sciences, Wiesbaden, Germany

Abstract. We present an efficient method to deblur images for information recognition. The method is successfully applied directly on mobile devices as a preprocessing phase to images of barcodes. Our main contribution is the fast identifaction of blur length and blur angle in the frequency domain by an adapted radon transform. As a result, the barcode recognition rate of the deblurred images has been increased significantly.

Keywords: Blind deconvolution, Image restoration, Deblurring, Motion blur estimation, Barcodes, Mobile devices, Radon transform.

1 Introduction

Increasingly, mobile smartphone cameras are used as alternative input devices providing context information – most often in the form of barcodes. The processing power of smartphones has reached a state to allow to recognise all kinds of visually perceptible information, like machine-readable barcode tags and theoretically even printed text, shapes, and faces. This makes the camera act as an one-click link between the real world and the digital world inside the device [9]. However, to reap the benefits of this method the image has to be correctly recognised under various circumstances. This depends on the quality of the captured image and is therefore highly susceptible to all kinds of distortions and noise. The photographic image might be over- or underexposed, out of focus, perspectively distorted, noisy or blurred by relative motion between the camera and the imaged object. Unfortunately, all of those problems tend to occur even more on very small cameras.

Blurry image taken by user   Preprocessing (blur removal)   Information recognition

Fig. 1. Image deblurring as preprocessing phase for information recognition

First, cameras on smartphones have very small image sensors and lenses that are bound to produce lower quality images. Second, and more important, the typical single-handed usage and the light weight of the devices make motion blur a common problem

G. Csurka et al. (Eds.): VISIGRAPP 2011, CCIS 274, pp. 105–119, 2013.

of pictures taken with a smartphone. In many cases, the small tremor caused by the user pushing the trigger is already enough to blur the image beyond machine or human recognition.

In order to make the information that is buried in blurry images available, the artefacts caused by the blur have to be removed before the attempt to extract the information. Such a preprocessing method should run in an acceptable time span directly on the device. In this paper, we present a method that identifies and subsequently removes linear, homogeneous motion blur and thus may serve as a preprocessing phase for information recognition systems (see figure 1).

2   Related Work

Undoing the effects of linear motion blur involves three separate basic steps: Calculating the blur direction, calculating the blur extent, and finally using these two parameters to deconvolute the image. Since the quality of the deconvolution is highly dependent on the exact knowledge of the blur kernel, most publications focus on presenting new ways for blur parameter estimation. While some of the algorithms work on a series of different images taken of the same scene [4,16,7], our method attempts to do the same with only a single image.

2.1   Blur Angle Calculation

We focus on methods in the frequency domain, as methods in the spatial image domain suffer from large estimation errors [18] and are computationally expensive. An image blurred by uniform linear camera motion features periodic stripes in the frequency domain [2]. These stripes are perpendicular to the direction of motion (see figure 2). Thus, knowing the orientation of the stripes means knowing the orientation of the blur. In [8], an elaborate overview of the diverse methods for estimating linear motion blur in the frequency domain is presented. One possibility to detect the motion angle is the use of steerable filters, which are applied to the logarithmic power spectrum of the blurred image. These filters can be given an arbitrary orientation and therefore they can be used to detect edges of a certain direction. Since the ripples in the image's power spectrum are perpendicular to the direction of motion blur, the motion angle can be obtained by seeking the angle with the highest filter response value [12]. Unfortunately, this method

Fig. 2. Barcode image linearly blurred by 45° and its logarithmic power spectrum

delivers inaccurate results. Another method of computing the motion direction analyses the cepstrum of the blurred image [13,5,21]. This is based on the observation that the cepstrum of the motion blur point spread function (PSF) has large negative spikes at a certain distance from the origin, which are preserved in the cepstrum of the blurred image. Drawing a straight line from the origin to the first negative peak and computing the inverse tangent of its slope provides an approximation of the motion angle. However, the method only delivers good results in the absence of noise, because image noise will suppress the negative spikes caused by the blur. In addition, calculating the cepstrum requires another time-consuming inverse Fourier transform. A third approach are feature extraction techniques, such as the Hough or Radon transform [17]. The Hough transform requires a binarisation of the log spectrum [10]. Since the highest intensities concentrate around the center of the spectrum and decrease towards its borders, the binarisation threshold has to be adapted for each individual pixel, which is computationally prohibitive. In addition, stripes tend to melt into each other at the origin and become indistinctable. This would require an expensive adaptive thresholding algorithm that is appropriate for every possible ripple form [18]. The Radon transform can be applied directly on the unbinarised spectrum. It delivers a two-dimensional array in which the coordinate of the maximum value provides an estimate of the blur angle. The Radon transform delivers the most stable results [8]. However, it needs a huge amount of storage space and computation time.

2.2   Blur Length Calculation

Again, most of the algorithms estimate the blur length in the frequency domain, where it corresponds to the breadth and frequency of the ripples. The breadth of the central stripe and the gaps between the ripples are inversely proportional to the blur length. One way of computing the blur extent is to estimate the distance from the origin where the two negative peaks become visible in the cepstrum. After rotating the cepstrum by the blur angle, these peaks appear at opposite sides from the origin and their distance to the ordinate can easily be determined [5,21]. Another way collapses the logarithmic power spectrum onto a line that passes through the origin at the estimated blur angle. This yields a one-dimensional version of the spectrum in which the pattern of the ripples becomes clearly visible, provided that the blur direction has been calculated exactly enough. By taking the inverse Fourier transform of this 1-D spectrum, which can be called the 1-D cepstrum, and therein seeking the coordinate of the first negative peak, the blur length can be estimated [10,12]. As with the angle estimation, these two methods have their specific disadvantages: In the first method, calculating the two-dimensional cepstrum is a comparatively expensive operation, while the second method is once again highly susceptible to noise.

2.3   Image Deblurring

Knowing the blur parameters, an appropriate PSF can be calculated. This blur kernel can be used to reconstruct an approximation of the original scene out of the distorted image [8]. Unfortunately, traditional methods like Wiener or Lucy-Richardson filter tend to produce additional artefacts in the deconvoluted images [3]. These artefacts occur mainly at strong edges and along the borders of the image. Some methods have been developed to overcome that issue [15]. However, these methods always involve some sort of iterative optimisation process, which makes them inappropriate for the use in time-critical applications. Luckily, there is no need to get rid of all the artefacts, as long as the information contained in the image is recognisable. However, it has to be taken into account that the deconvolution artefacts may still hinder or complicate the recognition process.

3   The Image Degradation Model

When a camera moves over a certain distance during exposure time, every point of the pictured scene is mapped onto several pixels of the resulting image and produces a photography that is blurred along the direction of motion. This procedure can be regarded as a distortion of the unblurred original image, i.e. the picture taken without any relative movement between the camera and the imaged scene. The blurring of an original image $f(u,v)$ equates to the convolution with a PSF [2]. In the case of linear homogeneous motion blur, this PSF $h(u,v)$ is a one-dimensional rectangular function [10]. In fact, it is a line segment through the origin. Its angle φ to the x-axis is equal to the direction of motion. Its length L equals the distance one pixel is moved by the motion. The coefficients in $h(u,v)$ sum up to 1, thus the intensity being $1/L$ along the line and 0 elsewhere. With the knowledge of the correct motion parameters, the PSF is

$$h(u,v) = \begin{cases} \frac{1}{L} & \text{if } (u,v)\begin{pmatrix} \sin(\varphi) \\ \cos(\varphi) \end{pmatrix} = 0 \text{ and } u^2 + v^2 < \frac{L^2}{4} \\ 0 & \text{otherwise} \end{cases} \tag{1}$$

It has to be taken into account that in the majority of cases, the original image is distorted by additional, signal-independent noise. This noise can be modelled as an unknown random function $n(u,v)$, which is added to the image. Hence, $i(u,v) = f(u,v) * h(u,v) + n(u,v)$ describes the blurred image. Because the convolution becomes a multiplication in the frequency domain, the Fourier transform of the blurred image equates to $I(m,n) = F(m,n) \cdot H(m,n) + N(m,n)$. This multiplication could theoretically be reversed by pixel-wise division. With the proper PSF, the undistorted original image could then be obtained through inverse Fourier transform, which is called *inverse filtering* [6]. However, this only works if there is zero noise. In the presence of noise, only an approximation

$$\hat{F} = \frac{I(m,n)}{H(m,n)} = \frac{F(m,n) \cdot H(m,n) + N(m,n)}{H(m,n)} = F(m,n) + \frac{N(m,n)}{H(m,n)}$$

of the transformed original image can be obtained. Note that $\hat{F}$ cannot be reconstructed without the knowledge of the transformed noise function N. In addition, the small coefficients in $H(m,n)$ make the term $N(m,n)/H(m,n)$ very large and superpose the actual original image beyond recognition [6]. To avoid that, a method of inverse filtering is needed that explicitly takes the noise signal into account. The Wiener deconvolution is such a method, which is based on the well known Wiener filter [20] for noise suppression in signal processing.

4   The Image Deblurring Algorithm

In our algorithm a given blurred input image is analysed to determine the direction
and length of the camera movement that caused the blur. These two motion parameters
are used to calculate a point spread function modelling the blur. Regarding the blur as
a linear convolution of the original image with that blur kernel, it can be removed by
reversing this operation. The algorithm focuses on efficient computation and is therefore
suitable for resource-limited environments.

First, in section 4.1 a *preprocessing* step, which converts a relevant part of the respective greyscale image to the frequency domain with FFT, is introduced. Then, in section 4.2
the *blur direction* is determined by performing a Radon transform on the logarithmic
power spectrum of the blurred image. The power spectrum features some ripples in its
centre, which run perpendicular to the direction of motion. The computation time of the
Radon transform is significantly decreased by customising it to fit the structural conditions of the spectrum. Next, in section 4.3 the *blur length* is estimated by measuring
the breadth of the central ripple within the log spectrum, which is inversely proportional
to the sought-after blur length. This is done by collapsing the spectrum onto a line that
passes through its origin at an estimated blur angle. Then the resulting one-dimensional
log spectrum is analysed to find the first significant local minimum. This approach does
not require any further costly Fourier transforms. In the last step in section 4.4, the PSF
is calculated and a simple Wiener filter is used to *deconvolute* the image.

4.1   Preprocessing

Estimating the blur parameters requires some preprocessing. First, the colour image
obtained by the smartphone camera is converted into an 8 bit-greyscale picture. This
can be done by averaging the colour channels or by weighting the RGB-parts according
to the luminance perception of the human eye [1].

Next, a square section is cut out of the centre of the image. For the FFT to be easily
applicable, the size should be a power of two. In practise, sizes of 512×512 and $256 \times
256$ pixels have shown to maintain a reasonable balance between stable high quality
results and computational cost. The period transitions from one image border to the next
often lead to high frequencies, which become visible in the image's power spectrum as
vertical and horizontal lines. Since these lines may distract from or even superpose
the stripes caused by the blur, they have to be eliminated by applying a windowing
function before transforming the image. The Hanning window w_H offers a good trade-
off between forming a smooth transition towards the image borders and preserving
a sufficient amount of image information for the parameter estimation. For a square
image of size M, the Hanning window [1] is calculated as

$$w_H(u,v) = \begin{cases} \frac{1}{2}\cos(\pi r + 1) & \text{if } r \in [0,1] \\ 0 & \text{otherwise} \end{cases} \quad \text{with } r = \sqrt{\left(\frac{2u}{M}-1\right)^2 + \left(\frac{2v}{M}-1\right)^2} \,.$$

After that step, the windowed image is transferred into the frequency domain. To facilitate the identification of particular features of the Fourier spectrum, its logarith-
mic power spectrum is computed. Taking the log power spectrum $s(u,v) = \log|I(m,n)|$

helps to balance the rapid decrease of the coefficients of the Fourier spectrum from the center towards the borders. Since the interesting features are around the centre of the spectrum, the following operations can be performed upon a centred 256×256-window, which reduces computation time.

4.2 Blur Direction Determination

As a result of the above operations, the power spectrum exhibits a pattern of stripes parallel to a line passing through its origin at an angle θ, which corresponds to the motion angle φ as $\theta = -\varphi$. Thus, estimating the direction of these stripes means knowing the motion angle. To do so, a Radon transform is performed by shooting a certain amount of parallel rays for each possible angle θ through the image, adding up the intensities of the pixels hit by each ray and subsequently storing the sums in a two-dimensional accumulator array. The high intensity values along the sought-after stripes lead to local maxima within this array, and the corresponding array indices reveal the parameters (radius and angle) of the detected lines. The precision of the algorithm depends on how fine the angle domain $\theta = 0 \ldots \pi$ is divided into a number of n_θ steps. 360 steps provide an accuracy of $0.5°$, which is sufficient for image reconstruction and subsequent information extraction.

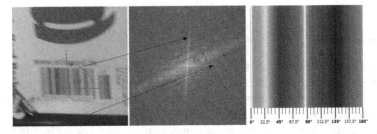

Fig. 3. The periodic structures of the barcode lead to additional features in the power spectrum and create distracting maxima in the Radon accumulator array

If the position of the sought-after feature is unknown, then there is no alternative but to try every possible distance for each angle (see figure 4(a)). Because in our case the central stripe runs through the origin, the radius is always 0 and the detection procedure can be simplified. In principle, it is sufficient to shoot one ray per angle through the origin of the spectrum and determine the angle with the highest sum (see figure 4(b)). Unfortunately, this method usually fails in practise. Periodic structures are common in e.g. barcodes and high-contrast edges occur for example along the border of a white sheet of paper photographed against a dark background. In the spectrum they manifest as additional lines (see figure 3). Since these distracting parts tend to have very high frequencies, they can easily lead to wrong estimations. Therefore, a criterion is needed which helps to separate the "wrong" features from the "right" ones. Fortunately, the breadth of the central stripe caused by the blur is inversely proportional to the blur length. This means that for typical cases of motion blur up to 50-70 pixels, the blur stripe is much broader than the distracting other stripes. At the same time, it is also more diffuse, meaning that it spreads its energy over its breadth. The correct angle can reliably be estimated by looking for maxima within the expected breadth from the origin only (see figure 4(c)). This is a nontrivial problem, because the blur length and with it the expected breadth b are not known. Since taking a value for b that is significantly larger than the actual breadth would lead to an inaccurate estimation, the best result can be achieved by choosing b according to the largest expected blur length (which corresponds to the smallest expected ripple breadth). The blur length is equal to the size of the spectrum divided by the half of b. Hence, for a length of 60 pixels, b equates to $\frac{1}{30}$ of the spectrum width.

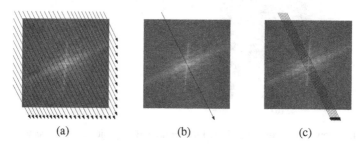

(a)   (b)   (c)

Fig. 4. Different versions of the Radon transform. The arrows denote the rays shot through the image for one angle. In (a) every possible radius is taken into account, (b) and (c) are customised to the expected structure of the power spectra.

The result is an array with $n_\theta \cdot b$ sums. Determining the correct blur angle out of this array is done by searching for the w consecutive angles whose sums add up to the highest total sum. Each of these sums consists of b single values, according to the number of rays sent through the image for each angle. Having found these w angles, the maximum out of all $w \cdot b$ single values is determined. The angle to whose sum this maximum value has contributed is the desired angle of camera motion. A range of $3°$ has proven to be sufficiently large to ensure that the correct angle is selected. Thus, the number of consecutive angles can be calculated out of the angle resolution n_θ as $w = n_\theta/180 \cdot 3$.

4.3   Blur Length Determination

The blur length is also calculated by analysing the logarithmic power spectrum of the blurred image. Here, it is the breadth of the central ripple running through the origin that has to be estimated. This breadth is inversely proportional to the blur extent and therefore can be used to calculate it. Unlike the majority of other algorithms, the estimation requires no further Fourier transform. To determine the breadth of the central stripe, a one-dimensional version of the spectrum is calculated. This is done by collapsing the intensity values of the spectrum onto a line running through the origin perpendicular to the blur ripples. The intensity of each pixel is summed up in an array according to its distance d from that line. In order to do so, d has to be discretised first. Since simple rounding may lead to imprecise results, [12] proposes another approach where the intensities are proportionately divided into two array indexes according to the decimal places of their distances from the projection line. He also suggests to normalise the projected spectrum by dividing each sum by the amount of pixels that went into it. That way, the sums do not necessarily decrease towards the borders of the array, because fewer pixels contribute to them. In addition to these two improvements, [8] proposes to mirror the array in its centre and to add the values to the respective other side. Due to the fact that the blur ripples should be symmetric, this suppresses noise and at the same time clarifies the interesting features.

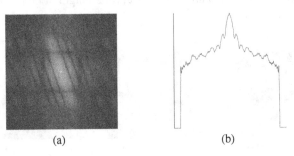

(a)   (b)

Fig. 5. Log power spectrum of a blurred image (a) and its projected 1-D spectrum (b)

The resulting 1-D spectrum exhibits a prominent peak in its centre which matches the central blur ripple in the 2-D spectrum (see figure 5). The zeros, or rather the gaps, between the individual stripes manifest as local minima in the collapsed spectrum. To identify the maximum in the centre of the spectrum, a search to the right (either direction would be possible because of the symmetry) is performed until the values become higher instead of smaller, i.e.

$$P(x_0) < P(x_0 + 1) \ . \tag{2}$$

Out of this first local minimum x_0, one can easily calculate the breadth of the blur ripple by doubling its distance to the maximum. Unfortunately, this simple approach usually fails in the presence of noise. With blur that has been developed under realistic conditions, small deflections show up in the spectrum. Thus, the collapsed spectrum is not monotonically decreasing up to the sought-after first local minimum and the approach described in (2) is bound to fail. To solve this problem, we propose to define a distance s within which the values must not become bigger than at the potential minimum, i.e.

$$P(x_0) < P(x_0 + 1) < P(x_0 + s) \ . \tag{3}$$

Since the parallel ripples in the spectrum become smaller and more dense to the same degree the causing movement is faster, the choice of a proper value for s is not an easy one. On the one hand, it has to be larger than the maximal breadth of the noise deflections it strives to suppress. On the other hand, it has to be smaller than the minimal breadth of the next ripple, which is half as broad as the one in the centre. This means that s has to be individually computed according to the characteristics of the present spectrum. With increasingly larger blur lengths, the values in the spectrum decline more rapidly towards the sides. This is why the calculation of the slope m between two points

$Q_1 = (x_1, y_1)$ and $Q_2 = (x_2, y_2)$, which both lie on the central peak, is a promising approach. To be on the safe side, we presume a maximal blur length of 100 pixels, which would make the breadth of the entire peak $1/50$ of the width $\sqrt{2}M$ of the spectrum. Hence, x_1 is set to be at the centre $M/\sqrt{2}$ and x_2 at a distance of $1/100$ of the spectrum width from there. The resulting slope

$$m = \left| \frac{y_2 - y_1}{x_2 - x_1} \right| = \left| \frac{P(x_2) - P(x_1)}{\frac{1}{100}\sqrt{2}M} \right|$$

grows with increasingly larger blur lengths. At the same time, the deflections become smaller as the slope becomes steeper, which means that smaller blur lengths are more susceptible to noise than larger ones. Thus, $s = 1/m \cdot f$, where f is an appropriate correction factor.

For a spectrum with a size of 512×512 pixels, we found that dividing the slope by a correction factor of 5 worked best. Since the breadths of the peaks depend on the size M of the projected power spectrum, this results in a correction factor of $f = M/2560$:

$$s = \frac{1}{m} \cdot f = \frac{1}{m} \cdot \frac{M}{512 \cdot 5} = \frac{M}{2560 \cdot m} \ .$$

When the correct minimum x_0 has been found according to equation (3), the breadth b of the peak is calculated as

$$b = 2 \cdot \left(x_0 - \frac{M}{\sqrt{2}} \right) \ .$$

Because b is inversely proportional to the length L of the camera motion, the reciprocal of b is used. Thus, the blur length is calculated by dividing the size of the spectrum by the half of b yielding $L = 2 \cdot M/b$.

It is possible that the algorithm fails to detect a local minimum. This is mostly due to a faulty calculation of the distance s or the collapsed spectrum exhibiting no prominent peaks. The latter is the case when the angle has not been estimated exactly enough in the previous step, which leads to an incorrect projection line orientation.

4.4   Deconvolution

Knowing the two blur parameters, an adequate PSF can be calculated according to equation (1). Then both the PSF and the original, unaltered image have to be transformed into the frequency domain so that the deconvolution can be carried out. The Wiener deconvolution filter as it is presented in [10] is given by

$$\hat{F} = \frac{H^*(m,n) \cdot I(m,n)}{H^*(m,n) \cdot H(m,n) + K} \ ,$$

where $H^*(m,n)$ is the complex conjugate of $H(m,n)$ and K is a constant that can be approximated by the reciprocal image width $1/B$. In order to obtain the reconstructed, deblurred image, the result eventually has to be transformed back into the image domain.

Provided that the information in the pictured object consists solely of monochrome elements, it might be reasonable to binarise the reconstructed image. Good results can be achieved with the thresholding algorithms of White [19] and Bernsen [14]. Since most of the locally-adaptive thresholding methods require a lot of computation time, this method is better used in environments that are not time critical. However, if the photo is consistently lit so that a viable global threshold can be found, the method of Otsu [11] might also be applicable.

5   Evaluation

In order to evaluate how accurate and reliable the motion parameter estimation works, two different classes of input data have been used. The first category consisted of images with artificially generated motion blur. To do so, 11 different motifs had each been convoluted with 30 different PSFs. These PSFs had been constructed from all possible combinations out of five different, randomly chosen angles and six different, likewise random lengths according to the definition given by equation (1). This way, a total of 330 test images were created. The original motifs comprised real photography as well as completely digitally created pictures, all of a size of 512×512 pixels.

Nine of the images showed different kinds of barcodes. The benefit of artificially created blur is that the exact motion parameters are known beforehand and can therefore easily be compared to the ones determined by the algorithm. Yet it can not predict whether the method works for photos taken under real conditions. Hence, the second class consisted of real, unaltered photographs. For these pictures, five different barcodes had each been photographed five times. In order to simulate realistic conditions, they were made using a smartphone camera, manually moving the phone in different speeds and angles during exposure time. The shots were also taken under different light conditions in order to vary the shutter speed.

5.1   Artificial Blur

For the artificially blurred images, the angle estimation continuously produced stable results. The algorithm could estimate the angles up to an accuracy of 5° for 92.71% of the test images. In most of the cases where the estimation delivered incorrect results, this was caused by additional features in the power spectrum induced by periodic structures or high-contrast edges. The accuracy of the angle estimation is to some degree dependent on the intensity of the blur: If the ray within which the Radon transform sums up the intensity values is smaller than the stripe it strives to detect, multiple maxima occur at adjacent angles. Since shorter blur lengths lead to broader stripes, the accuracy decreases with the blur length, as can be seen in table 1. Only taking into account pictures with blur lengths greater than 50 pixels leads to an increase of the detection rates for 0.5° accuracy of 40% of the images. Out of the pictures with blur lengths greater than 30 pixels, nearly 100% could be detected correctly with an accuracy of 4°.

The blur length estimation also worked reliably, provided that the angle had been calculated correctly. In the case of an exact angle estimation in the range of 0.5° around the desired value, 95.73% of the blur lengths could be determined with an accuracy up

Table 1. Angle detection rates for angles with artificial blur

accuracy up to	maximal blur length					
	all	≥ 25 px	≥ 30 px	≥ 40 px	≥ 50 px	≥ 70 px
0.5°	35.56%	41.82%	45.00%	48.48%	50.00%	47.27%
1.5°	64.13%	74.55%	79.09%	84.24%	87.27%	89.09%
2°	76.60%	86.55%	90.91%	94.55%	94.55%	94.55%
3°	86.32%	96.36%	97.27%	98.18%	97.27%	96.36%
4°	89.06%	98.55%	99.55%	99.39%	99.09%	98.18%
5°	92.71%	99.27%	99.55%	99.39%	99.09%	98.18%
7°	95.44%	99.64%	99.55%	99.39%	99.09%	98.18%
10°	95.44%	99.64%	99.55%	99.39%	99.09%	98.18%
∅ deviation	3.01°	1.36°	1.28°	1.25°	1.36°	1.82°

to 5 pixels. As shown in table 2, this rate decreases to 79.43% for an angle estimation accuracy of 5°. Given these numbers, the percentage of images where both the angle and the length could be estimated with an accuracy of up to 5° or 5 pixels, is 73.56%. Nevertheless, the high portion of correctly estimated blur lengths with the exact knowledge of the blur angle shows that the method for blur length estimation presented in this paper works well. The accuracy however decreases for greater blur lengths, which is once again due to the breadth of the central ripple: In a spectrum of the size of 256 pixels, it is 26 pixels broad for a blur length of 20 pixels. If the blur length is doubled to 40 pixels, the breadth is halved accordingly to 13 pixels. For a blur length of 80 pixels, the stripe is merely 6 pixels broad. The breadth of the ripple converges towards the resolution limit and the accuracy with which it can be determined inevitably decreases.

5.2   Real Blur

To allow the verification of the blur parameters estimated for photos taken under real conditions, the angles of the ripples appearing in the images' power spectra were measured manually. The same was done for the blur lengths using plots of the 1-D spectra. Since the estimation of the blur length is impossible without the exact knowledge of the corresponding blur angle, in cases where the angle estimation had failed the spectra were recreated using the manually measured data. In other words, corrective actions were taken in order to make separate statements about the estimation accuracy of both parameters.

The test material presented here can only attempt to provide evidence of the algorithm's performance under real conditions. On the one hand, the amount of images is much smaller than that with the artificially created blur. On the other hand, even the images taken with a smartphone camera were likewise created "artificially", since they all had been taken with the explicit intent to create linear motion blur. Yet, it can be stated that the method generally works for motion blur caused by actual movement of

Table 2. Length detection rates for artificial blur

accuracy up to	maximal accuracy of the angle estimation						
	0.5°	1.5°	2°	4°	5°	10°	all
1 px	15.38%	17.54%	17.86%	18.77%	19.02%	19.43%	18.84%
2 px	49.57%	45.97%	46.03%	46.08%	47.21%	48.09%	46.20%
3 px	74.36%	66.35%	63.10%	61.43%	62.30%	62.74%	60.49%
4 px	95.73%	82.94%	78.57%	76.11%	76.39%	76.43%	73.56%
5 px	95.73%	84.83%	81.75%	79.18%	79.34%	79.62%	76.90%
7 px	99.15%	90.52%	86.51%	83.96%	83.93%	84.08%	81.76%
10 px	99.15%	92.89%	88.89%	87.71%	87.87%	87.90%	86.63%
∅ deviation	6.08 px	6.46 px	9.24 px	8.99 px	8.74 px	8.62 px	9.08 px

a physical camera. Table 3 shows that for 16 out of the 25 images, the motion angle could be estimated with a 5°-accuracy, which still is a detection rate of roughly 60%. The lengths could be estimated accurately to 5 pixels in 14 out of 25 cases. When the exact angles from the manual measuring were used, this rate increased to 22 out of 25 (88%).

Table 3. Comparison between the manual measuring and the values determined by the algorithm for the 25 test images. Deviations of more than 5 pixels are highlighted

	angle man.	angle alg.	length man.	length alg.
	179.0°	180.0°	9.23 px	20.48 px
	174.0°	177.5°	15.28 px	18.96 px
	75.0°	78.5°	8.53 px	2.67 px
	142.0°	146.0°	14.42 px	14.63 px
	45.0°	49.0°	14.63 px	15.52 px
	150.0°	98.0°	11.38 px	11.38 px
	90.0°	90.5°	25.6 px	25.6 px
	42.0°	86.0°	8.46 px	9.31 px
	1.0°	1.5°	20.9 px	85.33 px
	63.0°	86.5°	16.0 px	16.52 px

	angle man.	angle alg.	length man.	length alg.
	91.0°	90.0°	9.23 px	46.55 px
	7.0°	0.5°	15.28 px	8.53 px
	156.0°	1.5°	11.38 px	11.38 px
	62.0°	93.0°	10.04 px	11.64 px
	59.0°	61.5°	14.42 px	14.22 px
	178.0°	1.5°	14.22 px	14.63 px
	91.0°	90.5°	15.75 px	15.06 px
	12.0°	3.5°	6.4 px	4.92 px
	140.0°	177.0°	14.03 px	4.92 px
	171.0°	173.0°	8.83 px	8.83 px

5.3 Image Reconstruction

In the last step, the algorithm uses the determined motion parameters to remove the blur artefacts. The images in figure 6 clearly show that the reconstruction is able to produce good results: Text that could not even be identified as such becomes legible again, and individual elements of the barcodes become clearly distinguishable. Figure 6(b) shows

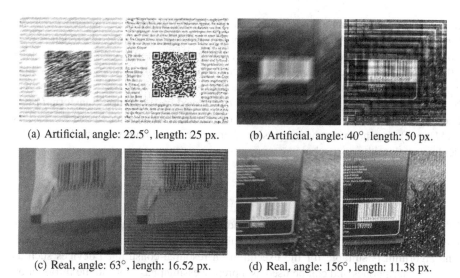

(a) Artificial, angle: 22.5°, length: 25 px.   (b) Artificial, angle: 40°, length: 50 px.

(c) Real, angle: 63°, length: 16.52 px.   (d) Real, angle: 156°, length: 11.38 px.

Fig. 6. Images blurred by artificial ((a), (b)) and real ((c), (d)) linear motion and their respective deconvolution results

that even with very large blur lengths good results are possible. While the results are of course better with the artificial blur, the naturally blurred images also could be successfully deblurred in many cases.

To determine whether the deblurring allows for increased detection rates of barcode scanners, some test images were passed through the open source ZXing-Decoder before and after the reconstruction. Out of the artificially blurred images, 50 were chosen where the barcode elements were distinctively visible. With these 50 images, the detection rates of the ZXing-Decoder could be increased by 30.6%. An additional binarisation of the resulting images using the method of Bernsen could increase the success rate by another 4.1%. There, among the images with less than 15 pixels blur length the increase was 41.7% in total. Extrapolated onto all images that could have been recognised theoretically, this gives a rate of 8.1%. Note, that even then the percentage of images on which the reconstructed information is recognisable with the naked eye is much higher. Obviously, the scanning algorithm cannot handle the reconstructed input images. This is most likely due to the additional artefacts and diffuse edges caused by the deconvolution [15].

5.4 Performance

The algorithm has been implemented in Java in order to conduct the experiments. It was first run on a standard desktop PC (3 GHz Intel Pentium D with 2 GB RAM) using JavaSE 1.6 and then ported to JavaME in order to test it on a real mobile device. In the test run, the whole process (preprocessing, blur parameter estimation and deconvolution) took about 500 ms for all images to be completed on the desktop computer. The exact same calculation took a total of about 22 seconds on a last generation mobile device (*Sony Ericsson k800i*), which is more than 40 times longer. While some parts (e.g. the windowing) ran about 23 times slower on the smartphone than on the desktop PC, the FFT took 90 times as long. For the FFT the comparatively much slower floating point arithmetic makes itself felt. However, note that next generation hardware offers higher integer performance, much better floating point support, and faster Java run time environments. An analysis on the desktop computer revealed that the FFT by far required the longest CPU time (36%), followed by the Radon transform (18%) and the calculation of the power spectrum (8%). Since the complexity of the FFT is $O(M \log M)$, dependent on the image size M, this also determines the complexity of the deblurring algorithm as a whole.

6 Conclusions and Future Work

In this paper, a novel method combining and adapting existing techniques for the estimation of motion blur parameters and the subsequent removal of this blur is presented. The algorithm is suitable for the execution on resource-constrained devices such as modern smartphones and can be used as a preprocessing phase for mobile information recognition software.

The algorithm uses the logarithmic power spectrum of a blurred image to identify the motion parameters. It introduces a new, specially adjusted and therefore time-saving version of the Radon transform for angle detection where features are only sought after within a certain distance around the origin. The blur length is detected by analysing a one-dimensional version of the spectrum. No cepstrum and hence no further FFT are required. The estimated parameters are then used to form a proper PSF with which the blurred image can be deconvoluted. To do so, a Wiener filter is employed.

It was found that the motion angle estimation worked with a 5° accuracy for 92.71% of 330 artificially blurred images. The blur length determination delivered correct results with a maximum error of 5 pixels in 95.73% of all cases. For images blurred by real movement of an actual camera, these rates amounted to roughly 60% and 88%, respectively. The algorithm was implemented in Java to run on desktop computers as well as mobile devices. The algorithm terminated within 500 ms on an standard desktop computer and took around 40 times longer on an older smartphone. While sub second performance on smartphones is not to be expected any time soon, execution time within a few seconds on modern hardware should be attainable.

The application of the presented algorithm makes some previously unrecognised barcodes to be recognised by the ZXing decoder. However, the additional artefacts caused by the deconvolution itself often hinders the recognition in other cases. Yet, after the deconvolution, completely blurred text become legible again, and individual barcode features become clearly distinguishable in many of the cases where decoding failed. This gives reason to surmise that a successful recognition might be possible if the decoders were able to cope with the singularities of the reconstructed images. Or, deconvolution methods that suppress the emergence of artefacts could be explored.

References

1. Burger, W., Burge, M.J.: Digital Image Processing – An Algorithmic Introduction Using Java. Springer, Heidelberg (2008)
2. Cannon, M.: Blind deconvolution of spatially invariant image blurs with phase. IEEE Transactions on Acoustics, Speech and Signal Processing, 58–63 (1976)
3. Chalkov, S., Meshalkina, N., Kim, C.-S.: Post-processing algorithm for reducing ringing artefacts in deblurred images. In: 23rd International Technical Conference on Circuits/Systems, Computers and Communications, ITC-CSCC, pp. 1193–1196. School of Electrical Engineering, Korea University Seoul (2008)
4. Chen, L., Yap, K.-H., He, Y.: Efficient recursive multichannel blind image restoration. EURASIP J. Appl. Signal Process. 2007(1) (2007)
5. Chu, C.-H., Yang, D.-N., Chen, M.-S.: Image stabilization for 2d barcode in handheld devices. In: 15th International Conference on Multimedia, MULTIMEDIA 2007, pp. 697–706. ACM, New York (2007)
6. Gonzalez, R.C., Woods, R.E.: Digital Image Processing. Pearson Education Inc. (2008)
7. Harikumar, G., Bresler, Y.: Perfect blind restoration of images blurred by multiple filters: Theory and efficient algorithms. IEEE Transactions on Image Processing 8(2), 202–219 (1999)
8. Krahmer, F., Lin, Y., McAdoo, B., Ott, K., Wang, J., Widemann, D., Wohlberg, B.: Blind image deconvolution: Motion blur estimation. Technical report, University of Minnesota (2006)
9. Liu, Y., Yang, B., Yang, J.: Bar code recognition in complex scenes by camera phones. In: Fourth International Conference on Natural Computation, ICNC 2008, pp. 462–466. IEEE Computer Society, Washington, DC (2008)
10. Lokhande, R., Arya, K.V., Gupta, P.: Identification of parameters and restoration of motion blurred images. In: SAC 2006: Proceedings of the 2006 ACM Symposium on Applied Computing, pp. 301–305. ACM, New York (2006)
11. Otsu, N.: A threshold selection method from gray-level histograms. IEEE Transactions on Systems, Man and Cybernetics 9(1), 62–66 (1979)
12. Rekleitis, I.: Visual motion estimation based on motion blur interpretation. Master's thesis, School of Computer Science. McGill University, Montreal (1995)
13. Savakis, A.E., Easton Jr., R.L.: Blur identification based on higher order spectral nulls. In: SPIE Image Reconstruction and Restoration (2302) (1994)
14. Sezgin, M., Sankur, B.: Survey over image thresholding techniques and quantitative performance evaluation. Journal of Electronic Imaging 13(1), 146–168 (2004)
15. Shan, Q., Jia, J., Agarwala, A.: High-quality motion deblurring from a single image. ACM Trans. Graph. 27(3), 1–10 (2008)
16. Sorel, M., Flusser, J.: Blind restoration of images blurred by complex camera motion and simultaneous recovery of 3d scene structure. In: Proceedings of the Fifth IEEE International Symposium on Signal Processing and Information Technology, pp. 737–742 (2005)
17. Toft, P.: The Radon Transform – Theory and Implementation. PhD thesis, Electronics Institute, Technical University of Denmark (1996)
18. Wang, Y., Huang, X., Jia, P.: Direction parameter identification of motion-blurred image based on three second order frequency moments. Measuring Technology and Mechatronics Automation, 453–457 (2009)
19. White, J.M., Rohrer, G.D.: Image thresholding for optical character recognition and other applications requiring character image extraction. IBM J. Res. Dev. 27, 400–411 (1983)
20. Wiener, N.: Extrapolation, Interpolation, and Smoothing of Stationary Time Series. Wiley, New York (1949)
21. Wu, S., Lu, Z., Ong, E.P., Lin, W.: Blind image blur identification in cepstrum domain. In: Computer Communications and Networks, ICCCN 2007, pp. 1166–1171 (2007)

Part III

Information Visualization Theory and Applications

Human Centered Design in Practice: A Case Study with the Ontology Visualization Tool Knoocks

Simone Kriglstein[1] and Günter Wallner[2]

[1] University of Vienna, Faculty of Computer Science, Rathausstraße 19, 1010 Vienna, Austria
simone.kriglstein@univie.ac.at
[2] University of Applied Arts, Institute of Art and Technology
Oskar Kokoschka Platz 2, 1010 Vienna, Austria
guenter.wallner@uni-ak.ac.at

Abstract. Ontologies make it possible to understand, analyze, exchange or share knowledge of a specific domain and therefore they are becoming popular in various communities. However, ontologies can be very complex and therefore visualizations can support users to understand the ontology easier. Moreover, graphical representations make ontologies with their structure more manageable. For an effective visualization, it is necessary to consider the domain for which the ontology is developed and its users with their needs and expectations. This paper presents the development process of Knoocks (Knowledge Blocks) - a visualization tool for OWL Lite ontologies - which was implemented with the help of the human centered design process. The presented case study underlies the importance of repeated usability evaluations during the development process to identify weak points of the design and missing features which are relevant for the intended users.

Keywords: Ontology visualization, OWL Lite, Knoocks, Usability evaluation, Comparison study, Human centered design.

1 Introduction

Ontologies were becoming popular in various communities and disciplines over the past few years. The reason for their popularity is that they define concepts and relations which can be used as a skeletal foundation to model and to represent knowledge of a domain [3,24]. The study of Cardoso [2] shows that the vast majority of the participants use ontologies to share and to communicate information between people or software agents. OWL [26] is among the most popular languages to describe ontologies with OWL Lite being a sublanguage of OWL. The three main components of OWL Lite are: classes, instances and properties. Classes present the relevant concepts and describe the abstract model of the domain. For every class, instances present individual objects of this class and properties represent relationships between instances (object properties) or they relate instances to datatypes (datatype properties).

To make ontologies more manageable and understandable for humans, different ontology visualization tools were developed over the past few years (see e.g., [5,11]). Visualizations allow users to see and analyze the structure and dependencies within ontologies in a transparent way or allow them to detect new information which they were

G. Csurka et al. (Eds.): VISIGRAPP 2011, CCIS 274, pp. 123–141, 2013.

not aware of before [17]. Furthermore, graphical representations of ontologies can also be helpful to support users in their decisions. For example, they allow domain experts to control if the concepts and their dependencies are correctly implemented and to decide if modifications will be necessary. The study of Kriglstein [8] has shown that the participants used many different ontology visualization tools for their work. This may be due to the wide variety of applications and forms of ontologies which reflects that different users have different needs and that different domain specific tasks exist. Therefore, it is important to know the context and domain to find the best solution to model and visualize an ontology. Many of the existing tools focus either primarily on the visualization of relationships and properties between classes (e.g., OntoViz) or on the hierarchical structure (e.g., CropCircles) and instances (e.g., treemap view of Jambalaya). This restriction on certain elements of the ontology limits ontology experts but on the other hand allows domain users to use such tools for specifics tasks (as shown in Section 4). For an effective usage of such tools, it is necessary to consider requirements which are relevant for ontology visualization (e.g., [8,14]). For example, it is essential that the visualization allows users to efficiently compare subclasses and their instances with each other. In addition to these requirements, it is important to consider potential users and the concepts of the domain during the development process to make sure that the visualization satisfies users' needs, tasks and expectations. Therefore, strategies of human computer interaction (e.g. usability studies) were becoming more and more popular for the evaluation of visualizations over the past few years [10,13].

Based on these observations we adapted the human centered design process (defined by ISONORM 13407 [32]) to develop an ontology visualization tool – called **Knowledge Blocks** (Knoocks) – to integrate the information of classes, instances and properties in one single tool to allow users to analyze OWL Lite ontologies more easily. For this purpose, Knoocks provides an overview which allows users to observe relationships on the class level, to analyze classes with their subclasses, and to see the distribution of instances within the ontology. In addition to the overview, Knoocks also contains a detail view, which concentrates on the visualization of instances in connection with their classes and properties. Many visualization tools also have technical interfaces which make them only understandable for ontology experts which have a lot of experience with these tools (e.g., abbreviations for the drawing settings in OntoViz). However, it is essential to find out what different user groups expect from the visualization and in which context the visualization approach can support them. Our intention was to develop an ontology visualization which is suitable for both groups: ontology experts (users who develop and maintain the ontology) and domain users (users who only want information about the concepts of their domain).

In this paper we present the development process of Knoocks and its evaluation with focus on usability as well as comparison studies with other visualization tools. The remainder of this paper is structured as follows. Section 2 gives a short overview of visualization approaches for ontologies and Section 3 describes the development process of Knoocks with its four iterations. Section 4 presents the evaluation as well as a discussion of the results. The paper is concluded in Section 5.

2   Related Work

A number of visualization tools for OWL ontologies were developed in the past few years. These tools adapted well-known information visualization techniques. For example, several of the existing visualization tools (e.g., TGVizTab [1] and OntoViz [20] which are both plug-ins for Protégé [21]) present subclass-of relationships and object properties between concepts as node-link visualizations. Node-link representations are an intuitive way to make interconnections within the ontology transparent. However, if the graph contains a large number of classes, instances and relationships, it can happen that the graph becomes crowded and cluttered and therefore the analysis of the ontology is more difficult. In contrast to the node-link representation, container approaches are often used if the focus of the ontology visualization is on the instances and on the hierarchical structure. For example, CropCircles [27] visualizes subclasses as circles which are nested inside the circle of their parent class. Similar to the node-link representation, it is not easy for the user to get a quick overview with a container approach if the ontology contains a large number of instances or classes. A combination of node-link approaches and container approaches is another possibility to visualize ontologies. For example, Jambalaya [22] – also a plug-in for Protégé – provides different views with different visualization techniques. In addition to views which represent the relationships between the concepts purely as node-link representation, one view provides the adapted treemap approach of Shneiderman [19] which allows users to rapidly jump between classes or instances. Another view uses a nested graph to visualize classes and their instances and a node-link approach to display object properties. A good overview of existing ontology visualization techniques can be found in [5,11].

3   Development Process

For the development of the ontology visualization tool Knoocks we adapted the human centered design process (see Figure 1). The process starts with the development of an ontology which needs to be visualized (e.g., to evaluate the ontology structure). For the development of an ontology visualization it is necessary to analyze the domain, the purpose of the ontology and potential users. Based on the outcome of this step, the requirements for developing a prototype can be defined. Requirements are measurable benchmarks for the evaluation, which specify design goals and primarily describe what the visualization should provide. For the development of Knoocks we considered usability and interface design aspects [4,12,18] as well as specific ontology visualization requirements. These requirements – as listed below – are based on a user requirement analysis with ontology experts [8] and literature studies (e.g., [14]).

Visibility of the Structure. The visualized structure should support effective management of ontologies. It should be possible to compare subtrees with each other and to see the size and depth of each subtree. The visualization should allow users to quickly scan all information with minimal cognitive effort.

Visibility of Classes. Because classes describe the concepts of the ontology, it is essential to get a good overview of them and to understand the relations between

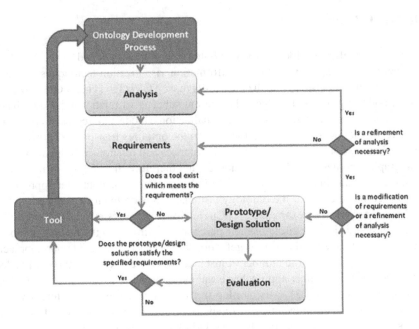

Fig. 1. Design process

the concepts. The visualization should unmistakably distinguish between different classes.

Visibility of Instances. Based on the fact that instances represent data and therefore are often more important to the end-user than the underlying concept, the visualization should also consider instances. It should obviously visualize which classes contain which instances.

Visibility of Relationships. The visualization should clearly show the defined interconnections between the classes and their instances. For good differentiations between the relationships, it is necessary to represent the different types in a distinguishable way (e.g., every type has its own color).

Based on the specified requirements the next step of the design process is to develop the visualization. Our main objective in the design of Knoocks was to improve the accessibility of instances and simultaneously allow users to grasp and analyze the structure and interconnections of OWL Lite ontologies. We use a combination of a container approach to represent instances and a node-link approach to depict object properties. The hierarchical structure of classes is similar to the Icicle Plot concept [28]. The major advantage of the Icicle Plot is that the clustering of objects is easily noticeable [28]. The study of Barlow and Neville [29] shows that the participants' performance with the Icicle Plot was equivalent to the node-link representations. They stated that the orientation (top-to-bottom or left-to-right) of the Icicle Plot approach was familiar to them, because a similar orientation is also used by common node-link approaches. For the representation of instances, we were also inspired by intended lists, because the list representation is familiar to the user and allows quick scanning of the elements without overlapping. For the representation of non-hierarchical relationships (object properties) we adopted node-link representations. Although they need more space in general than other approaches (e.g., treemap), they are a very intuitive way to show the connections between two nodes. This allows users to clearly differentiate between hierarchical and non-hierarchical relationships. In contrast to existing ontology visualization approaches like, for example, Jambalaya or TGVizTab which either focus on a high-level view of the ontology or on details of individual nodes, it was important for us to visualize both views simultaneously. Although, Jambalaya has the possibility to choose between different visualizations only one visualization is visible at a time and switching between them requires recalculations which can be cumbersome if the ontology is large.

The evaluation step of the design process has the goal to identify if the prototype matches the defined requirements. If modifications are necessary, the next iteration starts by altering the requirement specification, by refining the data of the analysis step, or by modifying the prototype. The process is repeated until the result of the evaluation is satisfactory in regard to the defined requirements. The developed visualization of the ontology allows users to detect new information and can influence the further development process of the ontology.

We will give a short overview about the development process of the latest version of Knoocks in the next subsections which – as of this writing – required four iteration cycles. The findings of the evaluations are described in more detail in Section 4.

3.1   First Iteration Cycle

In the first iteration cycle we concentrated on the design of the representation of subclass-of relationships and instances (for details see [30]). A block (see Figure 2) is the main entity in our approach. Such a block is constructed for each class which is directly connected to OWL:Thing. It is basically a logical container that groups classes, which are connected by subclass-of relationships, in a hierarchical left to right manner. In other words, a class c_s placed to the right of another class c_p is a subclass of c_p. The instances of a class are listed within their class and thereby users see the instances of every class directly without overlapping. If an instance belongs to multiple classes (multiple inheritance) then the instance is listed in each respective class. The size of a rectangle depends on the size of its subclasses and the number of contained instances.

3.2   Second Iteration Cycle

After the basic block structure was well received by the users (see evaluation in Section 4) we implemented the two views – overview and detail view. Depending on which of the two views is from more interest, the user can select which one will be displayed in the main window (cf. C in Figure 2) and which one will be shown in the preview window (B in Figure 2).

The overview (in Figure 2 currently located in the preview window) shows all blocks arranged in a radial pattern and is well suited to grasp the overall structure of the ontology. Colored curves depict the relations (object properties) between instances. These curves are actually meta-edges, because they bundle relations according to common classes and property type (reflected by the color of the curve) to avoid cluttering the

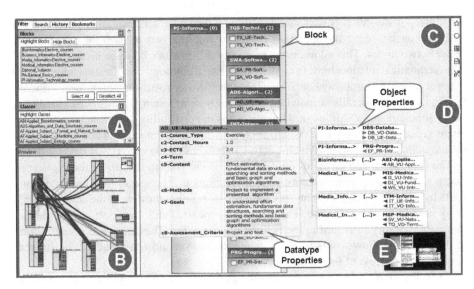

Fig. 2. The fourth and current version: (A) toolbox which includes the search/filter, history and bookmark functions, (B) preview window, (C) main window, (D) vertical toolbar and (E) thumbnail

view with a lot of individual curves. The thickness of the curve corresponds to the number of contained relations. If the mouse is moved over a line, a relation table with all connected instances appears. To get a better view, it is possible to select which relationship types are visible and which are not.

After clicking on a block in the overview, its detail view is presented in the other window and only relationships, which are relevant for this block, are visible. The detail view only shows one block at a time and therefore can be used to closely examine the individual instances with their associated properties. The detail view shows the instances of every class. Clicking on an instance opens separate tables for datatype properties and object properties (which can also be seen in Figure 2). The object property table allows to directly jump to a connected instance, which means that the detail view is automatically focused on the respective instance. The direction of the relationship is presented as arrow symbol and the color of the symbols reflects the type of the relationship. A thumbnail (cf. *E* in Figure 2) of the block in the lower-right corner helps to see the structure of the whole block and allows to navigate quickly within the detail view. The length of texts is restricted to a certain number of characters, otherwise the text is truncated with "..." and tooltips show the full text. Of course, users can switch the views between the main and the preview window to enlarge the view which is of more interest.

Furthermore, the impression of hierarchy – one of the elementary concerns by users – was improved by adding arrows between subclasses. These arrows also allow to expand and collapse the underlying subclasses which further improved the understanding of the left-to-right hierarchy (see Figure 3, right).

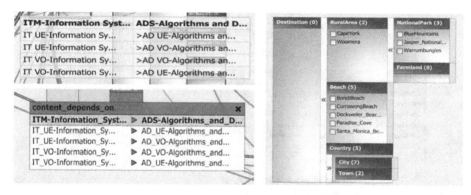

Fig. 3. Left: Comparison between the object property table from the second version (top) and the redesigned table from the fourth version (below). Right: Subclasses can be collapsed or expanded by clicking on the arrows located to the right of each class which contains subclasses.

3.3 Third Iteration Cycle

Based on the results of the user study of the second version we included several modifications. For example, double-clicking on a block will now automatically open the detail view of this block in the main window. Formerly, this was only possible with a specific *switch* button located in the upper-right corner of the preview window. The intensity of the color of a class in the overview reflects the number of contained instances. Another modification is that the relation table can also be pinned down after the user clicks on the associated curve in the overview. The color of the relation table header and of the arrows corresponds now to the color of the object property (Figure 3 (left) shows the modifications in detail). Each table was extended with a close button (one of the major confusions in the second version). Furthermore, blocks in the overview can also be individually arranged by the user in case they are not satisfied with the automatic circular alignment.

Additionally, we extended the prototype with history, bookmarks, search and filter functions (*A* in Figure 2) as well as a setting window which allows, for example, to set the maximum text length. The history function records every jump from one instance/class to another instance/class and allows users to track their progression through the ontology. Furthermore, bookmarks allow users to select instances that are of interest and to jump back to them at anytime. Additionally to the object property filter, user can also highlight blocks and classes to quickly locate them or they can be hidden if they are not from special interest. Furthermore, a new search function allows users to find specific instances or classes of the ontology. For a thorough description of the third version see also [9].

3.4 Fourth Iteration Cycle

In the last iteration cycle, we extended Knoocks with additional features for better user support which will be discussed in detail in the following. One of the main concerns in the evaluation of the third prototype, in regard to the datatype property table was

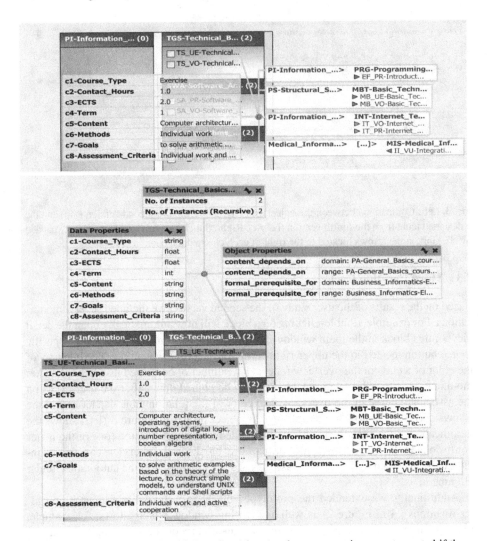

Fig. 4. Comparison between the third version (above), where text entries were truncated if they exceeded a certain length and the fourth and current version (below) which displays the complete entries. Note also the new header of the property table which now shows the name of the instance or class it belongs to and buttons to collapse and close the table. To enhance readability the opacity of the tables has been reduced. The lower image also shows the new class information tables which were not available in the previous version.

that the table does not list the internal datatype (e.g., integer or string) of a property. This issue has not been addressed by domain users so far but we agree that this is an important information for ontology developers and they can now be accessed via tooltips if the mouse is placed over the name of the property. The ontology developers also complained that it is not possible to retrieve general information of a class, in particular information about contained datatype and object properties. This information

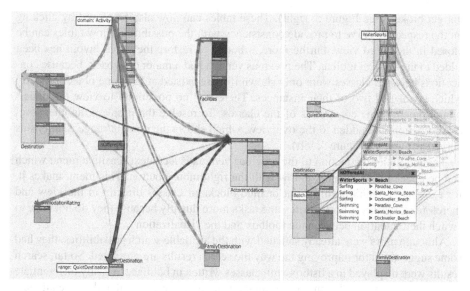

Fig. 5. Left: Domain/range relationships are visualized as curved arrows which point from the domain to the range. The direction is further accentuated by varying the width of the curve from thin (domain) to thick (range). As it is the case with object property curves (right image), the color reflects the property type. Hovering the mouse over such a curve shows the name of the property, the domain and the range. Right: Clicking on a curve opens a table which shows all relations between instances of the two connected classes. As schematically shown these tables can be moved along the curve.

is now accessible by clicking on the class name itself which did not have an effect previously. Furthermore, the internal datatypes for each datatype property are shown. This way it is now possible to inspect all datatype properties assigned to a class, because previously only datatype properties which really had a value assigned were visible in the datatype property table of the instance.

In the previous version long texts were truncated in tables and the complete text was only shown in a tooltip if the mouse was placed over such an entry. Whereas our intention was to avoid that a single table occupies too much space this proved to be inapplicable in same cases, especially if all values of a property start with a certain substring (as it is, for example, the case in Figure 3). Users were therefore not able to differentiate the values without accessing the tooltip and therefore had a hard time to remember which property has which value. The revised version gives the user the possibility to expand or collapse the tables to review the complete text or to minimize it (see Figure 4 for a comparison). As can be seen in Figure 4, the new table also displays the name of the instance to which the table belongs and, next to it, a close button. These changes were introduced because, if multiple tables were open, users lost track which tables belonged to which entity.

In regard to the overview some minor changes have been introduced. Relation tables can now be moved along a curve which allows users to avoid overlapping to a certain degree and simultaneously ensures that the connection between curve and table does not get broken (see Figure 5, right). These tables can now also be closed by clicking on the respective curve to provide consistency with the possibilities how tables can be closed in the detail view. Furthermore, a button to restore the radial layout has been added to the vertical toolbar. The previous version had a major drawback, because connections between classes were only shown if there existed at least one object property which connected two of their instances. There was no possibility to view the underlying domain/range constraints of the classes. To resolve the problem, another level of abstraction was added to the overview, which shows the domain/range relations as curved arrows (see Figure 5, left).

Another major distinction to the previous version is a context sensitive menu which can be opened in the main window with the right mouse button. This menu makes it, for example, possible to highlight or hide blocks or classes directly in the view and therefore allows users to perform some tasks more fluently because they do not have to switch their attention between the toolbox and the visualization.

Although users were already satisfied with the available search possibilities, they had some suggestions for improving the way the search results are presented. So far, search results were displayed in a listbox with classes written in boldface to easily differentiate them from instances. Clicking on a search result automatically centered the detail view on the respective entity in question and highlighted it with a yellow border. However, if the entity was located in a hidden block nothing was shown in the detail view which led to confusion among users. We now indicate entities located in hidden blocks to remedy the problem. In addition, entities in highlighted blocks or classes are colored to signalize that they may be from greater significance to the user. Furthermore, we refined the navigation of the tool by supporting keyboard shortcuts for important functions, like search and the new screenshot feature. Navigation in the detail view is now also possible by dragging the mouse (and with the arrow keys), because we observed that most users tried at first to navigate this way instead with the thumbnail view in the lower right corner. Finally, the colors of the object properties are now definable by the user, because this way they can accentuate specific properties by assigning appropriate colors.

4   Evaluation

The main motivation to conduct user tests was to find out more about the usability of the developed prototype in each iteration cycle to make sure that the development goes into the right direction and to compare Knoocks with other visualization tools. The evaluation of the first prototype in the early development phase of Knoocks served as an initial test instrument to find out about the advantages and drawbacks of the representation of the hierarchical structure and their instances in comparison with other visualizations techniques. The focus of the user tests of the later prototypes was to detect usability problems and to compare Knoocks with other visualization tools. Furthermore, results of the evaluation were analyzed to find out which functionalities need further improvements and to check if users missed important features.

4.1   Methods

For the evaluation, a combination of the following methods was used: task scenarios, observations in combination with thinking aloud, questionnaires and semi-structured interviews.

To test the efficiency of Knoocks and to compare it with other tools, users had to solve several tasks which were based on scenarios. One set of tasks required to identify specific instances and their datatype properties. Another set of tasks concentrated mainly on the dependencies between instances and between classes. To evaluate the structure of blocks, we asked them to identify, which blocks have the most/least classes or which classes contain the most instances. Although certain core tasks stayed the same for each prototype (e.g., which instances belong to a certain class, find a specific instance) additional tasks were introduced in each iteration because of the increasing number of features (e.g., find a specific instance with a certain datatype property). Users had as much time as they needed to solve the tasks with each tool. While users solved the tasks, they were observed and encouraged to think aloud to make their behavior and decisions more transparent.

In addition to the observation of the subjects and thinking aloud protocols, they were also asked to state how helpful the visualization was for executing each task. For this purpose, we applied a 7-point Likert scale [33] from "not helpful" to "very helpful". Furthermore, subjects were asked to explain their decisions and to give suggestions for possible improvements. After the subjects had finished their tasks, they rated the design of the graphical representation (e.g., bad or good color combination) and they were asked about the strengths and weaknesses of the visualization.

For the evaluation of the second and fourth prototype, we additionally adapted the usability questionnaire, as defined by Prümper [15]. The usability questionnaire was originally developed to evaluate software prototypes in regard to the seven dialog principles of ISONORM 9241/110 [4]: suitability for the tasks, self-descriptiveness, controllability, conformity with user expectations, error tolerance, suitability for individualization and suitability for learning. In general, the questionnaire includes five items for each of the seven principles and has a 7-point bi-polar format from "- - -" (very negative) to "+++" (very positive). Not all items are relevant or meaningful for the visualization and therefore we only used items, which reflect the scope of the visualization.

The motivation to compare Knoocks with other visualization tools was to detect advantages as well as drawbacks between the tools. Furthermore, it was from interest to analyze how well users interacted with the different visualization approaches. For the comparison studies, we have chosen the following visualization approaches: CropCircles, TGVizTab, OntoViz and the nested graph view of Jambalaya. CropCircles is a container approach, which represents the subclass-of relationships between classes as nested circles. Our motivation to compare Knoocks with CropCircles was the different representation of the hierarchical structure of the classes. In contrast to CropCircles, TGVizTab and OntoViz visualize the structure of ontologies as node-link representation. Both approaches represent classes and instances as nodes and subclass-of relationships and object properties as edges. The reason to compare Knoocks with Jambalaya was their similarity, because the nested graph view of Jambalaya presents the hierarchical structure with its instances as container approach and the object properties as node-link representation. To make the results comparable, the subjects solved similar tasks for each tool. Additionally, the order of tasks and tools was changed for each testing session to avoid that a specific order influences the results.

Before the participants started with the tasks, they got a short introduction to the most important functionalities of the tools. After the subjects had finished their assignments, we asked them which visualization they preferred in regard to their expectations and user friendliness (specifically, which tool was most helpful, which one was the most understandable tool and which tool met their expectations best).

4.2 Sample

For the evaluations we used an ontology that defines a bachelor of computer science curriculum which includes 86 classes, 122 instances, 2 object properties and 8 datatype properties. We used such a kind of ontology because we were able to get a large number of participants in that particular domain. Contrary, it was very hard to get participants in other domains, especially experts (e.g., in medicine). Furthermore, it supported the ongoing efforts at our university to make the curriculum structure more transparent for students and lecturers.

Motivated to evaluate the fundamental idea and to detect misinterpretations or unclear elements of the visualization, we tested Knoocks with potential users of the domain and with ontology developers. In each iteration cycle we used different subjects to make sure that previous experiences with Knoocks do not influence the results.

First Iteration Cycle. The findings of the first evaluation are based on six students and the testing sessions for each participant took about 40 minutes. For the comparison study in the first iteration cycle, the participants solved similar tasks with CropCircles and the nested graph view of Jambalaya.

Second Iteration Cycle. The results of the second evaluation are based on 22 participants (15 students and 7 lecturers). The testing sessions for each participant took about 90 minutes.

Third Iteration Cycle. Three ontology developers evaluated the prototype in regard to usability and functionality. Although this is a rather small number of participants, we received valuable qualitative feedback and the testing sessions for each participant took about 180 minutes. For the comparison study, we chose TGVizTab and the nested graph view of Jambalaya.

Fourth Iteration Cycle. The prototype were evaluated by 16 subjects (9 students and 7 lecturers) and the testing sessions for each participant took about 120 minutes which include also the comparisons with Jambalaya and OntoViz.

4.3 Results

In general, the findings of the observation and thinking aloud protocols showed that the concepts of Knoocks and especially the hierarchical layout of the blocks was clear and immediately understandable. The color combination was rated as good and the design was considered to be well-balanced. The following strengths of Knoocks were named most frequently during the user tests:

Clear Overview and Detail View. The layout of blocks allowed to quickly see the subclasses and the instances of classes. Furthermore, the switching between the overview and the detail view, the circular arrangement of blocks in the overview and the visibility of both views at the same time were named as helpful to get a good overview about the ontology.

Easy to Learn and Understand. The participants found Knoocks and its functionalities intuitive, easy to learn and to memorize.

Clear Structure and Relationship Views. The representations of object properties in the overview was clear and gave a fast impression of the relationships of the ontology. The visualization of properties of an instance in the detail view provided a clear overview about the dependencies between the instances.

Additional Support for Analysis. The different filter and search possibilities, as introduced in the third version, were mentioned as very helpful, e.g., to find specific instances or classes or to set the users' focus on specific blocks or object properties. The visual coding was named as a further strength, e.g., the color coding to present the number of instances or the thickness coding to visualize the number of connections between classes.

These strengths are in line with the expectations of almost all participants which they have in regard to ontology visualization tools and are also in accordance with the revealed user expectations in [8].

The following sections discuss the findings of the usability study and comparison study between the three tools in detail.

Usability Evaluation. Although the results of the user tests showed that the subjects rated Knoocks in each stage predominantly positive, the modifications, which were based on the detected usability problems, were the reasons for noticeable improvements in Knoocks' usability in each stage. The findings which are listed below are not exhaustive but were the most relevant ones for the further development process.

First Iteration Cycle. The elementary problem was that the direction of the hierarchy was ambiguous. However, the block structure allowed them to get a quick overview and to locate instances without problems.

Second Iteration Cycle. During the second evaluation we observed that users tried to double-click on a block to enlarge it. This might be the case, because the icon of the switch-button was not clear enough for many participants. However, they appreciated the possibility to choose which view is shown in the main window. It was intuitive for them to click on an instance to retrieve detail information (object and datatype properties). Though, most of the users had problems to close the details again, because there was no explicit close button. Most of them found the truncated texts annoying, especially if multiple instances began with the same letters as it was the case in our test ontology. The representation of properties was well received by the participants, because it allowed them to compare different instances in regard to their properties. This was further supported by the possibility to drag and drop these tables. One of the most missed features was a search function, because they stated that currently the tool is nice for browsing but is not suitable for finding a

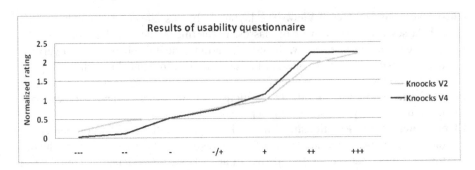

Fig. 6. Normalized results of the rating of the seven dialog principles from "- - -" (very negative) to "+++" (very positive) for the second and fourth prototype

specific instance. As further improvement, they stated they would like to be able to also move/highlight/hide blocks in the overview.

Third Iteration Cycle. The changes were well received by the users. However, ontology experts complained that information about the internal types (integer, string, etc.) of datatype properties is missing. They also missed general information about a class, like the number of contained instances or which object properties are supported by this class. The search results were partly confusing because the list representation made no difference between hidden, highlighted or normal blocks.

Fourth Iteration Cycle. Although the node-link representation of object properties and that the thickness of their curves reflects the number of connections was clear, several subjects stated that the thickness alone is insufficient with increasing number of represented relationships. Therefore they would prefer to additionally see the number of connections as label for each curve. Furthermore, they found that the color coding of classes to show the number of instances is a good way to quickly get an overview of the distribution of instances within the ontology. The possibility to jump between instances and their highlighting was noted as very helpful. However, more than half of the subjects missed the highlighting of instances or classes in the detail view, because the time, which showed the highlighting, was too short or the instance in question was occluded by open properties. All participants found the search function very helpful, especially because it allowed them to find instances or classes which conform to a specific datatype property (e.g., to find all courses which were held in the third term).

The improvement of the usability was further underlined by the results of the usability questionnaire, as can be seen in Figure 6. A closer look at the different dialog principles shows that the participants rated the fourth prototype better than the second, especially in regard to the following three principles (see also Figure 7 for details):

Suitability for the Task. Reasons for the better rating are the new filter and search function. Moreover, the handling of the fourth version was rated as easier, because of the additional support of keyboard shortcuts, the modifications of the property representations and the context sensitive menu.

Self-descriptiveness. Relevant improvements, amongst others, are that the complete text in the datatype property tables is now visible at first glance, that the name of

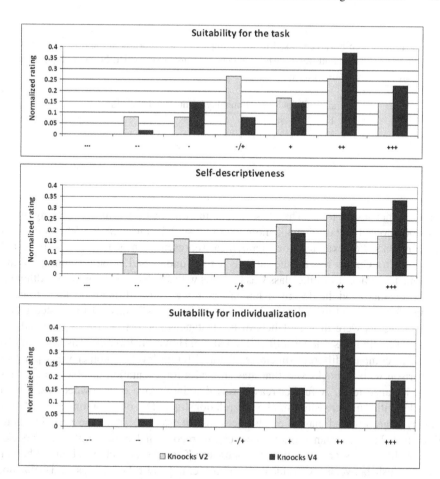

Fig. 7. Normalized values of the rating of three dialog principles for the second and fourth version

the instance along with a close button is shown in the property table and that a double click on a block automatically opens the detail view in the main window.

Suitability for Individualization. The possibility to move blocks and relation tables individually, to customize colors for object properties and to set the maximum label length are reasons for the better rating of the fourth version.

Comparison Study. For the comparison studies different kind of tasks had to be solved by the participants. This would include tasks like: find a specific instance, identify dependencies of an instance, find out which instances belong to a certain class or identify to which class a specific subclass belongs to. Table 1 summarizes which tools have been used for the comparison in which iteration of the development process.

The comparison studies showed that most subjects found that Knoocks was easy to learn and provided a better general overview about the ontology and its object properties

Table 1. Tools which have been used for the comparison of Knoocks at the different stages of development. In the second iteration no comparison study was carried because the evaluation concentrated mainly on usability issues.

Iteration	CropCircles	Jambalaya	OntoViz	TGVizTab
1	×	×		
3		×		×
4		×	×	

than the other tested tools. The observations in combination with the thinking aloud protocols showed that users made more incorrect assumptions with the other tools than with Knoocks. For example, the hierarchical representation of the classes as nested circles in CropCircles was for the subjects hard to understand in the beginning and the performance to find a specific class was lower as with Jambalaya or Knoocks. Although the participants liked the design of Jambalaya, it was rather difficult for them to get a general overview and to find specific classes or instances in case of the nested graph layout. Reasons were that the labels of the instances and classes overlapped and the zooming function was rated as difficult to handle. However, zooming was necessary to be able to compare different subclasses from different levels. Another weak point in comparison with Knoocks was that they missed a representation of object properties on the instance level. A further reason was that Jambalaya overcrowded easier than Knoocks with an increasing number of relationships. The observations showed that if many edges crossed classes or instances then it was harder for the participants to click on a class or instance or, respectively, to read their labels. Similar to Knoocks they also liked the search function. In contrast to Knoocks, the subjects found it harder to distinguish between hierarchical and non-hierarchical relationships in TGVizTab, because of missing visual differentiations. The missing visual differentiations between non-hierarchical relationships were also the reason why the subjects had problems to distinguish the different object property types in OntoViz. Moreover, the representation of object properties was stated as confusing, because the edges were too long and the number of edge crossings was too high. Furthermore, they found it hard to memorize the abbreviations for the drawing settings in OntoViz. The search algorithm was also not clear at the beginning, because it was necessary to type the class name exactly or via wildcard symbols. Moreover, it was not possible to search for specific instances.

In summary, the comparison studies showed that tools with a rather technical interface (OntoViz and TGVizTab) had been rated lower than the ones with a more accessible interface (Jambalaya and Knoocks). This was also confirmed by the ranking of the tools in regard to user friendliness and expectations which yielded the following results for the last iteration circle. 79% ranked Knoocks on the first place, whereas 18% ranked Jambalaya on the first place. However, 78% voted Jambalaya on the second place followed by Knoocks with 11%. OntoViz on the other hand was ranked on the third place by 95% of all participants.

5 Conclusions

Visualizations support users to generate knowledge about the presented data and make the ontology more understandable and manageable. To make the work with ontologies more effective, the needs of users play an essential role for the design of the visualization. Usability evaluations of visualizations help to get feedback what works well and what needs further improvements. However, only one usability test at the end of the development process is in many cases not sufficient. Therefore we adapted the human centered design process which is a well-known approach in human computer interaction to develop Knoocks - a visualization approach for OWL Lite ontologies. Knoocks allows users to analyze the structure of classes with their instances and properties in one single tool. The tool is primarily developed for users who want information about concepts of their domain as well as for users who develop and maintain ontologies. The case study demonstrated that the involvement of potential users during the development process allowed us to integrate feedback immediately which was very valuable to keep the development on the right track and had a positive impact on the usability. This significantly simplified working with the visualization tool. Another advantage gained from the human centered design process was that Knoocks was in accordance with the requirements and expectations, which users had in regard to ontology visualization tools.

The comparison between Knoocks with CropCircles, OntoViz, Jambalaya and TGVizTab showed that the handling of OntoViz caused most problems. Although, participants liked the nested graph view in Jambalaya, most of them preferred the layout of Knoocks. Reasons were that Jambalaya only visualizes one set of subclasses or instances for a class in more detail and that the visualization easily overcrowds with an increasing number of object properties. One participant explicitly noted that the handling and functionalities of Jambalaya seemed more complex than the handling and functionalities of Knoocks. The results of the comparative study with these tools emphasize the significance of the usability in regard to the handling and rating of the tools.

One of our next steps is to verify how the requested functionalities or design elements which were difficult to understand (e.g., to add labels for showing the number of connections between classes in the overview) in the fourth prototype can be included in the next version. Knoocks is currently being developed as a plug-in for Protégé to combine our visualization approach with the editing functionality of Protégé.

References

1. Alani, H.: TGVizTab: An Ontology Visualization Extension for Protégé. In: Knowledge Capture (K-Cap 2003). Workshop on Visualization Information in Knowledge Engineering (2003)
2. Cardoso, J.: The Semantic Web Vision: Where Are We? Intelligent Systems 22(5), 84–88 (2007)
3. Fensel, D.: Ontologies: a silver bullet for knowledge management and electronic commerce. Springer, New York (2001)
4. International Organization for Standardization: ISO 9241-110:2006 Ergonomics of human-system interaction – Part 110: Dialogue principles (2006)

5. Katifori, A., Halatsis, C., Lepouras, G., Vassilakis, C., Giannopoulou, E.: Ontology visualization methods—a survey. ACM Computing Surveys 39(4) (2007)

6. Katifori, A., Torou, E., Halatsis, C., Lepouras, G., Vassilakis, C.: A Comparative Study of Four Ontology Visualization Techniques in Protege: Experiment Setup and Preliminary Results. In: Proc. of the International Conference on Information Visualization, pp. 417–423. IEEE Computer Society (2006)

7. Kriglstein, S.: Analysis of Ontology Visualization Techniques for Modular Curricula. In: Holzinger, A. (ed.) USAB 2008. LNCS, vol. 5298, pp. 299–312. Springer, Heidelberg (2008)

8. Kriglstein, S.: User Requirements Analysis on Ontology Visualization. In: International Conference on Complex, Intelligent and Software Intensive Systems. 2nd International Workshop on Ontology Alignment and Visualization, pp. 694–699. IEEE Computer Society (2009)

9. Kriglstein, S., Wallner, G.: Knoocks - A Visualization Approach for OWL Lite Ontologies. In: International Conference on Complex, Intelligent and Software Intensive Systems. 3rd International Workshop on Ontology Alignment and Visualization, pp. 950–955. IEEE Computer Society (2010)

10. Kulyk, O.A., Kosara, R., Urquiza, J., Wassink, I.: Human-Centered Aspects. In: Kerren, A., Ebert, A., Meyer, J. (eds.) Human-Centered Visualization Environments. LNCS, vol. 4417, pp. 13–75. Springer, Heidelberg (2007)

11. Lanzenberger, M., Sampson, J., Rester, M.: Visualization in Ontology Tools. In: Proc. of the International Conference on Complex, Intelligent and Software Intensive Systems. 2nd International Workshop on Ontology Alignment and Visualization, pp. 705–711. IEEE Computer Society (2009)

12. Nielson, J.: Usability Engineering. Morgan Kaufmann, San Francisco (1994)

13. North, C.: Toward Measuring Visualization Insight. IEEE Computer Graphics and Applications 26(3), 6–9 (2006)

14. Noy, N.F., McGuinness, D.L.: Ontology Development 101: A Guide to Creating Your First Ontology. Technical report, Stanford Knowledge Systems Laboratory and Stanford Medical Informatics (2001)

15. Prümper, J.: Test It: ISONORM 9241/10. In: Proc. of HCI International (the 8th International Conference on Human-Computer Interaction) on Human-Computer Interaction: Ergonomics and User Interfaces, vol. I, pp. 1028–1032. L. Erlbaum Associates Inc. (1999)

16. Rester, M., Pohl, M., Wiltner, S., Hinum, K., Miksch, S., Popow, C., Ohmann, S.: Evaluating an InfoVis Technique Using Insight Reports. In: Proc. of the 11th International Conference Information Visualization, pp. 693–700. IEEE Computer Society (2007)

17. Saraiya, P., North, C., Duca, K.: An Insight-Based Methodology for Evaluating Bioinformatics Visualizations. IEEE Transactions on Visualization and Computer Graphics 11(4), 443–456 (2005)

18. Shneiderman, B.: Designing the User Interface. Addison-Wesley (1998)

19. Shneiderman, B.: Tree visualization with tree-maps: 2-d space-filling approach. ACM Transactions on Graphics 11(1), 92–99 (1992)

20. Sintek, M.: OntoViz,
    http://protegewiki.stanford.edu/index.php/OntoViz

21. Stanford Center for Biomedical Informatics Research,
    http://protege.stanford.edu

22. Storey, M.A., Callendar, C., Lintern, R., Ernst, N., Best, C.: Jambalaya,
    http://protegewiki.stanford.edu/index.php/Jambalaya

23. Storey, M.A., Lintern, R., Ernst, N., Perrin, D.: Visualization and Protégé. In: Proc. of the 7th International Protégé Conference (2004)

24. Swartout, B., Patil, R., Knight, K., Russ, T.: Toward Distributed Use of Large-Scale Ontologies. In: Proc. of the AAAI 1997 Spring Symposium Series, Workshop on Ontological Engineering, pp. 138–148. AAAI Press (1997)

25. Vas, R.: Educational Ontology and Knowledge Testing. Electronic Journal of Knowledge Management 5(1), 123–130 (2007)
26. W3C: OWL Web Ontology Language Guide, http://www.w3.org/TR/owl-guide/
27. Wang, T.D., Parsia, B.: CropCircles: Topology Sensitive Visualization of OWL Class Hierarchies. In: Cruz, I., Decker, S., Allemang, D., Preist, C., Schwabe, D., Mika, P., Uschold, M., Aroyo, L.M. (eds.) ISWC 2006. LNCS, vol. 4273, pp. 695–708. Springer, Heidelberg (2006)
28. Kruskal, J.B., Landwehr, J.M.: Icicle Plots: Better Displays for Hierarchical Clustering. The American Statistician 37(2), 162–168 (1983)
29. Barlow, T., Neville, P.: A Comparison of 2-D Visualizations of Hierarchies. In: Proc. of the IEEE Symposium on Information Visualization 2001. IEEE Computer Society (2001)
30. Kriglstein, S., Motschnig-Pitrik, R.: Knoocks: New Visualization Approach for Ontologies. In: Proc. of the International Conference on Information Visualization, pp. 163–168. IEEE Computer Society (2008)
31. Martinez-Gil, J., Alba, E., Aldana-Montes, J.F.: Statistical Study about Existing OWL Ontologies from a Significant Sample as Previous Step for their Alignment. In: Proc. of the International Conference on Complex, Intelligent and Software Intensive Systems. 3rd International Workshop on Ontology Alignment and Visualization, pp. 980–985. IEEE Computer Society (2010)
32. International Organization for Standardization: ISO 13407:1999 Human-centered design processes for interactive systems (1999)
33. Likert, R.: A technique for the measurement of attitudes. Archives of Psychology 22(140), 1–55 (1932)

SmoothScroll: A Multi-scale, Multi-layer Slider

Michael Wörner[1,2] and Thomas Ertl[2]

[1] GSaME Graduate School for Advanced Manufacturing Engineering
University of Stuttgart, Stuttgart, Germany
[2] Institute for Visualization and Interactive Systems, University of Stuttgart, Stuttgart, Germany

Abstract. The SmoothScroll control is a multi-scale, multi-layer slider for the navigation in large one-dimensional datasets such as time series data. Presenting multiple data layers at gradually varying scales provides both detail and context information and allows for both fine-grained and coarse navigation and scrolling at different granularities. Visual data aggregation allows for multi-level navigation while the clear visual relation of the data layers aids the user in retaining a sense of both the current detail position and the immediate and global context. We describe SmoothScroll as well as related controls and discuss its application with the help of several usage examples.

Keywords: Navigation, Timelines, Distortion.

1 Introduction

The analysis of data is a central aspect of information technology. Often, data in itself is not overly useful, but very interesting pieces of information can be extracted from it. An online shop can use its order database to generate "you might also like" recommendations for customers. A dataset of experiment results might hint at which parameters are most relevant for the life expectancy of an engine. A lot of this can be achieved using automatic data analysis methods such as data mining or artificial intelligence. The field of visual analytics, however, argues that not all analysis tasks can be solved satisfactorily using automatic means alone, while the dimensions of many of today's datasets preclude a purely manual analysis. The combination of automatic data analysis, visualisation, and interaction can create systems that leverage both the computational power of computers and the understanding, the creativity, the experience, and the implicit knowledge of a human analyst.

One aspect of this is how to communicate vast amounts of information to the user. This is usually addressed with visualisation and aggregation, preparing a condensed, easy-to-understand display of relevant data. Another aspect is the way of navigating the data. It will usually be impossible to display the complete dataset all at once, so a system will usually present an aggregated overview, a selection of data items, or a combination of both. In order to explore the dataset, the user will then need a way of changing what is being displayed. In the simplest case, users can name precisely whatever it is they are looking for. No human could ever hope to read all the information on the internet, yet it is a trivial task to open a web page given its URL. The actual size of the internet and the actual number of web pages concern only the people managing the network

G. Csurka et al. (Eds.): VISIGRAPP 2011, CCIS 274, pp. 142–154, 2013.

infrastructure, not the user typing in the web address. Similarly, if we cannot name what we are looking for but can give a precise description of it, web search engines will usually take us there, again with little concern over how many web pages were actually crawled in the process.

Navigation becomes a whole lot more challenging once analysts are browsing a dataset in search for something that is "unusual" or "interesting". Often, they are not only interested in a certain data item but also in its context, possibly at various level of detail. Thus, they will usually want to "move" or "pan" or "scroll" through the dataset. Unlike the internet, many of these datasets have a clear notion of "forward" and "backward". With time-based data, for example, data items are ordered by time and may be navigated in a calendar-like fashion.

2 Related Work

In visual analytics, working with large datasets is often facilitated using the focus + context and overview + detail principles, sometimes in combination with a distorted display. Overview + detail [11], [9] describes the approach of presenting multiple visualisations of the same data at different levels of detail. By providing both high-detail information about the focus point and low-detail information about the data surrounding it, it aims at answering the questions "What am I looking at?", "Where in the data am I?" and "What else is there?" all at once. One common example is a calendar application that shows a larger day view and a smaller month view with an indicator highlighting the current day. The scale of the overview is often a trade-off between being too detailed, when the overview does not display useful context information, and being too coarse, when the overview is no longer useful for navigating the data.

The focus + context principle is similar to overview + detail but combines low- and high-detail information in a single view. The reduction in detail may be achieved by scaling down the visual representation of the data items, by aggregating data items to larger entities, or by a combination of both. The transition between the different levels of detail may be either abrupt or gradual. A gradual transition in detail can be achieved by distorting the view in a way that allocates a larger portion of the display to the focused data items and a smaller portion to those not in focus [8]. The classic approaches include the Fisheye view [5], which has been applied to one-dimensional [4] and two-dimensional [10] data alike. Using distortion, it is possible for all the data to remain visible without occlusion. Another advantage of this approach is that in comparison to the overview + detail concept it removes the need to relate information in different views. At the same time, however, the distorted space makes it very difficult to put item positions, distances and sizes into relation to each other.

The classical way of navigating through data on a computer is using the arrow keys on the keyboard. They allow for both precise and coarse navigation: Pressing the up key, for example, will usually move the display up by one data line. Pressing the page up key will move it by several lines, and pressing the home key will jump to the start of the data. While this may be sufficient and efficient in some cases, it does not allow for direct navigation to a certain region in the data. If, for example, a user is viewing a text file of an entire book and wants to jump to a certain chapter, this would require jumping to either the beginning or the end of the book and then pressing page up or page down until the respective chapter has been found. Also, the arrow keys themselves don't provide any context information on what portion of the data is currently displayed on screen.

In most contemporary computer applications, one-dimensional data navigation is handled using scrollbars or sliders. Just like arrow keys, they allow for precise and coarse navigation: Clicking one of the arrow buttons on either side of the scrollbar is the equivalent of pressing the up or down arrow key, while clicking between the arrow button and the thumb corresponds to pressing the page up or page down key. Additionally, scrollbars allow for direct navigation to a certain data position by dragging the thumb. They also provide context information to a certain extent in that the size of the thumb is an indication of what portion of the data is currently visible. This context information is strictly limited to position, however. To gain any insight into what kind of data lies beyond the current viewport, the user needs to navigate there and inspect it. This again gets slightly problematic when the scrollbar is attached to a very large dataset where moving the thumb by just one pixel results in a jump of hundreds of data items.

As a result, there is a need for navigation techniques that enable the user to reach distant parts of the data quickly and, at the same time, make precise adjustments to the current position. One proposition for such a navigational control is the Alphaslider [1] (Figure 1). It resembles a scrollbar, but its thumb is divided into three sections that correspond to fine, medium, and coarse granularity. When the user drags the thumb, the speed at which the data scrolls by is determined by the thumb section in which the user started the dragging operation. There is an alternative mode in which the granularity of the scrolling is determined by the speed of the mouse movement. In a third mode, the user can influence the scrolling granularity very precisely by moving the mouse pointer orthogonal to the scrolling direction. The farther away the cursor is from the slider, the coarser is the scrolling.

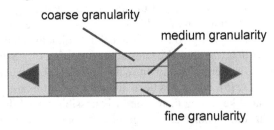

Fig. 1. The Alphaslider as described in [1]

This last idea has been explored further in the OrthoZoom Scroller [3] (Figure 2). The OrthoZoom control is similar to a normal scroll bar in that the user can scroll through the data by moving the mouse vertically. The speed of the scrolling is determined by the horizontal mouse cursor position. As the user moves the mouse cursor away from the scrollbar horizontally, the scrolling speed increases. Additionally, the OrthoZoom Scroller also scales the associated data display. As a result, the user has control both over how much detail or context is visible and about the granularity at which the current position moves through the data.

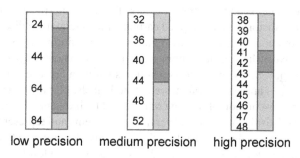

Fig. 2. The OrthoZoom Scroller as described in [3]

Concerning time-oriented data, [2] gives an overview over visual methods for analysing such data. The SIMILE project includes a web-based timeline widget [7], which supports multiple "bands" at different zoom factors. Most SIMILE timelines display two bands (one overview, one detail). When displaying one-dimensional time-based data on a two-dimensional screen, a matrix display [6] has been used to better utilize screen space. This has been combined with a degree-of-interest approach that selects an appropriate matrix resolution for different sections of data.

3   The SmoothScroll Control

Our own approach at developing a scalable slider control for the navigation of one-dimensional data is the "SmoothScroll" control, which we previously introduced in [12]. In this extended version, we also suggest several ways of handling cases in which the data items themselves consist of other items outside the navigated data dimenison. We had previously presented the example of a time line of pictures and now investigate ways of integrating metadata information on individual pictures into the timeline in Section 4.1. We added section Section 4.2 discussing the application to datasets with hierarchies that do not exhibit the strict regularity of timelines. We also show an example of a vertical control and how SmoothScroll could be used to scroll through structured text documents. Where we previously stated that other interpolation schemes may prove beneficial, we now provide a concrete example of an interpolation that reduces the scale differences between the most detailed layers in Section 5.2.

Our control extends some of the ideas presented in the Alphaslider and the Ortho-Zoom scroller. We, too, allow orthogonal mouse movements to influence the granularity of the scrolling. However, we do not use a single data display with a varying scale factor but show multiple layers of data at different yet fixed scales. The bottommost layer displays a small section of the data at a resolution that shows single data items in as much detail as is appropriate. The topmost layer shows the entire data range. The layers in between interpolate between these extremes. A highlight on each but the most detailed layer indicates which section of this layer covers the data range displayed on the detail layer. This facilitates tracing the focus position across different scales.

In the simplest case, the less detailed layers just scale down the data items. A more sophisticated approach, however, is to apply some sort of aggregation and use colour coding to relate data items on the different layers. The layer interpolation is similar to a focus + context data distortion as described earlier, with a gradual but discrete transition from a detailed to a coarse display. Having a discrete transition means data items are only distorted between layers, not within a single layer, where they are represented by rectangular shapes. Sizes and distances of items within a layer remain comparable. When the item shapes are large enough, we can add labels, glyphs, function graphs or any other visual representation of the data represented by the item. On the less detailed layer, an aggregated display item may cover many data items and represent them by one label. Because multiple scales are visible at the same time, the user can trace the current position across layers, across data scales and across aggregation levels.

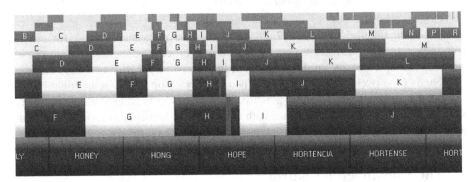

Fig. 3. The SmoothScroll control displaying a list of roughly 4000 names

Figure 3 shows the SmoothScroll control displaying a list of about 4000 names. The data is presented at three levels of abstraction: The bottommost layer displays individual names. The layers above it combine all names starting with the same letter into one data item that displays only this letter. The topmost layers only use colour to indicate sequences of names starting with the same letter, without actually identifying this letter. Looking at the display, you can tell we are looking at the name "Hope" and you can see what names directly precede and succeed it in the list. Following the red highlight of the data section visible in the bottommost layer, you also see that "Hope" is quite at the end of the names starting with h and you can see that those names are followed by roughly the same number of names starting with i and a long sequence of names starting with j. Looking at the top of the display, the h sequence is visibly one of the shorter sequences in the data set, although towards the end of the data, there are a few sequences that are even shorter.

To navigate to and investigate one of these short sequences, the user can click near it on one of the topmost layers. This will change the view to something like Figure 4 and reveal that in this example, the clicked position corresponded to the data item "Trudie". Now that the focus point is near the short sequence in question, the user can click in one of the lower layers to perform the precise navigation necessary to inspect single data items.

As is apparent from the shape of the stripes in Figure 3, the scale interpolation between layers is non-linear. In a way, a linear scale interpolation might seem more visually appealing, as it creates (imaginary) straight lines from the focus point area in the

Fig. 4. The SmoothScroll control after changing the focus point

overview layer to the edges of the detail layer. This linearity would make the relation between the detailed and the coarse data easily recognisable. However, this approach is not practical for large scale differences, because a linear interpolation on a sufficiently large dataset causes the scale factor to decrease rapidly, so that none of the intermediate layers display a significant part of the whole dataset. In the example of Figure 3, the total magnification factor is roughly 650 (about 6 items on the detail layer, about 4000 on the overview layer). If we apply linear scale interpolation, the scale increases by a factor of 95 in the first step from the topmost to the following layer. As a result, this second layer would display only about 1% of the total data. This configuration is not very useful in terms of orientation, and any navigation to data positions outside the immediate vicinity of the focus point would have to take place on the topmost layer.

As an alternative, we base our interpolation on a perspective projection and associate a distance $z(\lambda)$ with each normalized layer position $\lambda = \frac{l}{l_{max}}$ (l being the layer index with 0 representing the overview layer and l_{max} representing the detail layer). This distance determines a scale factor $s(\lambda) = \frac{e}{z(\lambda)+e}$ for every layer (e being an arbitrary "eye distance" between camera and screen), which translates to the pixel size of a data item on the corresponding layer. We want the overview layer to span all data items, so if S is the available display size in pixels, we require $s(0) = \frac{S}{n}$ (n being the number of data items). The item size on the detail layer, $s(1)$, can be freely chosen but should be large enough to display some sort of identification, such as a label. Using a linear interpolation of z values between $z(0) = \frac{e \cdot n}{S} - e$ and $z(1) = \frac{e}{s(1)} - e$ we get $z(\lambda) = z(0) \cdot (1 - \lambda) + z(1) \cdot \lambda$ and finally $s(\lambda) = \frac{S \cdot s(1)}{(1-\lambda)n \cdot s(1) + \lambda S}$.

We position each layer so that it displays the current focus point at the screen coordinate $x(\lambda)$. We require the overview layer to remain fixed: $x(0) = \frac{f}{n}S$ (where f is the index of the focused element). On the detail layer, we want the focus point to always be displayed at the centre of the control: $x(1) = \frac{S}{2}$. We determine the position of the intermediate layers using linear interpolation between these extremes.

Clicking on the control will move the focus point to the corresponding position, adjusting all layers accordingly. This allows for crude selections by clicking in the coarsest layer, precise selections by clicking in the most detailed layer, and many compromises between those two extremes by clicking in one of the intermediate layers. In order to browse through the data, the user may press and hold the second mouse button, causing smooth scrolling towards the mouse cursor position. Due to the different scales, the speed at which the focus point moves changes as the mouse pointer passes through different layers: The user can influence the speed of the movement by moving the mouse pointer vertically while scrolling through the data. This is similar to the zoom/pan control of the OrthoZoom Scroller, which has been evaluated to be very effective in [3]. An important difference is that the SmoothScroll control keeps the multi-scale context information instead of changing the scale of the single data display next to the slider. Even when moving through the data at high speeds, the bottommost layer will always display the current position at full detail and the topmost layer will provide global context information.

Navigating the data with the mouse gives a distinct three-dimensional effect. The bottommost layer moves quickly, whereas the layers above it move continuously slower. The topmost layer is stationary. This effect is similar to a motion parallax and, combined with the non-linear scale interpolation, gives the impression of looking into the distance. We think this might be a suitable visual metaphor and increased this impression by adding a subtle depth fog effect to the upper layers. We think that this visual continuity between the layers can alleviate the problem of non-linear scales being generally more difficult to understand than linear ones.

4   Glyphs and Highlights

Display items are not restricted to displaying a label but can use their rectangular area in any way suitable to represent the associated data. Displaying glyphs instead of text label uses less screen space and may convey information like item type or state more effectively. Figure 5 shows the SmoothScroll control displaying the data set provided for the first mini challenge of the 2010 IEEE VAST challenge. This (synthetic) data set consists of a number of text fragments from various sources (intelligence reports, newspaper accounts, e-mail messages, etc.). This data is displayed along a time scale with alternating background colours indicating months and thin vertical lines indicating days. Documents are visualised by brightening the background colour of the corresponding day and, on the more detailed levels, by displaying glyphs that indicate the number of documents created on that date and show the document type. Additionally, a full-text search for two search terms was performed and days that have documents containing the first term, the second term, or both of the terms are highlighted in green, red, and brown respectively. This gives a quick visual overview over the distribution of occurrences along the timeline. The multi-layer nature of the control makes it easy to navigate across the time scale and visually identify groups of occurrences that appear extraordinary. Once an interesting point in time is reached, the more detailed layers allow for precise selection of the relevant days and documents.

Fig. 5. The SmoothScroll control displaying documents along a timeline. Documents matching search terms are highlighted.

4.1 Multiple Aggregation Levels

By the nature of how our calendars work, time series data can be presented hierarchically in years, months, days, etc. Figure 6 shows the SmoothScroll control displaying a picture collection. We used the pictures stored on a digital camera and arranged them according to the date and time they were taken.

A picture collection is another typical example of data that is often navigated based on the creation time of the elements. For Figure 6, we used the pictures stored on a digital camera and arranged them according to the date and time they were taken. The alternating shades of grey on the top three layers indicate months. On the third layer, we add labels with the abbreviated month names. Starting from the fourth layer, additional shading indicates the day of the month. From the sixth layer, we add day labels. The bottommost layer finally displays hours of the day.

On the top six layers, the lower half of the layer visualises the number of pictures taken on a particular day. The upper half of each layer continues to provide temporal context. If at least one picture was taken on that date, a orange marker indicates the number of pictures, the brighter the shade of orange the more pictures. Note that the time resolution of these markers is independent of the underlying time resolution of the layer. Even though the top layers vary shades only at month resolution, the markers

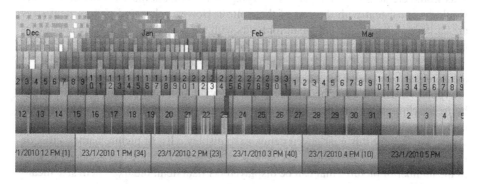

Fig. 6. A timeline of pictures

on these layers still give a rough impression of how pictures are distributed over the course of the month. Tracing the markers down, one can identify the actual dates for data items close to the focus point. On the two bottom layers, markers are drawn at hourly resolution. The text label on the detail layer displays both the exact hour and the number of pictures that were taken in that hour.

At this point, a user would probably want to be able to get metadata information on the actual pictures rather than just the picture count. However, for data presented in a timeline fashion as in Figure 6, the data items usually represent some unit of time, hours in this example. Using the aggregation rules, hours can be aggregated into days, which can be aggregated into months. The size of a month or day item is determined by the number of hours it covers. One straightforward way to insert single pictures into the hierarchy might be adding an additional layer that splits an hour item into a number of picture items and changing our underlying data item to be the picture, not the hour. Then, days and months would no longer be sized according to the number of hours they cover, but according to the number of pictures taken during that time. As a result, months in which no pictures were taken, would vanish from the display. Months with few pictures would be shorter than months with many pictures. Depending on the user's intent this may be a very useful aggregation, but the result would no longer be a smooth timeline.

We can achieve both an undistorted timeline and a layer with individual pictures by allowing different data models for different layers, so the bottom layer might display a sequence of pictures while the upper layers display a sequence of hours at various aggregation levels. It is possible to map data items between these layers, as each picture is associated with an hour during which it was taken, just as every hour is associated with a number of pictures. However, this loses the spatial relationship between the size of an item and the number of data items it represents. On the time layers, the size of an hour item is fixed, regardless of the number of pictures it represents. On the picture layer, the size of a picture item is fixed. As a result, continuity between these layers would be lost and scrolling would no longer be smooth.

In order to retain this continuity, it may be favourable to keep the hour as a reference unit for all layers and determine the size of a picture item by dividing the size that an hour item would have at the respective layer by the number of pictures in this hour. This would create a picture layer with varying item sizes, but the scrolling of the layer would be consistent with the rest of the control. However, because picture item sizes are variable and may get very small for hours with many pictures, there may not always be enough space to display meaningful metadata.

A third option is to not introduce a picture layer at all and add picture metadata to the hour items instead. This way, we can ensure a certain screen size. According to our interpolation scheme described in Section 3, the width of an item on the detail layer can be freely chosen. As for the height, we can extend our interpolation scheme to allow user-defined heights for certain layers and interpolate only the sizes of the remaining layers. We can use this guaranteed item size to display a list of picture names, creation times and file sizes, for example, as can be seen in Figure 7. While this is clearly limited in the number of pictures that can be displayed per data item, the fixed item size means we could integrate GUI elements that enable the user to scroll the list of pictures.

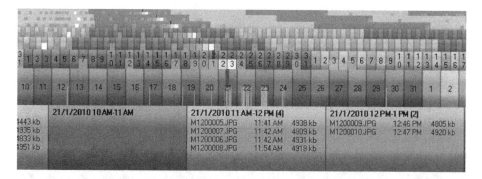

Fig. 7. The pictures timeline with an integrated list of pictures on the detail layer

Even with all these possibilities, however, it is not clear whether the control itself is the best place to present a wealth of information from outside the predominant data dimension. It is a common technique in visual analytics to combine multiple views of the same data and use brushing + linking to synchronize user actions, selections and highlights between them. Much in the same way, clicking on an hour item in this control might update a linked list view control to show details on the pictures taken during that hour.

4.2 Hierarchies and Vertical Display

In the timeline example, the aggregation of data items into less detailed items was very regular: Every day has 24 hours and every month has between 28 and 31 days. Hierarchies are not always this uniform, of course. In Figure 8, we configured the Smooth-Scroll control to display all the lines in Shakespeare's Hamlet. Our data items represent lines of text and we have aggregation levels of utterances (lines of text spoken by one character without being interrupted by another), scenes and acts. Since lines of text are, by their nature, horizontal entities, we rotated our control by 90°, so that the overview layer is on the left, the detail layer is on the right and the user scrolls vertically through the play.

The overview layer displays the five acts of the play. The next five layers represent scenes, followed by three layers of utterances and a detail layer showing lines of text. The scenes are shaded with alternating lightness and coloured to match the act they belong to. Utterances and lines of text are coloured according to which character speaks them. When there is enough room, the character is also identified by a text label on the second layer from the right. The large items on the utterance layers indicate long monologues by a single character. Thin stripes mark sequences where different characters exchange short utterances. The colouring also hints at which characters are predominant in the parts preceding and succeeding the current focus position.

Since our colouring for acts and scenes and our colouring for utterances and lines of text is different, we were looking for a visual clue that might convey to the user which utterances belong to which scenes. We decided to add coloured stripes to the left side of each utterance and line of text, with the colour of the stripe matching the respective scene. As in the previous example, we have made use of the possibility to

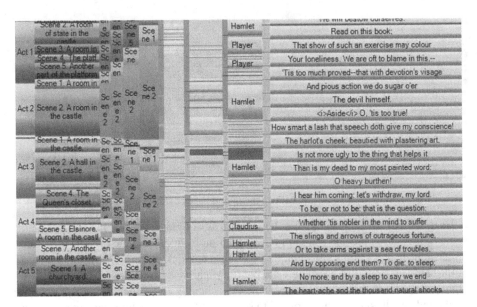

Fig. 8. Shakespeare's Hamlet in acts, scenes, utterances and lines of text

set certain layers to fixed sizes to ensure there is enough room for on-layer information. This mainly concerns the detail layer, which displays the lines of text, but we also extended the second layer to make room for displaying at least part of the scene title.

5 Discussion

5.1 Screen Space

While the SmoothScroll control has a number of benefits over other methods of one-dimensional navigation, there are drawbacks as well: The most prominent disadvantage is its screen space requirement. When compared to a simple timeline control, our control needs to be significantly higher (or wider in vertical mode) to display a reasonable number of layers. Where screen space is scarce, the benefits of more intuitive overview and navigation may not be as important as other information that could have otherwise been displayed to the user. This is especially true as there is a certain redundancy in the display, although this redundancy is essential to ensure the intended gradual scale progression.

The key to alleviating the screen space issue is reducing the redundancy. One approach is to use meaningful levels of abstraction and aggregation across layers, as in Figure 6 to provide an added benefit. Another idea is to make use of the spatial extent of the layers to display glyphs or textual information, as in Figure 5. One could also include a continuous line plot of one or more relevant values across the timeline. These overlays benefit from the same focus + context distortion as the rest of the timeline: The topmost layer shows a low detail representation of line plot values over the entire time span. We consider this possibility to add two-dimensional information a significant advantage over a layerless, continuous visualization, which corresponds to the special case of increasing the number of layers until one layer corresponds to one row of pixels on screen. When adding additional information to the layers, care must be taken not to overload the user with information. Displayed information should be consistent along layers, repeating the same information in order to aid in navigation and orientation. Displaying entirely unrelated pieces of information across the layers could both overfill the display with information and reduce the visual continuity between the layers. Also, aggregation schemes should be applied to on-layer information as well, in order to display less detailed representations of on-layer information on the upper layers.

5.2   Interpolation

While the interpolation we introduced in Section 3 is clearly superior to a linear one, it comes at the cost of a considerable scale difference between the two most detailed layers at the bottom of the control, which makes it hard at times to spot exactly which portion of the second layer is displayed in the most detailed layer. It may be better to use a non-linear interpolation of the z values across the layers. A bifocal transfer function [8] that ensures gentle scale changes on both the detailed and the coarse end might yield better results. In Figure 9, for example, we distorted the linear z progression to $z' = \frac{1}{2}(1 - cos(\lambda\pi))$, which causes smaller z increases at the bottom and at the top layers and steeper increases in the middle of the control.

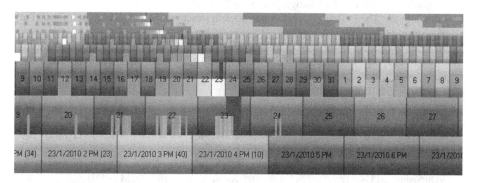

Fig. 9. An alternative interpolation function, which causes smaller scale differences among the detailed (bottom) layers (compare with Figure 6)

6   Conclusions and Future Work

We presented the SmoothScroll control, an intuitive slider control for the one-dimensional navigation in large datasets, as in the form of a timeline. It provides a focus + context view by dividing the timeline into multiple layers, each displaying the data at a different scale. There is an overview layer, which shows the entire dataset, and a detail layer, which shows a detailed view of a small portion of the data. Intermediate layers use non-linear interpolation to provide a distorted, two-dimensional view of the timeline. This facilitates both orientation and navigation in time-dependent data or other one-dimensional data. We also gave three application examples.

There is potential for future work, both in the features of the control itself and in its applications. The actual interaction with the control while navigating the data needs to be evaluated further. For mobile devices, kinetic scrolling (which continues for a time after the finger has been lifted) would probably better meet users' expectations. Extensive user studies will be necessary to identify visualizations which provide an enhanced data display and at the same time do not overwhelm the user with too many details. Configuring the control for other domains and datasets, such as personal calendar data, can be expected to unveil additional benefits and applications.

References

1. Ahlberg, C., Shneiderman, B.: The alphaslider: a compact and rapid selector. In: Proceedings of the SIGCHI Conference on Human Factors in Computing Systems: Celebrating Interdependence, p. 371. ACM (1994)
2. Aigner, W., Miksch, S., Muller, W., Schumann, H., Tominski, C.: Visual methods for analyzing time-oriented data. IEEE Transactions on Visualization and Computer Graphics 14(1), 47–60 (2008)
3. Appert, C., Fekete, J.: OrthoZoom scroller: 1D multi-scale navigation. In: Proceedings of the SIGCHI Conference on Human Factors in Computing Systems, p. 30. ACM (2006)
4. Bederson, B.: Fisheye menus. In: Proceedings of the 13th Annual ACM Symposium on User Interface Software and Technology, p. 225. ACM (2000)
5. Furnas, G.W.: The FISHEYE view: A new look at structured files. Readings in Information Visualization: Using Vision to Think, 312–330 (1999)
6. Hao, M., Dayal, U., Keim, D., Schreck, T.: Multi-Resolution Techniques for Visual Exploration of Large Time-Series Data. In: Eurographics/IEEE-VGTC Symposium on Visualization (2007)
7. Huynh, D.: SIMILE-Timeline (2006),
http://www.simile-widgets.org/timeline/
8. Leung, Y.K., Apperley, M.D.: A review and taxonomy of distortion-oriented presentation techniques. ACM Transactions on Computer-Human Interaction (TOCHI) 1(2), 126–160 (1994)
9. Robertson, G., Mackinlay, J.: The document lens. In: Proceedings of the 6th Annual ACM Symposium on User Interface Software and Technology, p. 108. ACM (1993)
10. Sarkar, M., Brown, M.: Graphical fisheye views of graphs. In: Proceedings of the SIGCHI Conference on Human Factors in Computing Systems, pp. 83–91. ACM, New York (1992)
11. Spence, R., Apperley, M.: Data base navigation: an office environment for the professional. Behaviour & Information Technology 1(1), 43–54 (1982)
12. Wörner, M., Ertl, T.: Multi-Dimensional Distorted 1D Navigation. In: Proc. of the International Conference on Information Visualization Theory and Applications, pp. 198–203 (2011)

Part IV
Computer Vision Theory and Applications

Palm Shape Comparison for Person Recognition

Irina Bakina*

Moscow State University, Moscow, Russia
irina_msu@mail.ru

Abstract. The article presents a new method for palm comparison based on the matching of palm shapes. The proposed approach allows comparison and recognition of palms with sticking fingers. The existing methods do not work correctly in this case, while it frequently appears in real environments (mostly among elderly people). The idea of the proposed method is to model a "posture" of test palm on reference palm. The form of flexible object is used for palm modeling. This representation provides a convenient tool for applying palm transformations and allows us to perform them in real-time mode. Low resolution webcams can be used for palm image acquisition. The article also introduces the application of person recognition based on the proposed comparison. At the end of the article the problem of improving recognition characteristics of palm is addressed. Particularly, it provides a bimodal approach that employs palm and voice features.

Keywords: Palm shape comparison, Flexible object, Alignment of palms, Person recognition, Combination of palm and voice features, Bimodal approach.

1 Introduction

The article presents a new method for palm shape comparison. Comparison is performed between reference and test palms. Reference palm is a model of person's palm stored in the form of flexible object [4]. This representation of reference palm is constructed for a "good" image of palm, i.e. it doesn't contain sticking fingers, long nails, rings or bracelets. Contrarily, test palm is a binary image of palm, which can contain sticking fingers, like on Fig. 1. Such a case appears while dealing with elderly people as sometimes it is difficult for them to separate fingers. The proposed method employs only palm shape information, interior is of no interest. So, non-expensive webcams can be used to obtain palm images.

The proposed method for palm comparison suggests analyzing shapes of transformed reference palm and test one. Transformation is performed for reference palm because it is a model of palm and we know its structure; while it isn't true for a test one. Generally, when person presents his/her palm for recognition by positioning it on a platform's surface, he/she can perform the following movements: shifts and rotations of palm; rotations of fingers. The used representation of reference palm allows these movements to be modeled and, finally, test and reference palms to be compared in the same "posture" [16]. Most existing approaches to palm recognition require to show palm the way

---

* The author thanks the Russian Foundation of Basic Researches, which has supported this work (grants $08 - 01 - 00670$ and $10 - 07 - 00609$).

G. Csurka et al. (Eds.): VISIGRAPP 2011, CCIS 274, pp. 157–171, 2013.

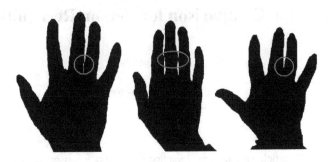

Fig. 1. Examples of palm images with sticking fingers

all fingers are well separated. The proposed method for palm shape comparison can operate in common cases with well separated fingers and, moreover, it suits for cases with sticking fingers.

Palm shape isn't really unique among people. So, one-to-many comparison (or identification) doesn't provide good recognition accuracy [3]. However, the reducing of identification problem to verification one may help. The possible way of doing this is combining palm shape features with other biometric data. As an example, a fusion of palm and voice features is considered in the article.

The article is organized as follows. Section 2 considers the background. In Section 3 the used model of palm is described, and its parametrization is introduced. Section 4 proposes method for automatic identification of model's parameters by the set of palm images. In Section 5 similarity measure and palm comparison algorithm are introduced. Section 6 describes the recognition system based on palm shape comparison. The results of the experiments carried out are in Section 7. Section 8 introduces the bimodal approach. Conclusion and future work are considered in Section 9.

2   Background

There are a lot of approaches to person recognition based on palm features. The first one, which is widely used nowadays, employs hand geometry features such as palm width, perimeter, area, lengths and widths of fingers, distances between finger joints, etc. This approach is introduced in several works — [6,7,8,9,10,13,15], etc. Generally, the works differ in a set of hand geometry features used, distance functions and classifiers applied. For example, in [15] information about width (measured at 40 locations) of index, middle and ring fingers is considered. In [10] feature vector is composed of 21 components — lengths of fingers, width of each finger at 3 locations, width of the palm. Also, several distance functions are compared. In addition to common hand geometry features special comparison is performed for finger tips in [6].

Another approach to person recognition based on palm features suggests transforming palm to predefined position and extracting shape-based features [5,11,12,14]. In this case a contour of palm is taken as a signal, to which independent component analysis, wavelet, cosine or other transforms are applied. But most of the existing approaches can operate only in situations when person presents palm in such manner that obtained image is "good". At least it means that fingers are well separated, i.e. don't touch each other.

Hand geometry features don't suit for person recognition in the case of sticking fingers, because we don't know the exact position of fingers and, therefore, can't calculate their characteristics correctly. However, shape-based approach gives hope to us, because the shape of palm is known, even when there are fingers touching each other.

Shape-based approach was introduced in several works. In [11] it is proposed to apply transform features for a normalized palm for recognition purposes. Normalization includes initial orientation of whole palm, orientation of fingers by their eigen values (fingers are rotated at their pivot points) and alignment of two palms by their centroids and pivot lines. The authors compare recognition accuracy for modified Hausdorff distance and two architectures of the Independent Component Analysis. The obtained correct identification and verification accuracies were about $98 - 99\%$ depending on the size of feature vector for the Independent Component Analysis.

Another approach is introduced in [5]. In this work it is suggested extracting five pairs of corresponding fingers and aligning them separately. Alignment for each pair of fingers is based on quasi-exhaustive polynomial search of point pair matching between two sets of points. Least-squares type distance is used to provide analytical solution to the alignment problem. The average distance between the corresponding points is used as measure of similarity of two palms. Threshold rule is applied for verification. FAR (False Accept Rate) and FRR (False Reject Rate) curves are presented for different values of a threshold. For the threshold equal to 1.8 the obtained FAR is about 2%, while FRR is near to 3.5%.

In [12] reference and test palms to be compared are transformed to a predefined position, where angles between fingers are fixed. This is done by performing rotations of fingers at their bending points. Then, the palms are aligned. After that normalized symmetric difference of their superposed silhouettes is calculated. Nearest neighbor approach and threshold rule are applied for classification. The obtained EER (Equal Error Rate) is about 5%.

In all these approaches reference and test palms are supposed to be of the same nature (set of contour points, flexible objects, etc). Generally, transformations are performed or can be performed for both of them. However, these approaches require no sticking fingers and long finger nails. Ring removal technique is introduced only in [11].

The idea proposed in this article is to construct a model of palm by the set of reference palm images. The model is active as it allows us to simulate different palm movements. During comparison reference palm is transformed to model the posture of test palm. The proposed similarity measure is based on the calculation of symmetric difference for superposed silhouettes of reference and test palms.

3   Model of Palm

The proposed model of palm uses the idea of flexible object, introduced in [4]. Generally, flexible object is a circular decomposition of binary image and set of transformations applicable to it. Let's consider basic definitions connected with the notion of flexible object.

3.1 Basic Definitions

Consider a set of points T on the Euclidian space $\mathbb{R}^2$ such that it is connected planar graph. The graph contains a finite set of vertices and continuous edges. Edges can intersect only at graph vertices. Each point $t \in T$ is associated with circle c_t with the center at this point.

Family of circles $C = \{c_t, t \in T\}$ is called the *circular graph*. Graph T is called the *axial graph* or *skeleton* of a circular graph. The union of circles $S = \bigcup_{t \in T} c_t$ with their interior is called the *silhouette* of a circular graph. So, silhouette of a circular graph is a closed connected set of points on the Euclidian space $S \subset \mathbb{R}^2$. The boundary of a circular graph is the envelope of all circles in the family C. The allowed set of transformations of a circular graph that preserve its topological structure and make the group, is called *deformations*. Denote a set of deformations by V. *Flexible object* $G = \{C, V\}$ is a circular graph and its set of deformations.

In the proposed approach to palm comparison it is possible to apply such transformations of flexible object that don't preserve its topological structure. So, let a set of deformations V be a set of transformations that make a group.

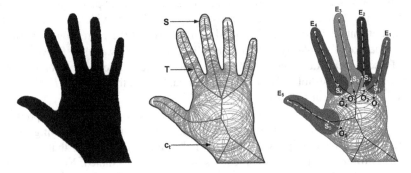

Fig. 2. Binary image of palm (on the left), its circular decomposition (in the center) and palm marking (on the right)

Fig. 2 shows an example of palm binary image (on the left) and its circular decomposition (in the center). Only circles c_t associated with graph vertices are drawn.

Circular decomposition can be constructed for any binary image by algorithm, introduced in [4]. Thus, to define the flexible object of palm it is necessary to describe the allowed set of transformations T.

3.2 Palm Transformations

In the proposed system person shows his/her palm by positioning it on a horizontal surface. So, basic movements of palm can only include, as it was described earlier, shifts and rotations of palm, rotations of fingers. In terms of circular decomposition these are shifts and rotations of circular graph, rotations of graph branches. The first two transformations can be easily applied to every flexible object. To define the third transformation additional information about palm structure is required. At least it is necessary to extract fingers and define their rotation points.

So, *model of palm* is a flexible object that have 5 branches of circular graph marked as fingers and 5 points marked as their rotation points. An example of palm model is shown on Fig. 2 on the right. The branches of circular graph, which correspond to fingers, are painted in different colors. Points $O_i, i = 1, \ldots, 5$ correspond to fingers' rotation points. Rotation of i-th finger is modeled in the following way: finger branch is rotated relative to point O_i as a whole. Transfer of axial graph vertices leads to transfer of circles with the centers at these points.

3.3 Palm Parametrization

It is supposed that a finger is a branch of circular graph that starts from vertex S_i of degree 2 or 3 and ends at vertex E_i of degree 1 (Fig. 2 on the right). Obviously, we can only specify point S_i, while E_i is defined automatically.

We propose to parameterize palm model by the vector of 10 components $p = (\{S_i, O_i\}_{i=1}^5)$. These parameters can be set manually by an expert. However, they can be calculated by the set of palm images, where palm is presented in different postures. The proposed algorithm is described below.

4 Model Parameters Identification

Let's consider that we have n palm images $I_1, \ldots, I_n$ of the same person, where palm is presented in different postures and fingers are well separated. For each image I_j we can construct palm model G_j with undefined vector of parameters p_j (unmarked model). The task is to calculate p_j for each model G_j based on the whole set of unmarked models $G_1, \ldots, G_n$.

The proposed method for model parameters identification consists of two basic steps:

1. Extraction of fingers (calculation of their tips and roots).
2. Calculation of their rotation points.

The first step is performed separately for each model G_j, while the method of rotation points calculation involves all models $G_1, \ldots, G_n$.

4.1 Extraction of Fingers

The method of fingers extraction was introduced in [16]. Here is the brief description.

First, we suppose that 5 longest branches of circular graph correspond to 5 fingers. Then, each branch is analyzed, tip and root of the corresponding finger is defined. The branch of the circular graph is considered from its branchpoint to leaf node. The first vertex to fulfil the restrictions on radius r of the circle and angle φ between two segments connecting the center of circle with its tangency points is treated as the root of a finger. Then, the branch is analyzed in opposite direction and similar restrictions are applied to extract the tip of a finger.

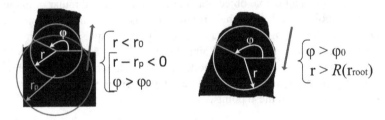

Fig. 3. Detection of root (on the left) and tip (on the right) of a finger

Fig. 3 illustrates the restrictions applied. Here, r is the radius of the current circle on the branch; φ is the angle between two segments connecting the center of a circle with its tangency points; r_p is the radius of the previous circle; r_0 and φ_0 are restrictive constants; r_{root} is the radius of the found root vertex; $R(x)$ is a function. In the current work $R(x) = 0.65x$.

Fig. 4 shows an example of tips P_i and roots R_i calculated by the described procedure. The line $P_i R_i$ connecting finger tip with its root is called *axis of finger*.

4.2   Calculation of Rotation Points

In this article we consider only rotations of fingers at joints between proximal phalanges and middle metacarpal bones. The idea is to find these points by the set of n unmarked palm models $G_1, \ldots, G_n$.

First, we suppose that rotation point of a finger lies on its axis $P_i R_i$. Let O_i be the rotation point of i-th finger. By $\boldsymbol{l} = (l_1, l_2, l_3, l_4, l_5)$ denote the vector of distances between tips and rotation points of fingers: $l_i = \rho(P_i, O_i)$, where ρ is Euclidean distance (Fig. 4 in the center). By $\boldsymbol{len} = (len_1, len_2, len_3, len_4, len_5)$ denote the vector of fingers' lengths: $len_i = \rho(P_i, R_i)$. The vector $\boldsymbol{len}$ is known, while $\boldsymbol{l}$ should be defined.

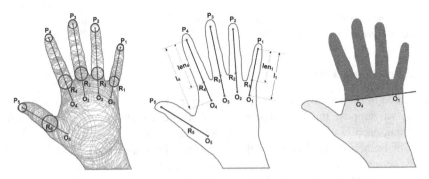

Fig. 4. Calculation of tips and roots (on the left), parametrization (in the center) and region for comparison

The first solution is to set $l_i = k \, len_i$, where k is method's parameter. For example, $k = 0.3$ was considered in [16]. The experiments showed that values of $k \in [0.25; 0.4]$ produce adequate results while modeling rotation of fingers. However, more accurate results in terms of recognition accuracy can be obtained if rotation points are calculated by the set of reference palm models.

Assume that there is a similarity measure $\mu^*(G_1, G_2)$ between two flexible objects G_1 and G_2. This measure is introduced later in Section 5. In general, it is a symmetric difference of superposed silhouettes for transformed flexible object G_1 and (not transformed) G_2. So, the value of μ^* implicitly depends on the choice of fingers' rotation points or vector l. Further, flexible object with rotation points specified by l, is denoted by $G(l)$.

It is obvious that palm models of the same person should be alike. We propose to measure similarity of n palm models by the following equation:

$$\mu_{av}(l) = \sum_{\substack{i,j=1,\ldots,n \\ i \neq j}} \frac{\mu^*(G_i(l), G_j(l))}{n(n-1)} \qquad (1)$$

The measure μ^* is asymmetric, i.e. $\mu^*(G_1, G_2) \neq \mu^*(G_2, G_1)$, and the number of ordered pairs is $n(n-1)$.

Thus, we can set the following optimization problem:

$$l^* : \mu_{av}(l^*) = \min_{l \in \mathbb{R}^5} \mu_{av}(l) \qquad (2)$$

This problem can be solved by methods for constrained and unconstrained minimization. For example, region of search can be reduced to spacial parallelepiped $l_i \in [0.2len_i; 0.5len_i], i = 1, \ldots, 5$.

In this work the problem (2) was solved by Nelder-Mead method [1] with parameters $\alpha = 1$, $\beta = 0.5$ and $\gamma = 2$.

As it was described above, the model of palm is parameterized by the vector $p = (\{S_i, O_i\}_{i=1}^5)$, where S_i is the starting point of i-th finger, and O_i is its rotation point. The points O_i are calculated by solving minimization problem (2). The point S_i is defined by the rule: it is the vertex of the corresponding finger's branch, nearest to the point O_i in terms of Euclidean distance. So, the parameters of existing models $G_1, \ldots, G_n$ are identified.

5   Palm Shape Comparison

Let's consider reference palm model G_1 (marked) and test palm model G_2 (possibly, unmarked). Test model is constructed for a test palm image. It can contain sticking fingers, so its vector of parameters p cannot be calculated. In this section we introduce similarity measure $\mu^*(G_1, G_2)$ and provide an algorithm for its calculation. The idea is to perform transformations over reference palm G_1 to provide the best superposition for silhouettes of G_1 and G_2.

Palm shape comparison process consists of two basic steps:

1. Initial superposition of palm models.
2. Matching of their silhouettes.

First, we introduce parametrization of palm transformations and then describe these steps in detail.

5.1 Parametrization of Transformations

Let's consider marked palm model G (Fig. 5). It should be noted that further we don't consider rotations of thumb, because its movements are more complex and can result in the significant change of palm shape (for example, skin changes between thumb and index finger).

First, we suppose that the structure of polygon $O_1O_2O_3O_4$ is fixed, i.e. lengths of its sides and angles between sides do not change during transformations.

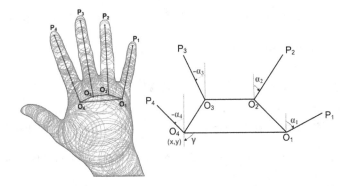

Fig. 5. Parametrization of palm transformations

Then, denote by $\alpha = (\alpha_1, \alpha_2, \alpha_3, \alpha_4, x, y, \gamma)$ the vector of transformation parameters, where α_i is the angle between finger axis P_iR_i and ordinate axis, (x, y) is the coordinates of point O_4, γ is the angle between line O_1O_4 and ordinate axis. So, shift of palm leads to the change of components x and y, rotation of palm leads to the change of angle γ (and angles α_i on the same value), rotation of i-th finger leads to the change of angle α_i.

5.2 Initial Superposition

Initial superposition of palm models G_1 and G_2 includes:

1. Superposition of tips of middle fingers.
2. Superposition of middle finger axes.
3. Exclusion of thumb region.
4. Exclusion of wrist region.

Thus, we superpose middle fingers of models and then draw the line connecting points O_1 and O_4 on a reference palm G_1 (see Fig. 4 on the right). The region of palm that lies below this line is excluded from future comparison.

Similarity measure for two superposed models G_1 and G_2 is calculated by the following equation:

$$\mu(G_1, G_2) = \text{Area}(S_1 \setminus S_2) + \text{Area}(S_2 \setminus S_1) \tag{3}$$

S_1 and S_2 are the silhouettes of the corresponding models G_1 and G_2; μ is measured in square pixels.

It is obvious that the initial superposition doesn't provide good matching of models, as it only eliminates the difference in their relative position and orientation (Fig. 6). The difference in the position of fingers is eliminated during matching process.

5.3 Matching

Denote by $v(\alpha) \in V$ the transformation of model G defined by the set of parameters α. Let $v(G, \alpha)$ be an object that is the result of transformation $v(\alpha)$ applied to model G. Let's introduce the similarity measure of reference model G_1 and test model G_2 by the following equation:

$$\mu^*(G_1, G_2) = \min_{v(\alpha) \in V_1} \mu(v(G_1, \alpha), G_2) = \mu(v(G_1, \alpha^*), G_2) \tag{4}$$

The idea is to find the transformation (with a vector of parameters α^*) that produces the best superposition of models' silhouettes.

The proposed initial superposition of models defines three components of vector α: x, y and γ. So, the measure μ^* depends on angles α_1, α_2, α_3 and α_4.

Minimization problem (4) can be solved by existing methods of numerical optimization. To construct initial approximation for α one can measure corresponding angles on the test palm G_2 and set them on the reference palm G_1. We used Nelder-Mead method with parameters $\alpha = 1$, $\beta = 0.5$ and $\gamma = 2$.

Fig. 6 shows some examples of matching for the palms of the same person and different persons. The average area of palm region is about 40000 square pixels, so the difference of 2000 square pixels makes up 5% of the whole area.

6   Person Recognition

The described above method for palm shape comparison is employed in the proposed recognition system. It is a real time application, the "Time & Attendance System", which traces the presence of students at the classes. This system works as follows.

Person positions his/her palm on a monochrome horizontal surface for recognition. Webcam, which is situated above person's palm, makes image of it. Fig. 7 shows the proposed system.

The acquired palm image, or test palm, is transformed to binary image and compared to database of reference palms. Database of reference palms consists of persons' palm models, and can include several models for each person. When test palm is compared

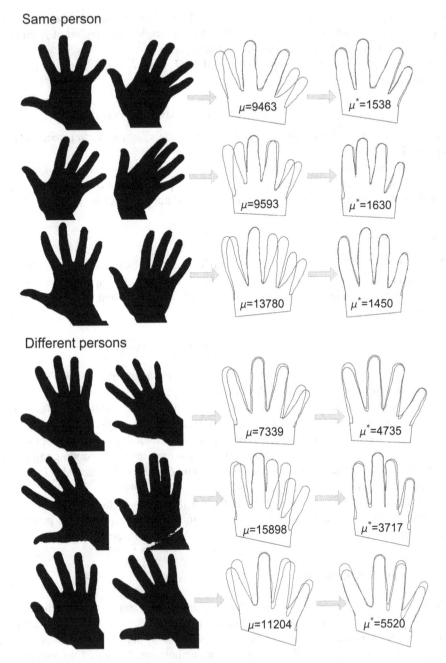

Fig. 6. Palms to compare (on the left), their initial superposition (in the center) and superposition after matching (on the right). The average area of palm region is about 40000 square pixels.

Fig. 7. Person recognition system

to reference palms of a particular person, the similarity of "reference" and "test" person is defined as the minimal distance between test palm and each of the existing reference palms of this particular person.

Then, simple threshold rule is applied to determine, if the presented test palm belongs to one of the users. In the case when database contains more than one similar person preference is given to the nearest one. If person isn't recognized as an insider within several seconds (while several palm images are made and passed for recognition), this person is treated as an outsider.

The acquired palm images are scaled for recognition. So, additional camera calibration is required.

7 Experiments

Experimental data contained 97 palm images of 22 persons. These images were divided into two groups — reference and test data. Reference data was composed of 45 palms (2-3 images for each user); so, test data contained 52 images.

Firstly, the distance between each test palm and each user (the minimal distance between test palm and each of the existing reference palms of this particular user) was calculated. It was done for different values of threshold. After that densities of distribution for inner- and inter-class distances were estimated. Every class is composed of all palms for a particular person. So, when test and reference palms belonged to the same person, the distance was considered to be inner; otherwise, it was inter-class distance. There were 61 intra-class and 1403 inter-class distances. The distance is measured in square pixels.

As a result, inner- and inter-class distances turned out to be really separable (see Fig. 8). In the next experiments recognition accuracy was estimated — FAR and FRR were calculated for verification and identification processes.

7.1 Verification

For each test palm verification was executed for different values of threshold. Incorrect verification was registered during FRR estimation, if the minimal distance

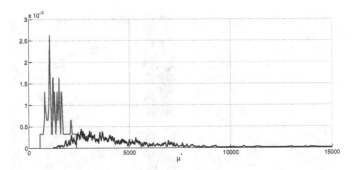

Fig. 8. Density of distribution for inner- and inter-class distances

between person's test palm and his/her reference palms was greater than the considered threshold. Incorrect verification was registered during FAR estimation, if the minimal distance between test palm and reference palms of another person was less than the considered threshold. Fig. 9 shows the obtained values of FAR and FRR for different methods of rotation points calculation (see Section 4): curve "30%" corresponds to setting $l_i = 0.3len_i$, while curve "nm" corresponds to solution of minimization problem (2).

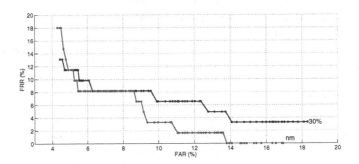

Fig. 9. FAR and FRR in verification process

The results show that the calculation of rotation points by the set of palm images (curve "nm") leads to better recognition. The proposed method can produce verification accuracy near to 99% when threshold value is about $1500 - 1600$. The obtained value of EER (Equal Error Rate) is about 0.5%.

7.2   Identification

Identification was executed for all test palms for different values of threshold. Incorrect identification was registered during FRR estimation, if the nearest reference palm, which met the threshold, didn't belong to the same person. Incorrect identification was registered during FAR estimation, if the list of nearest reference palms, which met the threshold, contained palms of other persons.

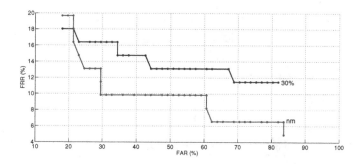

Fig. 10. FAR and FRR in identification process

Fig. 10 shows the obtained results for different methods of rotation points calculation (as before, curve "30%" corresponds to setting $l_i = 0.3len_i$, while curve "nm" corresponds to solution of minimization problem (2)). The minimal value of FRR is about 5%, and it is explained by the presence of really similar palms in database. The exclusion of similar palms produced better results with FRR about 0%.

Nevertheless, FAR remains high. Even when the nearest person from the database for the test palm is recognized correctly, there is amount of reference palms similar to test one (i.e. distances meet the threshold). And, mostly, it is the nature of this modality. Only palm shape isn't enough to produce reliable decision about person's identity. There can be different solutions to the problem of high FAR. One of them is combining different modalities.

8   Combining Modalities

We propose combination of palm and voice features to decrease the FAR value. In addition to presenting palm for recognition purposes, person is required to say a password. So, text-dependent person recognition can be applied [2].

Each person in the database is described by several reference models of palm and several records of password. Combination of modalities implements cascade model, where voice features serve as filter of knowingly unlike persons; and, then, recognition is performed over palm shape within a small group. Voice features are composed of cepstral coefficients, calculated for audio signal of password. DTW (Dynamic Time Warping) technique is used to compare passwords.

At first, test record of password is compared to records for each person in the database; and the list of k most similar persons is constructed. Then, identification is performed for test palm within the group of these persons. Bimodal recognition schema is shown on Fig. 11.

Experiments for bimodal recognition were carried out for a group of 20 users. As a result, there were 38 reference persons and 117 test objects. Experiments were carried out for different values of parameter k and threshold m. Table 1 shows the best obtained values of FAR and FRR for bimodal recognition.

As it is expected, bimodal approach shows better results than unimodal. Combination of two modalities allowed us to reduce the high value of FAR. For example, for

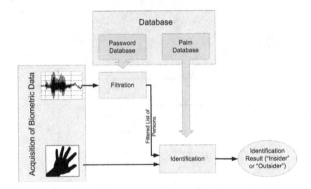

Fig. 11. Bimodal recognition schema

Table 1. FAR and FRR for bimodal recognition

k	m	$FRR, \%$	$FAR, \%$
3	1600	6.7	0
4	1600	6.7	0
5	1600	6.7	0
3	1700	4.2	0
4	1700	4.2	0
5	1700	4.2	0
3	1800	3.4	0
4	1800	3.4	5
5	1800	3.4	6.7
3	1900	1.7	1.7
4	1900	1.7	6.7
5	1900	1.7	8.4

several values of k and m it is equal to 0%. Also FRR is less than it was for unimodal identification. For $k = 3$ and $m = 1900$ we have $ERR = 1.7\%$.

9   Conclusions

The new method for person recognition by palm shape was proposed. The choice of palm shape is explained by the fact that there are people, who tend to show palm "poorly". In such cases (presence of sticking fingers, incomplete wrist, etc.) sometimes it is impossible to measure or generate palm features for future comparison correctly. The proposed method allows us to construct an active palm model by the set of good palm images, and employ it during comparison with test palm. The idea is to transform reference palm to provide the best superposition for silhouettes of reference and test palms.

Verification accuracy in terms of EER was shown to be about 5%. For identification purposes person palm shape isn't really unique, so FRR was near 5%. FAR remains high and can be reduced by combining palm shape features with other biometric data. One of the possible combinations with voice features, was illustrated. The best recognition accuracy for bimodal recognition was $EER = 1.7\%$.

The experiments were carried out on the prototype of the system. It is a real-time application, the "Time & Attendance" system, which traces the presence of students at the classes.

In the future it is supposed to implement matching of two palms, which will model the complex movements of thumb. Also, other decision rules should be studied (instead of simple threshold rule applied). The presence of some artificial things on palm (such as rings, bracelets, etc.) should be investigated.

References

1. Nash, J.C.: Compact Numerical Methods for Computers: Linear Algebra and Function Minimisation. International Series on Biometrics. Adam Hilger (1990)
2. Theodoridis, S., Koutroumbas, K.: Pattern Recognition, 2nd edn. Elsevier (2003)
3. Ross, A.A., Nandakumar, K., Jain, A.K.: Handbook of multibiometrics. International Series on Biometrics, vol. 6. Springer, Heidelberg (2006)
4. Mestetskiy, L.M.: Continious morphology of binary images: figures, skeletons, circulars. FIZMATLIT, Moscow (2009) (in Russian)
5. Anil, K.J., Duta, N.: Deformable Matching Of Hand Shapes For Verification. In: Proceedings of ICIP 1999, Japan, pp. 857–861 (1999)
6. Wong, A.L.N., Shi, P.: Peg-Free Hand Geometry Recognition Using Hierarchical Geometry and Shape Matching. In: Proceedings of IAPR International Conference on Machine Vision Applications, pp. 281–284 (2002)
7. Gonzalez, S., Travieso, C.M., Alonso, J.B., Ferrer, M.A.: Automatic biometric identification system by hand geometry. In: Proceedings of the 37th Annual International Carnahan Conference on Security Technology, pp. 281–284 (2003)
8. Boreki, G., Zimmer, Z.: Hand Geometry: A New Approach for Feature Extraction. In: Proceedings of the 4th IEEE Workshop on Automatic Identification Advanced Technologies, pp. 149–154 (2005)
9. Jianxia, W., Wanzhen, Z., Xiaojun, W., Min, Q.: The feature parameter extraction in palm shape recognition system. Journal of Communication and Computer 2, 25–28 (2005)
10. Covavisaruch, N., Prateepamornkul, P., Ruchikachorn, P., Taksaphan, P.: Personal Verification and Identification Using Hand Geometry. ECTI Transactions on Computer and Information Technology 1, 134–140 (2005)
11. Yoruk, E., Konukoglu, E., Sankur, B., Darbon, J.: Shape-Based Hand Recognition. IEEE Image Processing 15(7), 1803–1815 (2006)
12. Mestetskiy, L.M.: Shape Comparison of Flexible Objects. In: VISAPP, vol. 1, pp. 390–393 (2007)
13. Varchol, P., Levicky, D.: Using of Hand Geometry in Biometric Security Systems. Radio-Engineering 16, 82–87 (2007)
14. Su, C.-L.: Index, middle, and ring finger extraction and identification by index, middle, and ring finger outlines. In: Procedeengs of the International Conference on Computer Vision Theory and Applications (VISAPP), vol. 1, pp. 518–520 (2008)
15. Morales, A., Ferrer, M.A., Diaz, F., Alonso, J.B., Travieso, C.M.: Contact-free hand biometric system for real environments. In: EUSIPCO (2008)
16. Bakina, I.: Palm Shape Comparison for Person Recognition. In: Csurka, G., et al. (eds.) VISIGRAPP 2011. CCIS, vol. 274, pp. 157–171. Springer, Heidelberg (2012)

Bioinformatics-Motivated Approach to Stereo Matching

Jesus Martinez-del-Rincon, Jerome Thevenon, Romain Dieny,
and Jean-Christophe Nebel

Digitial Imaging Research Centre, Kingston University
Penhryn Road, Kingston-Upon-Thames, KT1 2EE, Surrey, U.K.
{Jesus.Martinezdelrincon,J.Thevenon,
R.Dieny,J.Nebel}@kingston.ac.uk

Abstract. We propose a framework for stereo matching that exploits the similarities between protein sequence alignment in bioinformatics and image pair correspondence in computer vision. This bioinformatics-motivated approach is based on dynamic programming, which provides versatility and low complexity. In addition, the protein alignment analogy inspired the design of a meaningfulness graph which predicts the validity of stereo matching according to image overlap and pixel similarity. Finally, we present a technique for automatic parameter estimation which makes our system suitable for uncontrolled environment. Experiments conducted on a standard benchmark dataset, image pairs with different resolutions and distorted images validate our approach and support the proposed analogy between computer vision and bioinformatics.

Keywords: Stereo correspondence, Dynamic programming, Sequence alignment, Bioinformatics, Parameter estimation.

1   Introduction

Stereo matching is an essential step in the process of 3D reconstruction from a pair of stereo images. Since it has many applications including robot navigation, security and entertainment, it has been an important field of computer vision for several decades. The problem of finding correspondences between pixels belonging to a pair of stereo images has been tackled using a wide range of techniques such as block correlations, dynamic programming, graph cut and simulated annealing; excellent literature reviews can be found in [1] and [2]. Among these techniques, those based on dynamic programming (DP) have proved particularly attractive. They provide good accuracy and are computationally efficient [3]: they are able to find the global minimum for independent scanlines in polynomial time.

Although the design of some of these DP algorithms was inspired by that of Needleman and Wunsch [4], e.g. [3], which was developed for alignment of protein sequences, to our knowledge, no author has exploited fully the analogy between protein and image correspondence. In this paper, we present a DP algorithm for stereo matching inspired by bioinformatics techniques. Not only does the bioinformatics

G. Csurka et al. (Eds.): VISIGRAPP 2011, CCIS 274, pp. 172–186, 2013.

analogy allow the design of an efficient stereo-matching algorithm, but it also permits investigating the limits of applicability of the algorithm in term of image overlap and pixel occlusion. This is illustrated here by producing dense disparity maps from images captured at different resolutions. Finally, we also propose a methodology allowing automatic configuration of all algorithm parameters.

The structure of this paper is organised as follows. After reviewing relevant literature, we detail our novel stereo matching algorithm. Then, experiments are conducted on a benchmark dataset, image pairs with different resolutions and distorted images to validate our approach. Finally, conclusions and future work are presented.

1.1   Related Work

First applications of DP to the problem of stereo matching produced sparse disparity maps using edge information [5] and [6]. In order to generate dense maps, correspondences between scanlines were computed using pixel colour values. This task highlighted complications which were not present when dealing only with edges: they include image noise, indistinct image features and half occlusion, e.g. object points which can be seen only in one of the two images. Statistical frameworks have been proposed to explicitly tackle these issues [7-10. Alternatively, Bobick et al. [11] suggested to pre-process images by producing a 'disparity-space image' based on block correlations and, then, use DP to find the optimal correspondences. In addition to rely on additional free parameters, all these approaches required additional calculations, which affect significantly the computational complexity of the stereo matching process.

Since traditional DP algorithms compute line-based global optimisations, they do not take into account vertical consistency between scanlines. Although some early methods attempted to address this issue [6,8,9,11], they only refine results produced from scanline optimisation. In order not to bias optimisation towards one direction, e.g. scanline, a new class of DP algorithms, which can be applied efficiently to tree structures, has been recently proposed [12,13]. Results show they are significantly more accurate than scanline based methods with only a marginal increase of computational cost.

In the last few years, the main emphasis has been on designing real-time solutions by adapting previous DP algorithms [14-16]. Eventually, the first FPGA hardware implementation of a DP-based stereo matching algorithm has just been proposed [3]. Its performance demonstrates DP-based approaches provide the best compromise between accuracy and speed.

2   Methodology

We propose a new matching algorithm particularly suitable for the scanline to scanline correspondence problem, which can be applied to pairs of rectified stereo images. First, we introduce the bioinformatics technique on which it is based. Then, we explain how it can be extended to image processing.

2.1   'Needleman-wunsch' Algorithm

The publication of the first 'Atlas of Protein Sequence and Structure' [17] which comprised the sequences of 65 proteins, arguably founded the field of bioinformatics. This gave researchers the opportunity to compare sequences to establish evolutionary relationship between proteins. Since protein sequences have an average length of 400 characters and mutate through substitution, insertion and deletion of characters, the alignment of a protein pair is not a trivial matter. The 'Needleman–Wunsch' algorithm [4] has provided an effective automatic method to produce an exact solution to the global alignment of two protein sequences. It is still at the core of the latest search engines [18, 19], which allow finding the best alignment between a given protein sequence and a large database such as UniProt [20], which contains more than 20 million entries.

The 'Needleman–Wunsch' (N&W) algorithm is based on a dynamic programming approach which optimises the global alignment of character strings according to a scoring function taking into account possible mutations. In practice, alignments are produced by, first, filling in a scoring matrix and, then, 'backtracking' from the highest score in either the last column or the last line of the matrix.

Each matrix cell stores the maximum value which can be achieved by extending a previous alignment (see Table 1). This can be done either by aligning the next character of the first sequence with the next character of the second sequence or extending either sequence by an empty character to record a character insertion or deletion ('indel').

In the case of character alignment, i.e. *diagonal* motion in the matrix, the score depends on their values. A reward, *match*, is allocated if the two characters are identical, otherwise a penalty, *mismatch*, is applied since this highlights a mutation (substitution). When a sequence is extended, i.e. from either *north* or *west*, this is also penalised, *gap*, because it reveals that a mutation (insertion or deletion) occurred. While completing the matrix, in addition to the score of each cell, the direction(s) from which the score is coming must be recorded since they are used in the 'backtracking' process.

The scoring matrix, M, is initialised by setting the initial score (top left cell) to zero and the first line and column according to cumulated *gap* penalties. Then, M is filled in using the following pseudo-code:

```
for i = 1 to length(sequence1)
{
    for j = 1 to length(sequence2)
    {
        north <- M(i-1,j) +gap
        if( character1 = character2 )
            diagonal <- M(i-1,j-1) +match
        else
            diagonal <- M(i-1,j-1) +mismatch
        endif
```

```
    west <- M(i,j-1) +gap
    M(i,j) <- max(north, diagonal, west)
  }
}
```

Once the matrix is completed, the optimal alignment is extracted using the 'backtracking' process (see Table 2). First, the highest score cell in either the last column or row is identified. Then, using direction information, a path to the origin of the matrix is constructed. Finally, this path is converted into an alignment. It is important to note that, although the algorithm always finds the best global alignment(s) for a given scoring scheme, there may be several alignments with the optimal score.

The whole process is illustrated with an example in Table 1 and 2, where the following scoring scheme is used: *match=2, mismatch=0 and gap=-1*. Representing gaps by '-', the resulting alignment is:

EDECE

AD-CE

Table 1. Extension of initial alignment. The new cell score is shown in blue; 3 possible scores are shown in green.

	-	E	D	E
-	0	$\to-1$	$\to-2$	$\to-3$
A	$-1^{\downarrow}$	$\searrow 0$	$\searrow-1$	$\searrow-2$
D	$-2^{\downarrow}$	$\searrow-1^{\downarrow}$	$\searrow 2$	$^{-1}_{1}1^{-3}$

Table 2. Completed scoring matrix and optimal path highlighted in red

	-	E	D	E	C	E
-	0	$\to-1$	$\to-2$	$\to-3$	$\to-4$	$\to-5$
A	$-1^{\downarrow}$	$\searrow 0$	$\searrow-1$	$\searrow-2$	$\searrow-3$	$\searrow-4$
D	$-2^{\downarrow}$	$\searrow-1^{\downarrow}$	$\searrow 2$	$\to 1$	$\to 0$	$\to-1$
C	$-3^{\downarrow}$	$\searrow-2^{\downarrow}$	$1^{\downarrow}$	$\searrow 2$	$\searrow 3$	$\to 2$
E	$-4^{\downarrow}$	$\searrow-1$	$0^{\downarrow}$	$\searrow 3$	$\searrow 2^{\downarrow}$	$\searrow 5$

2.2 Application to Stereo Matching

An analogy can be made between aligning protein sequences and matching pixels belonging to scanlines, since both tasks aim at establishing optimal correspondence between two strings of characters. In addition, the 'right' image of a stereo pair can be seen as a mutated version of the 'left' image: noise and individual camera sensitivity alter pixel values (i.e. character substitutions); and different view angle reveals previously occluded data and introduces new occlusions (i.e. insertion and deletion of characters). Consequently, the N&W approach is a very good starting point for developing a stereo matching algorithm, as seen in [3]. The novelty of this work is twofold. First, it takes full advantage of the protein sequence/scanline analogy by refining the N&W based stereo matching algorithm with the relevant extensions proposed in the field of bioinformatics. Secondly, this analogy is exploited further by producing a graph which suggests the limits of applicability of the algorithm in term of image overlap and pixel occlusion.

Scoring Matrix. Scoring matrices are filled in using scoring functions which quantify the cost of possible mutations. Different substitutions in protein sequences affect differently protein functions. However, this is not reflected in the match/mismatch dichotomy used in N&W. This was addressed by customising mismatch costs according to estimated rates of mutations between pairs of characters [17, 21]. Although it would be possible to perform a statistical study to establish the mutation frequency between pixel values, here we use a linear model which is context independent. The mismatch penalty of aligning a pair of pixels, where p_i and p_j are their values, is expressed by the absolute value of their difference, so that extending an alignment along the diagonal alters the global score by:

$$match - |p_i - p_j| \qquad (1)$$

In genetics, 'indels' are rare and dramatic events which usually have negative effect on protein functions. Although the N&W can penalise this type of mutations by associating them with a higher cost than substitutions, it does not take into account that an 'indel' of n characters is much more likely than n 'indels' of one character. For this reason, the initial scoring scheme was completed with a lower penalty for extended gaps, *egap*, which encourages gaps to cluster. We believe this concept is also valid in stereo matching where one would expect that a few occlusions of several-pixel length would be more frequent than a large number of 1-pixel occlusions: due to the nature of stereo matching, different camera viewpoints create occlusion areas associated with each object present in a scene. Accordingly, we implemented extended gaps in our algorithm.

As a consequence of these changes, our scoring matrix is filled in using the following pseudo-code:

```
for i = 1 to length(sequence1)
{
    for j = 1 to length(sequence2)
    {
        mismatch = -|IL(line,i) -IR(line,j)|
        if( M(i-1,j) is a gap )
            north <- M(i-1,j) +egap
        else
            north <- M(i-1,j) +gap
        endif
        diagonal <- M(i-1,j-1) +match +mismatch
        if( M(i,j-1) is a gap )
```

```
        west <- M(i,j-1) +egap
    else
        west <- M(i,j-1) +gap
    endif
    M(i,j) <- max(north, diagonal, west)
  }
}
```

Backtracking. The N&W backtracking process is straight forward. In the matrix, the cell with the highest score in either the last column or the last line of the matrix is identified. Then from that cell to the origin of the matrix, the global alignment is extracted using the stored direction information associated with each cell. This process usually produces a set of optimal alignments, see Fig. 1. Consequently, new information needs to be supplied to allow selecting a single solution. In bioinformatics, this is usually resolved by providing additional alignments involving other related sequences. They are used to produce a single multiple alignment which optimises all pair-wise alignment constraints [22-25].

Several strategies have been offered to deal with this issue in the context of stereo matching. Many suggest selecting the 'smoothest' solution in term of horizontal and vertical discontinuities along and across scanlines [9, 11]. Some are based on high confidence matches, such as edge intersections, which are identified during a pre-processing phase. These good matches are exploited as extra constraints in the choice of a unique solution [10, 11].

In this work, we follow the traditional bioinformatics approach. The general principle is that each scanline can be seen as a mutation of both the previous and the following lines. Therefore, alignments involving these lines can be used to select among several solutions by enforcing some vertical discontinuities.

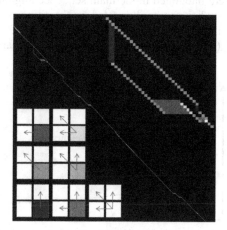

Fig. 1. Paths returned for a pair of scanlines. Colours – legend given in the bottom left – show valid direction(s) which can be followed to produce an optimal alignment. Zoom on an area with alternative paths is provided in the top right of the figure.

However, this approach is only valid if those lines are, indeed, mutations of the scanline of interest. Since usage of a neighbouring line does not ensure that the scanlines are related – there may be a horizontal edge – we impose that the pixel sequences used as constraints are composed of the mean values between the scanline and neighbouring line pixels. For instance, in addition to the alignment between the scanline, i, on the left image (l_i) and its corresponding line on the right one (r_i), we can calculate a constraining alignment between l_i and the average between r_i and r_{i+1}. Those solutions present in both alignments are more likely to be a correct solution. Following this reasoning, using all combinations between (l_i), (l_i+l_{i+1}), $(l_{i-1}+l_i)$, $(l_{i-1}+l_i+l_{i+1})$, and (r_i), (r_i+r_{i+1}), $(r_{i-1}+r_i)$, $(r_{i-1}+r_i+r_{i+1})$, and reading scanlines from right to left, a total number of 32 constraints are generated.

In practice, in order to reduce the added computational cost of this strategy, we generate only constraining alignments for the subsections of scanline pairs which display several optimal correspondences, see Fig. 1. Then, for a given subsection, each initial solution is scored according to the number of constraining alignments which reach the same solution. The solution with the highest number of votes is selected. In the case of a draw, it is chosen at random.

Scope. Traditional stereo matching algorithms are applied on rectified pair of images which share a 'sufficient' amount of overlap. To our knowledge, no statistically reliable study has quantified that amount. Since we use a bioinformatics-inspired framework, we propose to get an insight about this by investigating the confidence which is given to protein alignments according to the amounts of overlap and mutations.

Due to the availability of protein sequences, e.g. more than 20 million entries in UniProt [20], and its usage in major international projects such as the Human Genome Project (International Human Genome Sequencing Consortium, 2001), the validity of sequence alignments have been the subject of statistical and experimental studies [26-28]. Those statistics were integrated in the main sequence alignment servers [18, 19]. The outcome of these studies can be illustrated by the graph produced by Rost [28], where alignment meaningfulness is expressed according to the number of characters which can be aligned (i.e. overlap) and the percentage of characters with identical values (see Fig. 2).

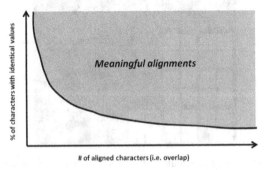

Fig. 2. Expression of protein alignment meaningfulness according to the number of characters which can be aligned (i.e. overlap) and the percentage of characters with identical values, adapted from [28]

In this paper, we propose to produce such a curve for stereo pair images and infer from it if alignments are meaningful.

3   Results

3.1   Experimental Setup

In order to validate our algorithm, most experiments are conducted using the benchmarking framework from Middlebury [1], [29], which has been largely accepted by the computer vision community for objective comparison of stereo matching algorithms. In addition, to demonstrate the versatility of our approach it is also applied to pairs of images where the second is a distorted version of the first one.

When several optimal solutions are returned by our algorithm, the selection of a unique solution is achieved by applying the 32 different constraints imposing scanline continuity. Finally, when specified, disparity maps are post-processed by a median filter (MF), which has been shown as a powerful and simple way to improve results [30].

Automatic Parameter Configuration. First score parameters, i.e. match, gap and extended gap, must be configured. Since they are sensitive to image characteristics, they need to be customised for each stereo pair. If the actual disparity map is known, an optimisation function can be applied to maximise matching accuracy. Although such process allows evaluating the best possible performance of an algorithm, it does not have practical applications.

Therefore, a methodology for automatic parameter configuration is required. We propose to generate a pseudo ground truth disparity map by establishing sparse pixel correspondences using the SIFT algorithm (Scale Invariant Feature Transform). Key points on corresponding scanlines are paired and used to calculate disparity values (code available at www.cs.ubc.ca/~lowe/keypoints/). However, since only a few pairs are detected (fewer than 100 for images from the Middlebury dataset), this initial set is not suitable for parameter optimisation. In order to increase this number, Delaunay triangulation is applied to estimate the disparity of more pixels (see Fig. 3). Using the key points as vertices, homographic transformations between both meshes can be calculated for each triangle. These transformations are then used to estimate a larger set of disparity values. Obviously, this approximation can only be considered as valid for small triangles: in this work, only triangles whose sides are shorter than 15 pixels are used. As Table 3 shows, those disparity values are very accurate since they have an average pixel error below 0.5. Consequently, such disparity maps can be considered as ground truth and used for parameter optimisation.

Table 3. Automatic ground truth generated for parameter configuration and its estimated error

	# of disparity points	Average error
Cones	657	0.36
Teddy	190	0.46
Venus	211	0.27
Tsukuba	600	0.45

Fig. 3. Delaunay triangulation of left and right images using the generated pairs of key points

3.2   Performances

Stereo-pair Correspondences. Fig. 4 shows raw disparity maps, i.e. without smoothing, obtained for the images used in the Middlebury framework. In Table 4, quantitative results are provided to validate our algorithm. The table quantifies the introduction of extended gaps (EG) and the procedure for automatic parameter selection (AP). In addition performances are provided for state of the art methods: the reference for scanline-based DP [11], tree-based DP which addresses inter-scanline coherence in the optimisation process [12, 13], and a segment-based stereo matcher [31].

Fig. 4. Disparity maps

When optimising parameters using the ground truth disparity map as other methods do, in its most advanced configuration (i.e. our approach +EG +MF) the proposed framework outperforms Bobick's [11]. Although, in terms of accuracy it cannot compete with the more computationally expensive approaches, ours could operate in real time as shown by [3].

Analysis of Table 4 shows that the inclusion of extended gaps suits the nature of occlusions since performances are significantly improved. Moreover, as expected, the application of a median filter on disparity maps, which introduces some inter-scanline coherence, increases accuracy. Finally, results obtained using the AP configuration demonstrates that, although performances are degraded compared to those produced by a system using optimal parameters, they are still satisfactory. For example, our approach outperforms Bobick's [11] in 3 image pairs out of 4.

These results confirm the validity of the analogy made between stereo matching and protein sequence alignment.

Table 4. Performance comparison

EG: with extended gaps, AP: with automatic parameter selection, MF: with median filter

%	Tsukuba (non occ)	Venus (non occ)	Teddy (non occ)	Cones (non occ)	All (bad pixels)
Klaus et al. 2006	1.11	0.11	4.22	2.48	4.23
Veksler 2005	1.99	1.41	15.9	10.0	11.7
Deng & Lin 2006	2.21	0.46	9.58	3.23	6.82
Bobick & Intille 1999	4.12	10.1	14.0	10.5	14.2
Our approach	6.67	12.0	15.5	12.7	18.6
Our approach +EG	6.74	10.7	14.1	11.0	16.7
Our approach +EG +MF	4.63	7.40	10.7	7.75	13.4
Our approach +AP +EG +MF	7.61	7.87	10.8	8.59	14.9

Stereo Matching Meaningfulness. Following the efforts of Rost [28] who experimentally defined a curve under which protein alignment may become meaningless (see Fig. 2), we have produced a similar graph plotting accuracy as a function of image overlap and pixel similarity to express the meaningfulness of matching an image pair.

In this section, we consider that the alignment between two scanlines L and R is meaningful if the optimal score obtained for this alignment according to the scoring matrix is the highest score that L can achieve against any scanline of the right image.

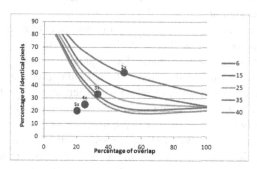

Fig. 5. Scanline correspondence errors according to overlap and pixel similarity. Red dots show where matching experiments between an image and its zoomed version (from 2x to 5x) would fit on this graph.

In the original paper by Rost, results were plotted in a graph showing the number of residues aligned versus the percentage of character similarity. In our particular case we can assimilate the number of aligned characters as the number of pixels matched between the images, or equivalently, the percentage of overlap between the images. Regarding the second axis, it can be understood as the percentage of identical pixels existing between both images.

Unlike in bioinformatics, pixel value changes have a continuous nature, Consequently, the estimation of pixel similarity between a pair of stereo images would depend on a threshold. In order to have an absolute control of all variables, the conditions of the matching experiments were simplified. Our algorithm was applied to match an image with a tranformed version of itself. Pixel identity was controlled by adding 'salt and pepper' noise to the image, while the percentage of overlap was simulated by removing the required number of pixel columns. On Fig. 5, points are connected according to the measure accuracy in terms of percentage of scanlines matching the correct scanlines (see Fig. 6). Thus, a set of curves were created highlighting the image pair characteristics required to obtain matching errors between 6% and 40%. As expected the shape of these curves is very similar to Rost's (Fig. 2), which reinforces the value of our analogy between stereo matching and protein sequence alignment. As in Rost's case, we believe the graph in Fig. 5 can estimate the meaningfulness of stereo correspondences using image overlap and the number of identical pixels as parameters.

In order to test this hypothesis, we propose to predict the outcome of matching image pairs captured at different resolution. On Fig. 5, we have plotted in red the estimated overlap and pixel similarity between images where the second one was taken with a zoom of 2x, 3x, 4x and 5x. Using the predictive accuracy suggested by the curve set, one can infer that matching with 2x or 3x image should provide meaningful results, whereas results obtained for pairs including a 4x or 5x zoomed image should be meaningless. These predictions are tested in the next section.

Matching Images Captured at Different Resolutions. First, to evaluate the predictions made from the meaningfulness graph, the 'cone' image and its zoomed versions were processed using our algorithm. Here, the extended gap feature is deactivated since the assumption it is based on is not valid when dealing with images captured at different resolutions. Each scanline of the standard image was aligned against all scanlines of the zoomed image. The alignment with the highest score in the scoring matrix is then automatically selected to determine matching scanline pairs.

Fig. 7 shows the results of this procedure for different zoom values. As expected, the performances worsen with zoom increase. In the case of x2 and x3 zooms, correspondences between lines are usually correct or shifted by only a few lines, correlations between actual and predicted corresponding scanlines are 0.997 and 0.643 respectively. However, matching using x4 and x5 zooms produces associations which are often meaningless as quantified by the calculated correlations, i.e. 0.495 and 0.209 respectively. These experimental results confirm the predictions formulated using the meaningfulness graph.

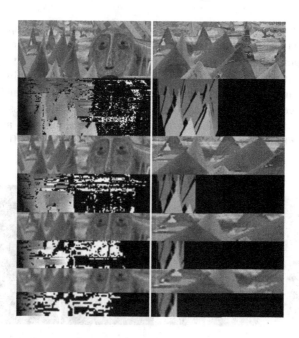

Fig. 6. a) Left and b) right images used for zoom x2, x3, x4 and x5, c) corresponding computed and d) ground truth

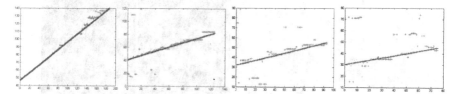

Fig. 7. Correspondences between lines on the standard and zoomed images for zooms of a) 2x, b) 3x, c) 4x and d) 5x: calculated (red) and ground truth (blue)

Although finding meaningful correspondences between lines is essential for accurate stereo matching, it is not sufficient to assess the quality of pixel matching itself. Consequently, we undertook a second experiment where we calculated pixel correspondences between the left and the right images of the 'cone' stereo pair, where the right image was subject to a zoom transformation. Here, we assume that line pairings between the left and right images are known. In practice, if dealing with static cameras, this can be calculated if the zoom ratio is known. Otherwise, the procedure described in the previous experiment can be used to initialise a line pairing optimisation algorithm. Colour images in Fig. 6 show pairs of images, i.e. a) and b) where the lines of the left image were removed so that both images have the same number of scanlines. Images c) and d) display calculated and actual disparity maps. In agreement with the previous experiment, only usage of x2 and x3 zooms produces meaningful results, even if, in the case of x3 zoom experiment, the accuracy is poor.

Distorted Images. Given the general nature of our framework, its application is not only limited to stereo matching scenarios. More diverse scenarios can be thought, for instance, the comparison of retouched images. Fig. 8 a) and b) show images before and after an intensive retouching process. Disparity maps generated by our algorithm (Fig 8c) reveal areas that have been worked on. For example, legs and chest area of the first character are thinner. In addition, values produced in the associated scoring matrices allow specifying the directions in which distortions were applied. This is illustrated in Fig 8d where left and right pixel shifts are identify by different colours.

Fig. 8. a) Original images, b) distorted images after retouching, c) disparity maps and d) disparity maps using colours (red from the left, blue form the right) to highlight disparity directions

4   Conclusions

The main contribution of this paper resides in the exploitation of the analogy between protein sequence alignment and image pair correspondence to design a bioinformatics-motivated framework to stereo matching based on dynamic programming. Not only does this approach offer accurate results with an algorithm which is suitable for real-time implementation, but it motivated the creation of a meaningfulness graph, which helps to predict matching validity according to image overlap and pixel similarity. This graph led to the application of the proposed method to the unexplored scenarios of stereo matching between images with different resolutions and before and after distortion. Experimental results reveal that good performance can be obtained when there is a ratio of 2 between the resolutions of a pair of images. Moreover, distortions are easily detected.

Another contribution of this work is an automatic procedure to estimate automatically all matching parameters. Conducted experiments showed that high quality sparse pixel correspondences generated by the SIFT algorithm could be extended using a Delaunay triangulation approach to generate a partial disparity map suitable for parameter optimisation.

In future work, we intend to exploit further the computer vision/bioinformatics analogy by considering video frames as leaves of a phylogenetic tree.

References

1. Scharstein, D., Szeliski, R.: A taxonomy and evaluation of dense two-frame stereo correspondence algorithms. International Journal of Computer Vision 47(1), 7–42 (2002)
2. Lazaros, N., Sirakoulis, G.C., Gasteratos, A.: Review of Stereo Vision Algorithms: From Software to Hardware. International Journal of Optomechatronics 2(4), 435–462 (2008)
3. MacLean, W.J., Sabihuddin, S., Islam, J.: Leveraging cost matrix structure for hardware implementation of stereo disparity computation using dynamic programming. Computer Vision and Image Understanding (2010) (in press)
4. Needleman, S.B., Wunsch, C.D.: A general method applicable to the search for similarities in the amino acid sequence of two proteins. Journal of Molecular Biology 48(3), 443–453 (1970)
5. Baker, H., Binford, T.: Depth from edge and intensity based stereo. In: IJCAI, vol. 81, pp. 631–636 (1981)
6. Ohta, Y., Kanade, T.: Stereo by intra- and interscanline search using dynamic programming. IEEE TPAMI 7(2), 139–154 (1985)
7. Geiger, D., Ladendorf, B., Yuille, A.: Occlusions and binocular stereo. In: European Conference on Computer Vision, pp. 425–433 (1992)
8. Belhumeur, P.N.: A Bayesian approach to binocular stereopsis. International Journal of Computer Vision 19(3), 237–260 (1996)
9. Cox, I.J., Hingorani, S.L., Rao, S.B., Maggs, B.M.: A maximum likelihood stereo algorithm. Computer Vision and Image Understanding 63(3), 542–567 (1996)
10. Torr, P.H.S., Criminisi, A.: Dense stereo using pivoted dynamic programming. Image and Vision Computing 22(10), 795–806 (2004)
11. Bobick, A.F., Intille, S.S.: Large occlusion stereo. International Journal of Computer Vision 33(3), 181–200 (1999)
12. Veksler, O.: Stereo correspondence by dynamic programming on a tree. In: Computer Vision and Pattern Recognition, San Diego, CA, USA (2005)
13. Deng, Y., Lin, X.: A Fast Line Segment Based Dense Stereo Algorithm Using Tree Dynamic Programming. In: Leonardis, A., Bischof, H., Pinz, A. (eds.) ECCV 2006. LNCS, vol. 3953, pp. 201–212. Springer, Heidelberg (2006)
14. Forstmann, S., Kanou, Y., Ohya, J., Thuering, S., Schmitt, A.: Real-Time Stereo by using Dynamic Programming. In: Computer Vision and Pattern Recognition Workshop, Washington, DC, USA (2004)

15. Wang, L., Liao, M., Gong, M., Yang, R., Nistér, D.: High-quality real-time stereo using adaptive cost aggregation and dynamic programming. In: 3D Data Processing, Visualization and Transmission, Chapel Hill, USA (2006)

16. Salmen, J., Schlipsing, M., Edelbrunner, J., Hegemann, S., Lueke, S.: Real-time stereo vision: making more out of dynamic programming. In: International Conference on Computer Analysis of Images and Patterns, Münster, Germany (2009)

17. Dayhoff, M.O., Eck, R.V., Chang, M.A., Sochard, M.R.: Atlas of Protein Sequence and Structure, National Biomedical Research Foundation, Silver Spring, Maryland (1965)

18. Altschul, S.F., Madden, T.L., Schäffer, A.A., Zhang, J., Zhang, Z., Miller, W., Lipman, D.J.: Gapped BLAST and PSI-BLAST: a new generation of protein database search programs. Nucleic Acids Research 25, 3389–3402 (1997)

19. Mackey, A.J., Haystead, T.A., Pearson, W.R.: Getting more from less: algorithms for rapid protein identification with multiple short peptide sequences. Molecular and Cellular Proteomics 1(2), 139–147 (2002)

20. Leinonen, R., Diez, F.G., Binns, D., Fleischmann, W., Lopez, R., Apweiler, R.: UniProt Archive. Bioinformatics 20, 3236–3237 (2004)

21. Henikoff, S., Henikoff, J.: Amino acid substitution matrices from protein blocks. Proceedings of the National Academy of Sciences 89, 10915–10919 (1992)

22. Higgins, D., Thompson, J., Gibson, T., Thompson, J.D., Higgins, D.G., Gibson, T.J.: CLUSTAL W: improving the sensitivity of progressive multiple sequence alignment through sequence weighting, position-specific gap penalties and weight matrix choice. Nucleic Acids Research 22, 4673–4680 (1994)

23. Notredame, C., Higgins, D., Heringa, J.: T-Coffee: A novel method for multiple sequence alignments. Journal of Molecular Biology 302, 205–217 (2000)

24. Edgar, R.C.: MUSCLE: a multiple sequence alignment method with reduced time and space complexity. BMC Bioinformatics 5, 113 (2004)

25. Lassmann, T., Sonnhammer, E.L.L.: Kalign - an accurate and fast multiple sequence alignment algorithm. BMC Bioinformatics 6, 298 (2005)

26. Karlin, S., Altschul, S.F.: Methods for assessing the statistical significance of molecular sequence features by using general scoring schemes. Proceedings of the National Academy of Sciences 87, 2264–2268 (1990)

27. Pearson, W.R.: Empirical statistical estimates for sequence similarity searches. Journal of Molecular Biology 276, 71–84 (1998)

28. Rost, B.: Twilight zone of protein sequence alignments. Protein Engineering 12(2), 85–94 (1999)

29. Scharstein, D., Szeliski, R.: High-accuracy stereo depth maps using structured light. In: IEEE Computer Society Conference on Computer Vision and Pattern Recognition, vol. 1, pp. 195–202 (2003)

30. Mühlmann, K., Maier, D., Hesser, J., Männer, R.: Calculating Dense Disparity Maps From Color Stereo Images, An Efficient Implementation. International Journal of Computer Vision 47(3), 78–88 (2002)

31. Klaus, A., Sormann, M., Karner, K.: Segment-based stereo matching using belief propagation and a self-adapting dissimilarity measure. In: ICPR, vol. 3, pp. 15–18 (2006)

32. Dayhoff, M.O.: Atlas of Protein Sequence and Structure. Suppl. 3, National Biomedical Research Foundation, Silver Spring, Maryland (1978)

33. International Human Genome Sequencing Consortium: Initial sequencing and analysis of the human genome. Nature 409, 860–921 (2001)

Hierarchical Grid-Based People Tracking with Multi-camera Setup

Lili Chen, Giorgio Panin, and Alois Knoll

Department of Informatics, Technische Universität München
85748 Garching bei München, Germany
{chenlil,panin,knoll}@in.tum.de

Abstract. We present a hierarchical grid-based tracking methodology for multiple people tracking in a multi-camera setup. In this system, frame-by-frame detection is performed by means of hierarchical likelihood grids, by matching shape templates through an oriented distance transform over foreground intensity edges, followed by clustering in pose-space. Subsequently, multi-target tracking is achieved by means of global nearest neighbor data association, with a fully automatic initialization, maintainance and termination strategy. We demonstrate our system through experiments in indoor sequences, using a four-camera calibrated setup. Moreover, in the paper we present the improvements obtained by means of a fast algorithm for computing the oriented DT, as well as using multi-part shape templates in place of a simple cylinder model, for a more precise localization.

Keywords: Edge-based background subtraction, Hierarchical likelihood grids, Oriented distance transform, Multi-view and multi-target tracking.

1 Introduction

Nowadays automatic visual surveillance is becoming increasingly popular, because of its wide applications in indoor and outdoor environments with security requirements. Usually there are two major problems in this system: one is to detect moving targets, and the other is to keep them tracked throughout the sequence. As the most representative application, detecting and tracking people is obviously the most challenging and attractive topic, due to people's huge variations in physical appearance, pose, movement and interaction. Therefore, people detection and tracking receives a significant amount of attention in the area of research and development.

Although some systems have been successfully developed towards this challenging task, it still remains difficult to detect and track multiple people precisely and automatically in a cluttered scene. This paper addresses the problem of employing a grid-based tracking-by-detection methodology. The primary goal is to develop a fully automatic system for tracking multiple people in an overlapping, multi-camera environment, providing a 3D output robust to mutual occlusion between interacting people.

As a commonly used technique for segmenting out objects of interest, background subtraction has achieved a significant success in fixed camera scenarios. Most of methods work by comparing color or intensities of pixels in the incoming video frame to the

G. Csurka et al. (Eds.): VISIGRAPP 2011, CCIS 274, pp. 187–202, 2013.

reference image [6,7]. However, it has the drawback of being susceptible to illumination changes, and provides a less precise localization. In contrast, we propose here an edge-based background subtraction, which employs Canny edge map together with Sobel gradients, because edges are more precisely and stably localized, to a better extent in presence of illumination changes.

A second contribution of our system is frame-by-frame detection by means of hierarchical likelihood grids. This scheme, adapted from [25], takes the advantage of multi-resolution grids that can, precisely and efficiently locate targets in cluttered scenes, without prior knowledge of their position. In particular, we compute the likelihood by edge matching through a fast oriented distance transform, which extends from our previous work [26], speeds up the computation by performing multiple searches along the given orientation while matching not only the location of edge points but also their orientation. And the likelihood is first computed on a coarse grid, then refined on the next level only the locations where likelihoods are higher than a given threshold. Subsequently, we perform state-space clustering on the high-resolution grid, in order to find the relevant peaks, possibly associated to people.

The third main issue consists in associating detected peaks to tracks, which is a classic data association problem. Several approaches have been developed for this purpose, the most representative ones being [13,14]; however, in place of complex methods, which require more complex models and parameter tuning, and further increase the computational complexity, our tracking module employs a Global Nearest Neighbor (GNN) approach in order to initiate, maintain and terminate tracks automatically.

The remainder of the paper is organized as follows: Section 2 reviews the state of the art and related work to our paper. Section 3 describes the general system overview with hardware setup and algorithmic flow of software. In Section 4, we provide the detailed detection procedure, including models, edge-based background subtraction, hierarchical grid evaluation as well as model-based contour matching and state-space clustering. Tracking by data association is presented in Section 5. The experimental results are discussed in Section 6. Finally, Section 7 summarizes the paper and proposes future development roads.

2   Related Work

A vast amount of literature has been published on people detection and tracking. We can mainly classify them into four categories: region-based approaches [21], based on the variation of image regions in motion; feature-based [17,22], that usually utilize information about color, texture, etc.; contour-based [18,19], that make use of the bounding contours to represent the target outline; and model-based methods [20,23] that explicitly require a 2D or 3D model of a person. However, a too detailed review is beyond the scope of our paper, therefore, in the following we will focus on people tracking-by-detection methodologies, more related to our work. There has been a number of literature on this approach [5,8,9], where detection of people in individual frame, as well as data association between detections, are the most challenging and ambiguous issues [4].

Template-based methods have yielded nice results for locating targets with no prior knowledge in a cluttered scene. In [1], the efficiency of this method is illustrated by using about 4,500 templates to match pedestrians in images. The core idea is using a Chamfer distance measure, so that matching a template with the DT image results in a similarity measure. Meanwhile this approach enables the use of an efficient search algorithm. However, if only computing the location of edge pixels without considering their orientation when computing distance transform, it inevitably leads to a high rate of false alarms in presence of clutter.

Another highlight of this system is the utilization of a template hierarchy, which is generated automatically from available examples, and formed by a bottom-up approach, using a partitioned clustering algorithm. It only searches locations where the distance measure is under a given threshold, so a speed-up of three orders of magnitude is demonstrated, compared to exhaustive searching.

This idea was taken further by [25], that however does not build the template hierarchy (or tree) by bottom-up clustering, rather by partitioning a state-space represented with an integral grid. The grid is hierarchically partitioned as the search descends into each region, so that regions at the leaf-level define the finest partition. This method is demonstrated to be capable of covering 3D motion, even with self-occlusion. Unfortunately, both approaches need a very specific model, only valid for a specific target.

Once the measurements have been obtained from the frame-by-frame detection, data association can be applied to solve the problem of measurement to track assignment. A simple nearest-neighbor approach [12] uses only the closest observation to any predicted state to perform the measurement update, it is commonly used for MTT systems because of its fast computation. More complex approaches, such as Joint Probabilistic Data Association Filter (JPDA) [13] combines all of the potential measurements into one weighted average, before associating it to the track, in a single update. By contrast, Multiple Hypothesis Tracking (MHT) [14] calculates every possible update hypothesis, with a track, formed by previous hypotheses associated to the target. Both methods are known to be quite complex, and require a careful implementation in terms of parameters; in particular, the latter cannot avoid the drawback of an exponentially growing computational complexity, with the number of targets and measurements involved in the resolution situation.

3 System Overview

In this section, we describe the hardware setup and present an overview of our tracking system. The overall setup is depicted in Fig. 1(a). Four uEye usb cameras are mounted overhead on the corners of the ceiling, each of them observing the same 3D scene synchronously. Furthermore, all the four cameras are connected to one multi-core PC. A necessary step before being able to get accurate 3D information, is calibration of the intrinsic and extrinsic camera parameters, that we perform with the Matlab Calibration Toolbox [1], with respect to a *world* coordinates system placed on the floor.

---

[1] http://www.vision.caltech.edu/bouguetj/calib_doc/

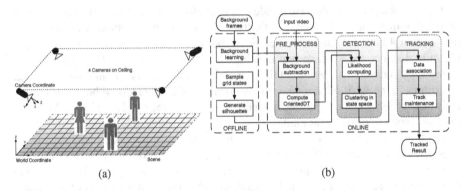

Fig. 1. System overview (a) Hardware setup (b) Block diagram of the tracking system

The tracking system is designed and implemented in the *OpenTL* framework[2] [2,10], which is a structured, general purpose architecture for model-based visual tracking. The block diagram is provided in Fig. 1(b), that consists of two main processing modules. Offline, we use a certain number of background frames to learn the background model. Moreover, grid states are sampled for each level, and the silhouettes are generated by projecting the external contours of the cylinder shape and keeping, for each contour and each camera view, a list of pixel positions and normals. Online, we have three main sub-modules: pre-process, detection and tracking.

In the pre-process part, for each camera view foreground contours are segmented by edge-based background subtraction, using the learned model. Afterwards, we compute an oriented distance transform onto this image, in order to match, for each template, both the location and the orientation of its contours. In particular, the oriented DT is efficiently computed over a finite set of orientations, so that the image is sampled over parallel scan lines that are pre-computed. The advantage of using both edge position and orientation, during background subtraction as well as template matching, is a strong reduction of false alarms.

Detection part first computes the likelihoods by matching projected templates and oriented DT for each camera view, where the likelihoods are computed on the coarse grid firstly, then refined on the next resolution only the locations where the likelihood is higher than a given threshold, the joint likelihoods can simply be multiplied then. The object-level measurements, or target hypotheses, are obtained by means of likelihood grid clustering, performed by Gaussian filtering of the high-resolution grid, and local maxima detection. Finally, the tracking module performs measurement-to-target association with the Global Nearest Neighbor approach.

4   People Detection

In this section, we provide more details about people detection, that serves as one of our key building blocks for our system.

---

[2] http://www.opentl.org

4.1   Construction of Template Hierarchy

The idea to construct a template hierarchy is inspired by the paper [25], as well as by the system developed by [1], extended to multiple views, multiple targets, and with a more general template.

Assuming there are L levels of search, the state space is partitioned with a coarse-to-fine strategy. A graphical illustration is shown in Fig. 2.

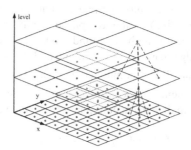

Fig. 2. Grid based state space with hierarchical partition

Each discrete region $\left\{R^{i,l}\right\}_{i=1}^{N_l}$, where N_l is the number of cells at level l, is sampled at its center, before the template hierarchy is generated. Meanwhile, we connect regions at a child level with its parent cell, by computing the nearest-neighbor in state-space, as well as its nearest neighbors within the same level, as it will be described in Section 4.4, in order to smooth the grid likelihoods.

After sampling the grid, templates are generated by rendering the 3D model at each state, under the respective camera projection. To more precisely match our target, the model chosen here is composed of 3 cylinders, where one cylinder is for the head, one for the torso, and one for the legs. The model undergoes (x,y) translation on the floor, while its silhouette is generated by projecting the external contour. An example of the model and a partial view of the hierarchy of silhouettes are shown in Fig. 3.

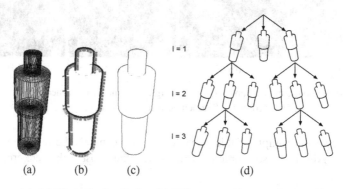

Fig. 3. Our model. (a) Discretized cylinder. (b) Silhouette with normals. (c) Silhouette without normals. (d) Hierarchy of the silhouettes.

For each silhouette, the position of each point as well as its normal is collected, as it will be described further in Section 4.3. As already emphasized, both grid sampling and template hierarchy generation are performed offline.

4.2   Background Learning and Foreground Segmentation

In order to match the image data with the templates, we first apply an edge-based background subtraction.

This approach can be divided into two phases: background learning (offline) and foreground segmentation (online). In the first phase, we utilize a certain number N of frames without people, to learn the background model. Let $\Theta_b(t), G_{bx}(t), G_{by}(t)$ respectively be the Canny edge map, Sobel x-gradient and y-gradient images, detected at frame $I_b(t)$. The Canny map Θ_b is accumulated by binary OR, from frame $\Theta_b^{(I)}(1), \ldots,$ $\Theta_b^{(I)}(N)$, while Sobel gradients are accumulated in a running average over the same frames. At the end, we normalize the accumulated Sobel image

$$G_{bx}^2 + G_{by}^2 = 1, \ \forall\,(x,y) \ . \tag{1}$$

Subsequently, standard distance transform is applied to the accumulated background Canny map, and thresholded to a few pixels, providing a binary mask $\Theta_{DT} \in \{0,1\}$, where potential background edges are found.

Online, from foreground Canny map and Sobel gradients $\Theta_f(t), G_{fx}(t), G_{fy}(t)$ of frame $I_f(t)$, we test the position and orientation of each edge pixel: edges $\Theta_f(t) \neq 0$ that lie near to a background edge $\Theta_{DT} \neq 0$ are candidate for removal. Then, we further test these edges for orientation with the Sobel masks, if the scalar product is higher than another threshold θ

$$\frac{G_{bx}G_{fx} + G_{by}G_{fy}}{\sqrt{G_{fx}^2 + G_{fy}^2}} > \theta \ . \tag{2}$$

the point is removed from $\Theta_f(t)$.

(a)	(b)	(c)	(d)

Fig. 4. Edge-based background subtraction. (a) Original frame. (b) Learned background model. (c) Unsegmented foreground edge. (d) Segmented foreground edge.

Fig. 4 shows an example of this procedure: as we can see, the resulting edge map robustly preserves the person contours, while discarding most of the background edges.

4.3   Template Matching with Fast, Oriented Distance Transform

The next step is to match foreground edges with the model silhouettes. One possibility would be to use the Chamfer distance transform on the edge map, that is tolerant to small shape variations, and has already been applied in several works, such as [1,24]. However, in case of images with considerable clutter, a significant rate of false alarms would be present. This problem can be reduced by matching not only the location of edge points, but also their orientation [3].

Therefore, an *oriented* distance transform, considering orientation of edge points, is more than necessary. It was first proposed in our previous work [26], where the oriented DT is defined by scanning the edge image through raster lines from top to bottom and from left to right. This method needs two scans for each raster line: one for finding edge pixels on the line, and the other for writing the DT values in the output image. In particular, all of the image pixels on each line must be read, before deciding whether any edge pixel is present, and then assign them DT values. However, if the line crosses no edge, no one of these pixels will have a valid DT value. Moreover, even for a valid scan line, most pixels have a DT which is higher than the validation gate, and therefore have no valid DT as well, but the line iterator can only proceed one pixel at a time, therefore wasting computational resources.

Here, we propose a significant faster implementation, that instead performs line scans starting directly from the *edge pixels*, and proceeding in both directions, until the desired distance. This is obtained by maintaining a double-linked, circular list of *exploring units*, two for each foreground edge pixel(which are in a limited amount, after background subtraction), that keep trace of the current DT value, and perform a single line iteration in each direction, execute one after the other through the circular list.

A single iteration consists of: one read operation, to check the current pixel, one write operation, and one increment of pixel position and DT value, for the next round. If a pixel has been already visited(i.e. its DT value is not infinity), or the DT value is beyond the validation gate, the unit is stopped and removed from the list, in order to not be checked again. By performing a single iteration per unit in a round, we make sure that two units, coming from two different edges but traveling along the same scan line in opposite directions, will meet exactly in the mid-point, and the DT values will be correctly assigned to the closest edge on the line.

When the list is empty, the algorithm terminates. Overall, this reduces the number of read/write/iterate operations to almost the minimum (only valid pixels are visited) except for the mid-point above mentioned, which will be *read* twice, by the two units that will terminate after each other. However, and in particular when the validation gate is reasonably small, this case is limited to a very small set of pixels. A pseudo-code of the fast oriented DT is shown in Algorithm 1, while Fig. 5 shows an example of results.

Once DTs are computed, template matching simply amounts to compute the likelihood, by summing up all values over the silhouette pixels, in the corresponding direction of the normal. To formalize the idea, a projected template s is represented by a set of pixel positions and normals $\{x_i, y_i, g_i\}_{i=1}^{N}$, obtained by re-projection through a 3×4 camera projection matrix P, where g_i selects the nearest $\gamma \in \Gamma$, from which the DT value will be taken. Therefore, the likelihood for state hypothesis s is given by:

Algorithm 1. Fast oriented distance transform

Initialization :
Fill the DT image with ∞, apart from 0 at the foreground edges.
Create a double $-$ linked, circular list of "exploration units", two for each foreg $-$
round edge pixel, going in opposite directions ($=$ line iterators).
Each unit consist of :
  $-$ A distance counter(initialized with 0);
  $-$ A line iterator(initialized with edge pixel position), with a given direction;
Main loop :
while *list is not empty* **do**
  Take current element of the list;
  Read DT value at (x, y);
  if $0 < DT(x, y) < \infty$ **then**
    Remove unit from the list;
  else
    Write the counter value into the DT image;
    Increment counter;
    if *counter $>$ validation gate* **then**
      Remove unit from the list;
    else
      Increment line iterator;
    end if
  end if
  Move to the next unit in the list;
end while

$$P(z|s) = \exp\left(-\frac{1}{2NR^2} \sum_{i=1}^{N} \min\left(DT_{\gamma(g_i)}(x_i, y_i)^2, D_{max}^2\right)\right). \qquad (3)$$

where $\gamma(g_i)$ denotes the closest available direction to the normal, and the sum is performed over all values $\{x_i, y_i, g_i\}_{i=1}^{N}$. R is the measurement standard deviation, and an outlier threshold is usually fixed at $D_{max} = 3R$, which is our validation gate for a more robust matching. Also notice that, in order to avoid problems with different scales, the sum is further normalized by N.

During the computation of likelihood, a coarse-to-fine search strategy is applied by evaluating it, at each level, only for locations where the parent cell likelihood is higher than a given threshold, which is usually obtained as the average likelihood [25]. For those cells where the parent likelihood is under the threshold, its value is simply inherited, thus saving a large amount of computation.

4.4   Likelihood Grid Clustering

In order to obtain the object-level measurements, or target hypotheses, after likelihood computation we employ a clustering procedure on the high-resolution grid, where each cluster is a local maximum, potentially corresponding to a person.

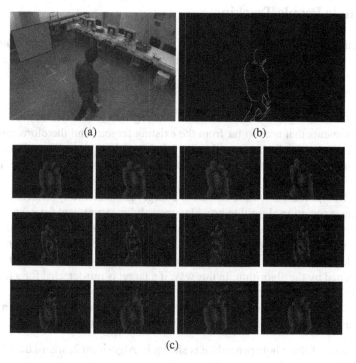

Fig. 5. Results of oriented distance transform (a) Original image (b) Foreground edge map. (c) Oriented DT results (at 12 discrete orientations).

This approach is similar to mean-shift, but explicitly done on discrete states. First of all, a Gaussian filtering is applied to the grid, where the isotropic Gaussian corresponds to the filtering kernel. For each cell s_i within the grid, we take the nearest neighbor s_j by looking at the connected states with distance $d_{i,j} = \|s_i - s_j\|$ up to a validation gate $D_{max} = 3\sigma_s^2$, where σ_s^2 is the measurement covariance in *state-space*, these neighbors are pre-computed in the off-line phase. For each neighbor, the Gaussian weight is also pre-computed by

$$W_{i,j} = exp(-\frac{d_{i,j}^2}{2\sigma_s^2}) \, . \tag{4}$$

the computed weights are also normalized to 1, so that the smoothed likelihood for state cell s_i is given by

$$P(z|s)_{weighted}(i) = \sum_{i,j} W_{i,j} \cdot P(z|s)(j) \, . \tag{5}$$

Subsequently, local maxima are detected (within the same neighborhood), to obtain the target hypotheses, or measurements. The final step will be to associate these hypotheses to tracks, as it will be described in next section.

5 Multiple People Tracking

In this section we deal with the problem of multi-target tracking, by associating measurements obtained from our detector to individual tracks, also performing automatic track initiation and termination.

In particular, our track management follows a strategy indicated in [11]:

- *Track Initiation.* In case of new targets entering into the scene, they will generate measurements that are too far from the existing targets, and therefore can be used to start new tracks. In this case, they are labeled with a unique ID, and a counter for the number of consecutive, successful detections for this target is also initialized to 1.
- *Track Maintainance.* During tracking, a target is successfully detected whenever the data association algorithm provides one valid measurement for it, so its counter is increased up to a maximum value (which can be taken as a confirmation time), while in case of misdetection it will be decreased. Those targets which are successfully detected over the confirmation time, can be considered as stable targets and maintained by the algorithm. In this way, if a target is misdetected for a few frames in case of occlusion, it can still be recovered until the counter goes to 0.
- *Track Termination.* When a target exits the scene, or after occlusion for a too long time, its misdetection counter goes to 0, and its track is terminated.

A pseudo-code of the whole procedure is shown in Algorithm 2, where the GNN algorithm is called in (line 25).

The data association problem consists in deciding which measurement should correspond to which track. Although our detection algorithm is fairly robust, it is also not person-specific, and therefore in a small indoor environment there are always ambiguities, arising from neighboring targets, as well as from missing detections and false alarms caused by background clutter. To this respect we employ the Global Nearest Neighbor (GNN) approach, that gives a good solution for this problem [15], while requiring relative low computational cost.

The first step of the GNN is to set up a distance (or cost) matrix: assuming that, at time t, there are M existing tracks and N measurements, the cost matrix is given by

$$D = \begin{pmatrix} d_{11} & d_{12} & \cdots & d_{1N} \\ d_{21} & d_{22} & \cdots & d_{2N} \\ \vdots & \vdots & \ddots & \vdots \\ d_{M1} & d_{M2} & \cdots & d_{MN} \end{pmatrix}. \tag{6}$$

where d_{ij} is the Euclidean distance between track i and measurement j, and $i = 1, 2, \ldots, M; j = 1, 2, \ldots, N$. In particular, d_{ij} is set to ∞ if it exceeds the validation gate, which is a circle with fixed radius around the predicted position, eliminating unlikely observation-to-track pairs. Moreover, it is commonly required that a target can be associated with at most one measurement (none, in case of misdetection), and a measurement can be associated to at most one target (none, in case of false alarms).

The GNN solution to this problem is the one that maximizes the number of valid assignments, while minimizing the sum of distances of the assigned pairs. To this aim,

Algorithm 2. Track management with GNN

```
 1: if nMeasurements = 0 then
 2:    for i = 0 to nTargets do
 3:      DecreaseCounter(target[i]);
 4:      if Counter(target[i]) > 0 then
 5:        MaintainTarget(target[i]);
 6:      else
 7:        TerminateTarget(target[i]);
 8:      end if
 9:    end for
10: else
11:    if nTargets = 0 then
12:      for j = 0 to nMeasurements do
13:        newTarget = CreateTarget(meas[j]);
14:        ResetCounter(newTarget);
15:      end for
16:    else
17:      for i = 0 to nTargets do
18:        for j = 0 to nMeasurements do
19:          D(i, j) = Distance(target[i], meas[j]);
20:          if D(i, j) > ValidGate then
21:            D(i, j) = ∞;
22:          end if
23:        end for
24:      end for
25:      (i ↔ j) = GNN(D);
26:      for i = 0 to nAssocTargets do
27:        if D(i, j(i)) ≤ ValidGate then
28:          MoveTarget(target[i], meas[j]);
29:          IncreaseCounter(target[i]);
30:          if Counter(target[i]) > MaxC then
31:            Counter(target[i]) = MaxC;
32:          end if
33:        else
34:          DecreaseCounter(target[i]);
35:          if Counter(target[i]) = 0 then
36:            TerminateTarget(target[i]);
37:          end if
38:        end if
39:      end for
40:      for j = 0 to nUnassocMeas do
41:        newTarget = CreateTarget(meas[j]);
42:        ResetCounter(newTarget);
43:      end for
44:    end if
45: end if
```

we adopt the extended Munkres' algorithm [16], where the input is the cost matrix D, and output are the indices (row, col) of assigned track-measurement pairs.

6 Experimental Results

We evaluated the proposed algorithms through pre-recorded video sequences, with multiple people entering and leaving the scene, as well as interacting with each other. The sequences have been simultaneously recorded from four cameras, as described in Section 3, with a resolution of (752×480), and a frame rate of 25 fps.

Before carrying out detection and tracking, state grids are set up at all levels, respectively 10×10, 20×20 and 40×40 from the coarsest to the finest, resulting in a total of 2100 grid cells, and the same amount of silhouette templates are sampled off-line. Since the area of interest is $(6m \times 4.2m)$, the corresponding grid on the finest level has a resolution of $(150mm \times 105mm)$.

Our current implementation of the fast oriented distance transform uses 12 discrete orientations, ranging from 0 to π, with the validation gate of 50 pixels. As it computes each orientation separately, they overall require about 0.12 sec/frame for four images, whereas the oriented DT in our previous work [26] is computed in 0.25 sec/frame. Therefore, we really speed up our oriented DT computation with our new algorithm.

Fig. 6 shows qualitative tracking results in a multi-camera environment, with a complex background. In particular, the top row shows foreground edges after edge-based background subtraction. Here 30 frames have been used for background learning, where the threshold θ mentioned in Eq. (2) is set to 0.9. The middle row shows likelihood values onto the finest grid, and the bottom row shows the corresponding tracking results after data association, with the projected cylinder silhouettes.

During data association, we keep a confirmation time of 10 frames (which is the maximum value for the consecutive detections counter) for keeping or removing tracks. As can be seen from the results, there are situations with significant occlusion from one or more views. For instance, at frame 345, each two targets are occluded from some views, however, since for the same pairs there are no occlusions from another camera view, all targets are successfully detected, thanks to the robustness of multi-camera fusion and oriented DT matching. The system also successfully handles targets entering and leaving the scene.

In order to better evaluate the performance of our system, we manually label the ground truth data for our sequences, and compare the results of our tracker, both in terms of position accuracy and robustness of detection. Ground truth trajectories, labeled on the finest grid, are depicted in Fig. 7(a), where we can see the challenges due to targets that keep close most of the time, with mutual interactions and position exchanges.

Fig. 7(b) shows the (X, Y) position errors of our tracking system. Although the above mentioned occlusions and dynamics, for each target the system can basically keep the track. For the temporal track lost case, compared to our previous work [26], it is improved to happens only 2 times per target over the 550 frames of sequence and can recover again very shortly afterwards. This is attributed to the utilization of updated 3-cylinder model. The leaded sub-tracks with different IDs have been also shown in Fig. 7(b) by the green boxes.

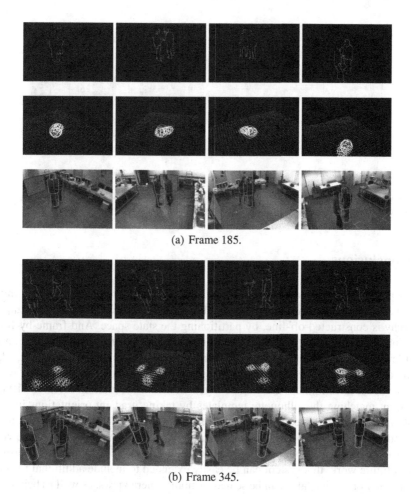

(a) Frame 185.

(b) Frame 345.

Fig. 6. Performance of 3D people tracking. Shown are edge-based background subtraction, likelihood grids, and the corresponding tracking results, on four camera views.

Overall these results indicate that, despite the cluttered situation, position errors are considerably low for all people, being most of the time under 100-$150mm$, that corresponds to one cell of the high-resolution grid. This is because of the local edge-based matching which, despite the simplicity of the model, is more precise with respect to global statistics such as color histograms, or histograms of oriented gradients.

The execution time of the whole tracking procedure is currently 2.8 FPS, on a desktop PC with Intel Core 2 Duo CPU (1.86 GHz), 1GB RAM and an Nvidia GeForce 8600 GT graphic card.

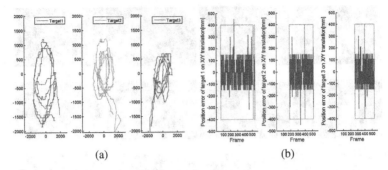

(a)   (b)

Fig. 7. Ground truth evaluation. (a) Ground-truth trajectories, sampled on the discretized grid. (b) Position error on X(red) and Y(blue) in world coordinates.

7   Conclusions

In this paper, we presented a novel system for multiple people tracking in a multi-camera environment, using a grid-based tracking by detection methodology. A template hierarchy is constructed off-line, by partitioning the state space. And frame-by-frame detection is performed by means of hierarchical likelihood grids and clustered on the finest level, followed by data association through the GNN approach. Moreover, edge-based background subtraction has been proposed for foreground segmentation, which is quite robust to illumination changes, together with a speeded-up oriented distance transform, matching the silhouette templates by taking gradient orientations into account, thus significantly reducing the rate of false alarms. Our system initiates, maintains and terminates tracks in a fully automatic way. Experimental results over the video sequences also show that our proposed system deals fairly well with mutual occlusions.

As a future work, this system can be easily extended to include additional features, such as color or motion, also can be scaled to more camera views, as well as being used for tracking different objects, for example 3D indoor tracking of flying *quadrotors*. In addition, the individual components can still be further optimized, both with respect to speed and performance, graphics hardware is possibly need to be exploited. Moreover, we plan to address the issue of heavy occlusions between people, taking place for longer periods. Re-identification after occlusions are going to be done by using more specific features, such as color or texture.

Besides these straightforward improvements, we also plan to test and extend our system to more challenging scenarios, such as outdoor tracking with multiple models (such as people and cars), as well as people tracking on mobile robots, with a non-static background and viewpoint.

References

1. Gavrila, D.M.: Pedestrian Detection from a Moving Vehicle. In: Vernon, D. (ed.) ECCV 2000. LNCS, vol. 1843, pp. 37–49. Springer, Heidelberg (2000)

2. Panin, G., Lenz, C., Nair, S., Roth, E., Wojtczyk, M., Friedlhuber, T., Knoll, A.: A Unifying Software Architecture for Model-Based Visual Tracking. In: IS&T/SPIE 20th Annual Symposium of Electronic Imaging, San Jose, CA (2008)

3. Olsen, C.F., Huttenlocher, D.P.: Automatic Target Recognition by Matching Oriented Edge Pixels. IEEE Transactions on Image Processing 6(1), 103–113 (1997)

4. Andriluka, M., Roth, S., Schile, B.: People-Tracking-by-Detection and People-Detection-by-Tracking. In: IEEE Conference on Computer Vision and Pattern Recognition (2008)

5. Wu, B., Nevatia, R.: Detection and Tracking of Multiple, Partially Occluded Humans by Bayesian Combination of Edgelet based Part Detectors. International Journal of Computer Vision 75(2), 247–266 (2007)

6. Stauffer, C., Grimson, W.E.L.: Learning Patterns of Activity using Real-Time Tracking. IEEE Transaction on Pattern Analysis and Machine Intelligence 22(8), 747–757 (2000)

7. Eng, H., Wang, J., Kam, A., Yau, W.: A Bayesian Framework for Robust Human Detection and Occlusion Handling using a Human Shape Model. In: International Conference on Pattern Recognition, pp. 257–260 (2004)

8. Okuma, K., Taleghani, A., de Freitas, N., Little, J.J., Lowe, D.G.: A Boosted Particle Filter: Multitarget Detection and Tracking. In: Pajdla, T., Matas, J(G.) (eds.) ECCV 2004. LNCS, vol. 3021, pp. 28–39. Springer, Heidelberg (2004)

9. Leibe, B., Schindler, K., Van Gool, L.: Coupled Detection and Trajectory Estimation for Multi-Object Tracking. In: International Conference on Computer Vision (2007)

10. Panin, G.: Model-based Visual Tracking: the OpenTL Framework. Wiley-Blackwell (2011)

11. Bar-Shalom, Y., Li, X.: Multitarget-Multisensor Tracking: Principles and Techniques. YBS Publishing (1995)

12. Bar-Shalom, Y., Fortmann, T.E.: Tracking and Data Association. Academic Press, San Diego (1988)

13. Fortmann, T.E., Bar-Shalom, Y., Scheffe, M.: Sonar Tracking of Multiple Targets using Joint Probabilistic Data Association. IEEE Journal of Oceanic Engineering 8(3), 173–184 (1983)

14. Reid, D.B.: An Algorithm for Tracking Multiple Targets. IEEE Transaction on Automatic Control 24(6), 843–854 (1979)

15. Konstantinova, P., Udvarev, A., Semerdjiev, T.: A Study of a Target Tracking Algorithm using Global Nearest Neighbor Approach. In: Proceeding of International Conference on Computer Systems and Technologies (2003)

16. Burgeois, F., Lasalle, J.C.: An Extension of the Munkres Algorithm for the Assignment Problem to Rectangular Matrices. Communications of the ACM, 802–806 (1971)

17. Fieguth, P., Terzopoulos, D.: Color-based Tracking of Heads and other Mobile Objects at Video Frame Rates. In: Proceedings IEEE Conf. on Computer Vision and Pattern Recognition, San Juan, Puerto Rico, pp. 21–27 (1997)

18. Roh, M.C., Kim, T.Y., Park, J., Lee, S.W.: Accurate Object Contour Tracking based on Boundary Edge Selection. Pattern Recognition 40(3), 931–943 (2007)

19. Nguyen, H.T., Worring, M., Van Den Boomgaard, R., Smeulders, A.W.M.: Tracking Nonparameterized Object Contours in Video. IEEE Trans. Image Process. 11(9), 1081–1091 (2002)

20. Andriluka, M., Roth, S., Schiele, B.: Monocular 3D Pose Estimation and Tracking by Detection. In: IEEE Conference on Computer Vision and Pattern Recognition (2010)

21. Khan, S., Javed, O., Rasheed, Z., Shah, M.: Human Tracking in Multiple Cameras. In: Proceedings of the 8th IEEE International Conference on Computer Vision, Vancouver, Canadam, pp. 331–336 (2001)

22. Li, L., Huang, W., Gu, I.Y.H., Tian, Q.: Foreground Object Detection from Videos Containing Complex Background. In: Proceedings of the 11th ACM International Conference on Multimedia, pp. 2–10 (2003)

23. Gavrila, D.M., Davis, L.S.: 3-D Model-based Tracking of Humans in Action: a Multi-View Approach. In: Proc. IEEE Computer Vision and Pattern Recognition, San Francisco, pp. 73–80 (1996)
24. Borgefors, G.: Hierarchical Chamfer Matching: A Parametric Edge Matching Algorithm. IEEE Trans. Pattern Analysis and Machine Intelligence 10(6), 849–865 (1988)
25. Stenger, B., Thayananthan, A., Torr, P.H.S., Cipolla, R.: Model-based Hand Tracking using a Hierarchical Bayesian Filter. IEEE Transactions on Pattern Analysis and Machine Intelligence 28, 1372–1384 (2006)
26. Chen, L., Panin, G., Knoll, A.: Multi-camera People Tracking with Hierarchical Likelihood Grids. In: Proceedings of the 6th International Conference on Computer Vision Theory and Applications. INSTICC Press, Algarve (2011)

The Spiral Facets: A Compact 3D Facial Mesh Surface Representation and Its Applications

Naoufel Werghi[1], Harish Bhaskar[1], Mohamed Khamis Naqbi[1], Youssef Meguebli[2], and Haykel Boukadida[2]

[1] Dept. of Computer Engineering, Khalifa University, Sharjah Campus, Sharjah, U.A.E.
naoufel.werghi@kustar.ac.ae, harishbhasky@gmail.com
[2] School of Science and Techniques, University of Tunis, Tunis, Tunisia
{youssefmeguebli,haykel.boukadida}@yahoo.fr

Abstract. In this paper we introduce the spiral facets framework as a novel mechanism of encoding 3D facial triangular mesh surface that incorporates crucial 3D face shape information by exploiting specific arrangement patterns of facets in the mesh model. The spiral facets framework is characterized by its simplicity and in the ability of adapting it for several useful applications within the domain of 3D face recognition. This paper will introduce the framework and study in detail the properties of the spiral facets that make it suitable for applications including frontal face extraction, estimation of face pose, facial feature extraction and face alignment. We validate the stability and the robustness of our framework against different system level parameters through experimentation with raw 3D mesh surfaces obtained from both globally available datasets and in-house 3D scanned data. Our results demonstrate that the spiral facets framework is a simple and compact representation that encompasses rich shape information that can be usefully deployed both locally and globally across the 3D face in comparison to other standard representations.

Keywords: 3D face descriptors, Spiral facets, Cubic spline, Feature localization, Geodesic curves, 3D face orientation.

1 Introduction

Visual surveillance and security systems for authentication or identification purposes most often require robust and accurate face recognition. Current methods of face identification using 2D image-based systems are restricted in their ability to cope with changing scale, position and orientation variations of the target. As an alternative technology, in more recent years, the 3D face images are investigated for this purpose. Some of inherent characteristics of 3D face image such as the richness and completeness allows this modality to be a promising alternative to other 2D face image-based systems. One of the main challenges in working with the 3D facial data is the growing need to faithfully encode raw 3D facial mesh surface into a simple, structured and compact facial representation.

Although there exist competing approaches to model 3D facial mesh surfaces, the object-centric representations have invited particular attention in recent years. These

G. Csurka et al. (Eds.): VISIGRAPP 2011, CCIS 274, pp. 203–224, 2013.
© Springer-Verlag Berlin Heidelberg 2013

representations are invariant to geometric transformations and have the potential to produce a reliable metric for facial shape comparison. The success of such representations not alone depends on how faithfully they can encode the characteristics of the face but also to remain as an unified framework for building related competing applications within face recognition domain such as face pose estimation, alignment, registration, etc.

In this paper, we propose a unified topological framework for encoding 3D facial mesh surface that is concise (encompasses dimensionality reduction, as a means of improving the efficiency, or allowing the data compression) and computationally efficient. The proposed framework is highly flexible to be adapted for several applications such as: facial landmarks detection, frontal face extraction, face shape description, face pose computation and face alignment.

2   Related Work

In the context of 3D face recognition, we can categorize the face shape representations into three classes, namely: Local features representation, global feature representation and hybrid representations.

Local feature representation methods employ features derived from local face surface (at a limited neighborhood). These attributes typically include curvature measures [1], and point signatures [2]. The derivation of local features is performed with differential geometry techniques that are intrinsically vulnerable to scaling and data deficiencies (e.g., non-uniform resolution, presence of noise).

In contrast to the local representation, in global representations, the facial features are derived from the whole 3D face data. Wu et al. [3] used vertical and horizontal profiles of faces and Xu et al. [4] derived invariant curve and surface moments from 3D face data. In these methods, matching is performed by evaluating the similarity between these entities. Other methods [5,6] superimpose the whole query 3D facial image with the stored instances in the database, and then evaluate the degree of overlapping to decide whether or not they match. These approaches are limited by their high computational cost. In [7,8] authors, extend the eigenfaces paradigm developed in 2D face recognition to the 3D case. This paradigm operates on a range or depth image in which the pixel intensity represents the 'z' coordinate. However, these methods have inherited some of the shortcomings of 2D face identification, particularly with regard to the face pose, self-occlusion and scaling. Other representations have been developed based on geodesic entities [9–11], these approaches aimed also to address face shape deformation. So did [12] with their deformable face model.

Finally, hybrid representation combines local and global facial features. These methods were motivated by psychological findings asserting that humans equally rely on both local and global visual information. Pan et al. [13] augmented the eigenface paradigm with face profile. Xu et al. [14] developed a face representation defined by a measure of the similarity between the 3D face image and a 3D face template, and local shape variation around local facial. landmarks (e.g., eyes and nose). Mian et al [15] employed a 2D histogram that encompasses rank-0 tensor fields extracted at local points of the facial surface and from the whole face depth map data.

3 Contributions and Structure

The main novelty and contributions of this paper emanate from the unified framework, its characteristics and importantly the ability to amend the framework to suit and be applied to face analysis tasks such as a) nose tip localization, b) frontal face extraction, c) 3D face shape modeling d) 3D face pose computation, e) nose profile identification, and f) face alignment. It is important to note that a majority of these applications are inherently required for accurate and robust face recognition. The framework extracts ordered structured patterns from 3D triangular mesh surface for a simple representation of facial surfaces. The discussed "spiral facets" representation is: a) simple and compact, b) generalized representation, c) computationally efficient that requires no form of mesh pre-processing. We acknowledge that there are a number of other representations of 3D facial surfaces in the literature and therefore, the characteristic features of our framework aforementioned would allow us distinguish from other close face shape representation such as [10, 11].

We begin by describing our framework of 3D facial surface representation in Section 4. We then elaborate different applications of the proposed framework in section 5 and conduct systematic experiments on varied datasets for nose tip localization 5.1, 3D frontal face extraction 5.2, face shape description 5.3, 3D face pose computation 5.4, face alignment 5.5 and nose profile identification 5.6. In Section 6 we present concluding remarks and directions of future work.

4 The Spiral Facets Framework

In our framework, we derive a 3D facial surface representation by constructing novel structured and ordered patterns in a 3D face triangular mesh surface. The triangular mesh surface representation though is simple, lacks an intrinsic ordered structure that allows the facets in the mesh to be browsed systematically. Consequently, storing the facets in the facet array is usually arbitrary and does not follow any particular arrangement. Therefore processing and analyzing triangular mesh surfaces are more complex compared with other intrinsically ordered shape modalities such as range images. According to our framework, we construct patterns exploiting topological properties of a triangular mesh surface. These patterns include concentric rings of facets that can also be arranged in a spiral-wise fashion.

Our framework has been inspired from the observation of the arrangement of triangular facets lying on closed contour of edges (Figure 1.a) . From this, we can categorize the facets into two groups: 1) facets having an edge on that contour that seem to point outside the area delimited by the contour (e.g. $fout_1$ and $fout_2$ in Figure 1.a). And 2) facets having a vertex on the contour that point inside the contour's area. The facets in the second group have an effect of filling gaps between facets in the first group. We call these two groups of facets as $Fout$ and $Fgap$ facets and together, they form a kind of ring structure. Using this ring facets we can derive a new group of $Fout$ facets that are one-to-one adjacent with the $Fgap$ facets of the previous ring, that will in-turn form the basis of the subsequent rings (Figure 1.b). We iterate this process to obtain a group of concentric rings. When the initial contour is composed of the edges of a given triangular facet, the rings will be centered at that particular facet (Figure 1.c). Moreover, by imposing the last facet in the current ring to be connected to the first facet in the subsequent ring, we obtain a sequence of facets arranged on a spiral-wise fashion, i.e. sequence of facets starting at the root facet and following a spiral path on the facial surface. We dubbed this arrangement "the spiral facet". (Figure 1.d). We also note that from the root triangle 3 different spiral facets can be generated depending on the chosen facet among the three facets adjacent to the root facet.

The algorithm for constructing a facet spiral starting at a given facet t is as follows:

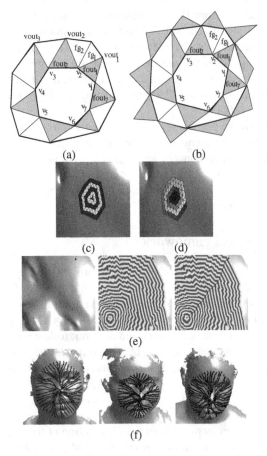

Fig. 1. a:$Fout$ facets (dark) on the contour $E_7 : (v_1, v_2, ..v_7)$. The $Fgap$ facets (clear) bridge the gap between pairs of consecutive $Fout$ facets. b :Extraction of the new $Fout$ facets. Notice that the new $Fout$ facets are one-to-one adjacent to the $Fgap$ facets. c: An examples of facet spiral and its concentring rings. d: The same facet spiral where the facets are arranged spiral-wise. e: Example of a geodesic path computation: The facet spiral is expanded from a source facet on the nose tip until the the destination facet is reached, then the geodesic path is extracted by tracing back the source facet. f: examples of geodesic paths between the nose tip and facets on a periphery ring of a facet spiral.

Algorithm GetSpiralFacets:
Rings = [t] , FoutFacets ← facets adjacent to t
For i=1: Number of rings
  GapFacets ← FillGap(FoutFacets)
  Ring ← FoutFacets + GapFacets
  Append Ring to Rings
  NewFoutFacets ← GetFoutFacest(GapFacets,FoutFacets)
  FoutFacets ← NewFoutFacets
End For

The algorithm $GetSpiralFacets$ has computational complexity of $O(n)$ where n is the number of facets in the facet spiral.

One of the main interesting characteristics of the spiral facets representation is that facets at a given ring are approximately at the same geodesic distance from the root facet. The geodesic distance can be approximated to $RingNumber \times L$, where $RingNumber$ is the ring's number in the facet spiral, and L is the average length of the triangle's edge. Therefore, it is possible to use the spiral facets as a low cost alternative for computing an approximation of iso-geodesic contours on the facial surface, compared to the standard $O(nlog(n))$ Dijkstra algorithm [16] (employed in [11]) and the $O(nlog(n))$ fast marching method [17] (used in [10]). We compute the geodesic path using the spiral facets in two distinctive stages (Figure 1.e) . In the first step, the spiral facets are expanded from a source facet until the destination facet is reached (i.e., found in the last ring). In the second step, the rings are browsed backwards, starting from the destination facet, and reiterated looking for the nearest connected facet in the previous ring until the source facet is reached. Since the algorithm $GetSpiralFacet$ intrinsically computes the connectivity between facets in adjacent rings, the second stage has a complexity of $O(RingNumber)$. (Figure 1.f) depicts facets on the geodesic paths between the nose tip and facets located at a given ring of the facet spiral.

We now review some of the characteristic features of the spiral-facets framework and bring them to perspective with some justifying claims. The features include: a) simplicity and compactness: the spiral facet representation is a single data structure, b) generalization: the facet spiral is a generalized representation of other popular 3D facial surface representations and it is possible that we can derive for example, the approximate geodesic rings structure from the spiral facet, c) processing efficiency: our representation also does not require any form of mesh pre-processing, whereas in most other method mesh regularization is often required and finally, d) computational complexity: out method is computationally more efficient. As we will explained in the end of Section 4, we infer a complexity of $(O(n))$ in comparison to $O(nlog(n))$ in [10, 11] which also requires a mesh regularization of complexity $O(n)$.

5 Applications

In this section of the paper, we exhibit the generality of the spiral facets framework by adapting it for several 3D face applications. One of the critical steps towards face recognition is the localization of features. In the initial attempt to localize 3D facial features using the "spiral facets" representation, we first present the nose tip detection application in Section 5.1. We substantially elaborate on this part since the rest of the applications depends on it. Next, we describe the algorithm to extract the frontal face from the raw 3D face scan by propagating rings starting from the detected nose tip in Section 5.2. Face shape description and pose identification are also important components particularly to model based matching of 3D faces. In Sections 5.3, 5.4 we explore an approach for face shape description and face pose computation using the spiral facets framework. Finally, we also exploit the geodesic properties of the spiral facets to extract the nose profile from 3D face scans in Section 5.6.

5.1 Nose Tip Detection

Face landmarks detection is critical to face recognition and nose tip detection in particular has a capital role due to its center position and saliency. A majority of 3D face analysis techniques are anchored to detecting the nose tip. The problem of nose tip detection has been approached using heuristic rules-based methods [18, 19]. Such methods requires a restricted face pose. This issue was addressed to some extent by shape descriptors-based methods [20, 21] that are specifically invariance to geometric transformation. However, the presence of noise has often affected the reliability of such systems. Statistical methods [22, 23] employed a landmarks model, obtained via training. This model is registered to the face data in order to get an approximate landmark locations, which are further refined in an iterative manner. This method inherits the problems of model registration; such as the need of prior pose information. Apart of [24] most approaches that dealt with face landmarks detection treated a pre-processed data, in which the 3D face surface has been cropped and smoothed. The method in [24] uses a hierarchical filtering scheme employing shape descriptors and a local nose tip shape model. The method is robust, but, revealed cases of false detection for some instance where clothing deformation matches the nose tip statistical model.

We propose an application of the 3D spiral facets for nose tip detection from raw 3D triangular mesh facial surfaces. Our method is inspired from the observation that the regions around some facial landmarks are characterized by low mesh quality. These result from gaps (in the nostrils) and reflection effects (at the eyes) (see Figure 2.a). To measure and assess the quality of the mesh surface, we present an original framework using which we extract a group of candidate triangular facets. In the second stage of our algorithm, we find the single facet that corresponds to the nose tip from the group of candidate triangle facets using a series of filtering steps.

Assessing the Regularity of the Mesh Tessellation. The term mesh quality is context driven and tightly linked to the subsequent use of the constructed mesh [25], therefore there is no standard framework for assessing the quality of triangular mesh surface for raw 3D facial surface scan. Our proposed technique measures to what extent a triangular mesh is close to an ideal mesh composed of equal-sized equilateral triangles at a given neighborhood. In such mesh, we can show easily that the number of triangles across the concentric rings that from the facet spiral follow arithmetic progression:

$$nrt(n + 1) = nrt(n) + 12 \tag{1}$$

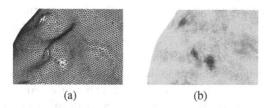

Fig. 2. a: A sample triangular mesh facial surface. Notice the mesh irregularities at the nostrils, and the the eyes areas. b: Computation of the error Δ_3 at each facet. Dark areas correspond to a large error.

where $nrt(n)$ and $nrt(n+1)$ are the number of triangles in the ring n and $n+1$ respectively. Therefore, the sequence $\hat{\eta}_n$ in an ideal mesh, starting at a root facet, is $[12, 24, 36, , 12n]$. This condition will not be satisfied at surface areas where the uniformity of the mesh tessellation is corrupted. Based on this, we propose the following local criterion for evaluating the mesh tessellation uniformity.

$$\Delta_n = \frac{\|\eta_n - \hat{\eta}_n\|}{\|\hat{\eta}_n\|}, \tag{2}$$

where η_n (respectively $\hat{\eta}_n$) is the sequence representing the number of triangles across a group of n concentric rings in a arbitrary mesh (respectively an ideal mesh). Figure 2.b depicts Δ_3 computed at each facet of a sample 3D raw facial data.

Cascading Filters. After computing the error Δ_n (Figure 3.b), we retain those facets having a Δ_n above a certain threshold. The group of facets extracted from this level of filtering (dubbed Group1), contains a majority of facets in the neighborhood of the nostrils and eyes and also other facets spread mostly across the ears, clothes and the periphery areas in the raw mesh surface (as in Figure 3.c). In the second level of our cascaded filtering implementation, we apply prior information derived from the topological characteristics of the raw face scan to extract the central facets corresponding to a potential landmark. As Figure 3.a shows, the face scan is composed of several fragmented manifold pieces which includes the face, parts of the hair, neck, and upper torso. We initialize a two-phase filter where in the first phase, facets from Group1 generating more than 18 rings are selected. By doing this, we capture facets located within the vicinity of the central face, and naturally discard those which are located at the surface periphery or at small surface fragments. We set the threshold to 18 as it is about half the maximum number of rings in a typical facial surface. In the subsequent phase, we select from the obtained facets those scoring the 10 highest number of rings (Figure 3.d). To these facets we add those locates at their neighborhoods (by expanding 4 rings-facet spiral around each one of them). We called the so obtained group of facets, Group 2 facets.

In the third level, we employ a model-based matching method based on the standard Geometric Histogram (GH) local shape descriptor [26]. The GH is a 2D accumulator that describes a pairwise relationship between a central facet and each of it surrounding facets within a given neighborhood. This relationship in the form of the angles (α)

between the central facet normals and all the other facets' normals, and the range of perpendicular algebraic distances (ρ) from the plane in which the central facet lies to all the other facets in the neighborhood. These measurements are entered in the discrete angle‑distance 2D accumulator, thus obtaining a kind of distribution that characterizes the relationship between the root facet and its neighbors. The neighborhood is constructed by generating a six-rings spiral facets around a central facet. At this level, the GH of each candidate facet is matched with the statistical model of GH of the nose tip neighborhood. This model is obtained from 100 face data samples, whereby we averaged the 100 GHs derived from their corresponding nose tip neighborhoods. The matching crite-

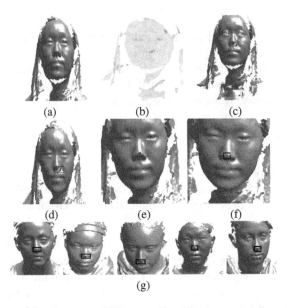

Fig. 3. Nose tip detection stages a: raw 3D face mesh surface. b: computation of the mesh quality criterion Δ_n. c: Selection of the facets scoring a Δ_n above a certain threshold. d: Elimination of the facets at the periphery areas and selection of the most central facets. e: Detection of candidate facets via Geometric Histogram matching. f: selection of the nose tip facet. g: Detected nose tips on some face samples.

rion used to evaluate the closeness of two GHs h_i and h_j is the Bhattacharya distance:

$$D^{ij}_{Bhattacharya} = \sum_{\alpha,\rho} \sqrt{h_i(\alpha,\rho)} \sqrt{h_j(\alpha,\rho)}. \qquad (3)$$

Since the nose tip can be located as an area rather a single point, and the matching is performed using an average model, we select the facets having a matching score at a given distance from the maximum. This set of facets, called Group 3, is defined by:

$$\mathcal{N} = \{t \setminus Max_D - 5\sigma \leq D_{Bhattacharyya}(GH_t, GH) \leq Max_D\} \qquad (4)$$

where sigma is the variance of Bhattacharyya distances between the GHs samples used for computing the mean GH model. Figure 3.e depicts and instance of this set. In the final level of our cascaded filtering implementation, we further refine the location of the nose tip by computing for each facet in Group 3, the rank-2 tensor field ([15])

$$T = \sum_{i=1}^{n} \frac{a_i r_i r_i^T}{A \|r_i\|^2} \tag{5}$$

where n is the number of facets in the facet's neighborhood. a_i is the area of the ith facet, r_i is a vector from its center to central facet's center and A is the total neighbourhood's area. T represents the covariance of r and encodes the local neighborhood variation which is reflected in its three eigenvalues. So in this level we select the facet having the largest eigenvalue as the one corresponding to the nose tip. Figure 3.(f,g) shows nose tips detected on some face samples.

5.2   Frontal Face Extraction

Using the same framework for assessing mesh quality,and exploiting the knowledge of the nose tip area, we present an extension to extract the frontal face area from the raw unprocessed 3D facial data. A popular technique to extract frontal faces discussed in the literature is using a cropping sphere centered at the nose tip (e.g. in [27, 28]). However such a technique is sensitive to scale variance. An alternative approach discussed in [29] uses 3D point clustering based on texture information. This method requires the texture map to be available, and is unstable for head orientations greater than $\pm 45°$.

In our approach, we exploit the spiral facets to develop an intrinsically scale-invariant method for frontal face extraction. Its implementation is as follows: For each facet t within a 5-ring size nose tip neighborhood, we generate a set of facets $\mathcal{R}(t)$ using the $GetFacetSpiral$ algorithm initialized at t and with the stop condition set to 'Rings reaches a border of the surface'. Following which, we merge all the sets $\mathcal{R}(t)$ into a single set $\mathcal{F}$ using:

$$\mathcal{F} = \uplus_{t \in \mathcal{N}} \mathcal{R}(t) \tag{6}$$

where $\uplus$ is the exclusive union. This procedure ensures a maximum coverage of the central face area.

An illustration of the frontal face extraction process is shown in Figure 4. In Figure 5, we show some results of frontal face extraction on 3D face data from our in-house 3D scanner.

5.3   Face Shape Description

we derive from the spiral facet, centered on the nose tip, a sequence of ordered, discrete, closed, contours , each comprising a clockwise ordered and uniformly sampled points. These contours are intrinsically invariant to rigid geometric transformation.

The contours extraction procedure is as follows: Let $p_1, ..., p_{n_k}$ a sequence of points representing the centers of the facets of the ring k, $k = 1 : \mathcal{M}$ of the spiral facet. A basic spatial smoothing is applied and followed by a cord-length parametrization, which is approximated by the following mapping:

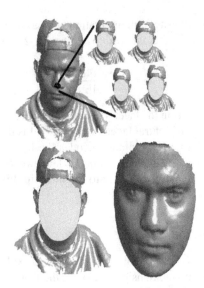

Fig. 4. Extraction of the frontal face area: from the each facet in the nose tip neighbourhood we propagate rings until a border is reached. Then we merge the obtained sets to get the frontal face area.

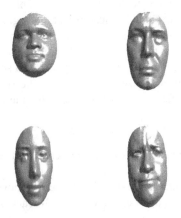

Fig. 5. Extraction of the frontal face area from raw images obtained from the in-house 3D scanner

$$\xi^{-1} : p_j \rightarrow \frac{\sum_{i=1}^{j} \|p_i - p_{i-1}\|}{\sum_{i=1}^{n_k} \|p_i - p_{i-1}\|} = t_j \tag{7}$$

ξ^{-1} maps the control points p_j onto the unit interval $[0, 1]$. t_j is the arc-length from the point p_1 to p_j, assuming that $\xi^{-1}(p_1) = 0$. Next, we parameterize the curves, using the inverse map, with a natural cubic spline interpolation [30]. We obtain a 3D cubic spline curve:

$$\Lambda_k(t) = [x_k(t), y_k(t), z_k(t)] \tag{8}$$

From each cubic spline curves Λ_k, $k = 1, ., \mathcal{M}$, Afterwards, we derive form the above continuous curve functions a set of uniformly and ordered sampled points via the following regular sub-sampling of the parameter t:

$$\Gamma_k = \Lambda_k(\frac{j}{12k}), j = 0, 1, ..., 12k \qquad (9)$$

With this sampling scheme the number of points across the contours Γ_k follows the same arithmetic progression of the number of facets across the spiral facet's rings in an ideal mesh. Figure 6 illustrates the different steps of the construction of a Γ contour. The Γ_k contours inherit from the spiral facet rings the iso-geodesic property. Therefore

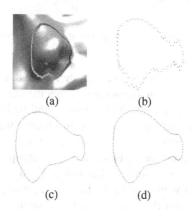

(a)   (b)

(c)   (d)

Fig. 6. a: Ring facet extracted using procedure described above, b: Curve generated from the centers of the ring facets, c: Continuous curve obtained from cubic interpolation and d: Discrete curve Γ generated by regular sub-sampling

they can be used as low-cost alternative of the iso-gedesic closed curves employed in [11], which do also require a mesh regularization.

Figure 7, depicts some examples of Γ_k contours superimposed on their corresponding facial surfaces. This Γ_k contours encapsulates the facial shape at a both local and global scale. Moreover, since they are attached to the facial surface, they can be augmented by the normals to to the face surface at each point . We presume that this representation is the only model that encodes such facial shape variation into a single mono-dimensional ordered structures.

5.4   Face Pose Computation

The computation of the face pose is a critical step to model based localization and recognition tasks. In this section, we brief on the details of how our framework is adapted to approximate the face pose of a 3D facial surface. By face pose, we refer to the coordinate system (O, u, v, w), attached to the face, in which the origin is the nose tip, and the axis are the gaze direction, the normal to the face symmetry plane, and the view up direction. In order to determine the face pose: we begin by grouping all the points that form the spiral facet rings' centers, and simply compute their principal axes via the standard PCA analysis. Since these points inherit the symmetry property with respect to face's symmetry plane, it is expected that the PCA method will produce axis that

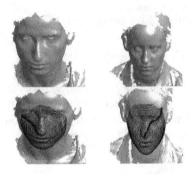

Fig. 7. Examples 3D face scans and the corresponding smoothed curves generated using cubic interpolation

match the face pose to a reasonably good extent. In Figure 8. we depict some examples of face pose axis plotted on the raw facial scans. From the face pose, we also derive the face symmetry plane, having as normal the vector v and including the nose tip. Some examples of the symmetry plane are illustrated in Figure 8(2nd row). We assess the pose estimation methods in two ways, 1) by aligning pairs of different face scans of the same individuals using their estimated poses and 2) by comparing the symmetry plane computed by our method with symmetry plan derived from ground truth data. The first experiment was conducted with a group of faces comprising instances of raw facial scan in neutral expression and their sad expression counterpart. The facial surface in this last group are cropped. Figure 8 (3rd and 4th row) shows some aligned instances. It is clearly observable that alignments exhibit an acceptable accuracy, and thus can be used for a suitable initialization for the iterative registration algorithms such as the iterative closest point method (ICP).

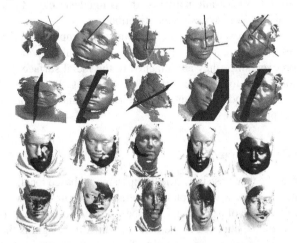

Fig. 8. Computation of the face pose (1st row) and deduction of the face symmetry plane for some face samples (2nd row). 3rd and 4rth rows:Alignment of cropped instances of faces exhibiting sad facial expression to their counterparts raw images in a neutral expressions.

In the following experiment, we compare the face orientations generated from the spiral facets to the smoothed discrete Γ contours. We anticipate that the regularization of the curve obtained through the smoothing process will enhance the accuracy and stability of the face pose estimates. In the Figure 9, we present some examples of 3D faces, their extracted Γ contours along with the orientation and symmetric plane. we have observed that the effect of smoothing the curve has a positive impact on the accuracy of pose estimation.

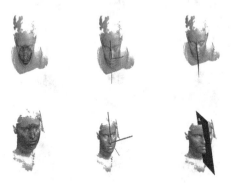

Fig. 9. Computation of the face pose (1st row) and deduction of the face symmetry plane for some face samples (2nd row) estimated using the Γ contours

In the second method of assessment, we consider symmetry plane estimation error as the angle between the the two normals of the estimated and the actual planes. We computed the estimation error for a group of 200 3D face instances (100 neutrals and 100 sads) and have found a standard deviation error of 2 degree for a mean error of 0.03 degree, and a maximum error of 4 degree.

In addition, we also assess the stability of the face pose estimate against increasing number of rings that define the the spiral facet. Here, we consider 100 sample images, 56 female and 44 male subjects at neutral positions. For each sample, we compute the face orientation for increasing percentages of the number rings starting 10% to 90% in steps of 20%. In Figure 10, we illustrate sample results of the aforementioned experiment. Rows 1 to 3 depict the face orientation with 30%, 50% and 70% of the maximum number rings and rows 4 to 6 shows the corresponding symmetry planes for different face samples (columns). As we can visually notice, the face pose stabilizes nearly at 50% of the maximum number of rings that is required to describe the facial surface.

We repeat the experiment relating the impact of the number of rings (or contours) on the face orientation on all the samples of our 3D face dataset but now with the Γ contours being used to compute the orientation. We can clearly notice from Figure 11 that the change in orientation with increasing curves is not as significant as in the previous case. Also importantly, we notice that the stability of the face orientation is achieved much faster (i.e. even at lesser number of curves we obtain more stable estimates of the face pose) than in comparison to the previous case discussed.

To further probe the issue of the stability of face pose, we construct histograms of the percentage of number of face images that exhibit stable face orientation against increasing percentage of the number of rings on distinguished male and female subjects

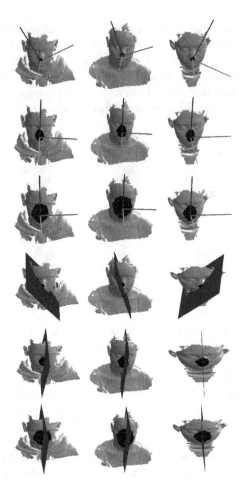

Fig. 10. Stability of the face pose (1-3 rows) and the corresponding face symmetry plane (4-6 rows) with increasing number of rings (20% rise) on different face samples (rows)

as in Figure 12 and in Figure 13. We measure stability in face pose as the difference in the angular distance between consecutive face pose estimates with increasing rings being lesser than a predefined threshold (which is 0.15 in our case). It is clear that over 92% of samples need just 70% of the maximum rings to produce stable face orientations and nearly 60% of samples need 50% of the maximum rings to produce stable face pose estimates. However, from Figure 13, we can see that at 50% of the maximum rings needed, nearly 85% of the samples exhibit a stable pose. Comparing the two bar graphs, it is evident that the regularized curves provide greater stability to the estimation of face pose than the former.

We have validated through our experiments so far that using Γ the contours, it is possible to extract more accurate and stable estimates of face pose in comparison to the original non-regularized rings. However, it is important to note that within the several Γ contours there is the possibility of variations that could cause the overall estimation to

Fig. 11. Stability of the face pose (1-3 columns) and the corresponding face symmetry plane (4-6 columns) with increasing number of rings (20% rise) on different face samples (columns) when measured using the discrete curve generated from cubic spline interpolation

be less accurate than what it can be. In order to investigate this issue further, we study the stability of the contours within themselves by estimating the variance of curves of the contour from its mean using Eigenvalue value analysis. From these measured eigenvalues, we extract shape descriptors in the form of ratios of eigenvalue values (λ_3/λ_1 and λ_3/λ_2) and we plot these descriptor estimates against increasing Γ contour index. The results of this process is presented in Figure 14.

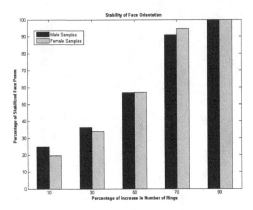

Fig. 12. Percentage of face with stabilized face orientation (y-axis) versus the percentage increase in the number of rings across male (blue) and female (yellow) samples

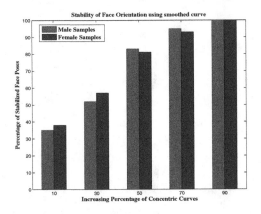

Fig. 13. Percentage of face with stabilized face orientation (y-axis) versus the percentage increase in the number of smoothed curves across male (red) and female (blue) samples

From the bar plots in Figure 14, we can see that curves between 1 and 13 exhibit maximum variations from their mean. We attribute these variations to the region from where these curves originate: which happens to be around the nose area which often exhibits irregular mesh tessellations.

5.5   Face Alignment

The process of face alignment is to put two faces on the same coordinates plane in order to prepare them for any authentication of recognition tasks. A number of different methods are used in order to align 3D faces. Popular approaches perform registration by establishing correspondences of contours and profiles that were extracted from the face. A majority of other techniques such as the global registration methods use of the iterative closet point (ICP) algorithm. In our proposed face alignment mechanism, we exploit the availability of our Γ contours generated from the spiral facets to perform

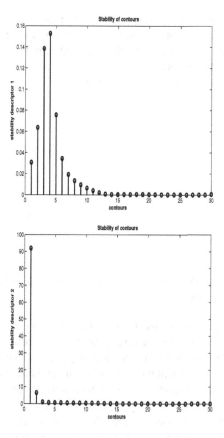

Fig. 14. Shape descriptors measuring the variance of the curves to their mean plotted against increasing number of rings

face alignment. In order to align two instances of 3D faces, we begin by generating the spiral facets on both the faces. We then derive the Γ contours from the facial rings through process illustrated in Section 5.3. We finally perform alignment by computing the rotation and translation components of the curves and map this geometrical transformation to align the face instances together.

Given two curves $\mathcal{P}$ and $\mathcal{Q}$ containing the points $p_1, p_2, , p_N$, and $q_1, q_2, , q_N$, respectively, we estimate the geometrical transformation component of rotation and translation as the one that aligns the two contours by minimizes the following least squares sum error:

$$f(R, T) = \sum_{i}^{N} ||p_i - Rq_{i+\tau} - T||^2 \qquad (10)$$

To estimate the translation parameter, we compute the vector that joins the nose tips of the subjects in the two 3D face instances. However, the rotational parameter is not as obvious to estimate as the correspondences between the two curves need not necessarily match. To find the best match of correspondences, we apply a circular shift parameter τ on the points q_i. In this way, at each shift, we compute the residual error using the sum of least squares and therefore select the shift with the least residual error. In the Figure 15, we illustrate the alignment of two face instances that belong to the same person (a) and the alignment of curves belonging to different subjects in (b) showing the error of alignment.

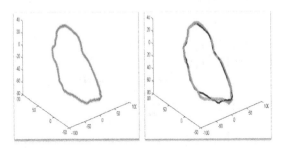

Fig. 15. Alignment of curves of two instances of the same person (a) and the alignment of curves extracted from different subjects (b)

We perform some experiments investigating the alignment approach proposed. In all our experiments for face alignment, we ignore the first 13 Γ contours (as we found them unstable according to the results above) and used the remaining contours for estimating the transformation. The experiment was carried on different 3D faces with and without expression. In Figure 16 and Figure 17, we tabulate some results of the alignment process. In both the tables, we align the neutral faces of subjects with itself, same face with expression and the 3D faces of other subjects. We notice that the alignment between the subject and itself (at neutral expression) is very low, followed next by the alignment of the same subject with different expressions.

	M2N	M2S	M3N	M3S	M4N	M4S	M5N	M5S	M7N
M2N	1.6079e-016	0.0476	0.2018	0.1718	0.0599	0.0617	0.1279	0.1178	0.0129
M3N			8.3267e-017	0.0057	0.1526	0.1699	0.0124	0.0140	0.0977
M4N					1.3816e-016	0.0075	0.2468	0.2200	0.0494
M5N							6.3441e-017	0.0066	0.0754
M7N									7.6862e-017

Fig. 16. Table containing the alignment error between the neural expressions of the different male subjects against their counter-parts. N-neutral expression and S-sad expression.

	F1N	F1S	F2N	F2S	F5N	F5S	F7N	F7S
F1N	8.88E-17	0.0058	0.0516	0.041	0.0409	0.0716	0.05	0.0473
F2N			1.80E-16	0.0059	0.0345	0.0175	0.0072	0.0086
F5N					4.27E-17	0.0256	0.0392	0.0388
F7N							2.30E-16	0.0042

Fig. 17. Table containing the alignment error between the neural expressions of the different female subjects against their counter-parts. N-neutral expression and S-sad expression.

5.6   Nose Profile Identification

As the final application of the spiral facets framework, we describe the problem of nose profile identification. We define the nose profile as a curve that joins the nose bridge with the nose tip across the face plane of symmetry. This curve follows the path of high curvature along the nose, which nearly coincides with shortest path between these two points. We extend our framework based on geodesic paths as described at the end of 4 to identify the nose profile. In effect, at it is shown in Figure 1.f, geodesic paths that join neighboring facets, in a given ring of the facet spiral, to the nose tip, get merged into a common path. This applies particularly for paths emanating at the central forehead where we can clearly observe the convergence of the paths at some level of the nose profile. We draw inspiration from this observation and use a frequency histogram that accumulates the occurrences of the facets at each path. The entries of this histogram include all the facets crossed by the paths. Based on this, we propose a nose profile detection method composed of the following steps: In a first step we select a ring $\mathcal{R}$ that passes through the forehead, which generally corresponds the last few rings, however in order to avoid border effects we choose the third ring from the last one as illustrated in (Figure 18.a). The chosen ring $\mathcal{R}$ intersects the symmetry plane at two points within two facets located at the forehead and chin areas. We then extract a portion of the ring $\mathcal{R}$ keeping the selected facets as the median as shown in Figure 18.b. In the third step, we generate a group of geodesic paths converging to the nose tip. These paths are represented by sequences of facets joining the two strips to the nose tip (Figure 18.c). From the two groups of facet sequences $\mathcal{S}_1$ and $\mathcal{S}_2$ we built two histograms that encodes the distribution of the facets across these paths (Figure 18.d). From each histogram we extract the two groups of facets having a score above a certain threshold (Figure 18.e) and in order to to select the valid group of facets; we perform a 3D line fitting to the facets' vertices in each group (Figure 18.f). Finally, we choose the line producing the least residual error (Figure 18.g) to correspond to the nose profile. Figure 18.h depicts some examples of detected nose profiles.

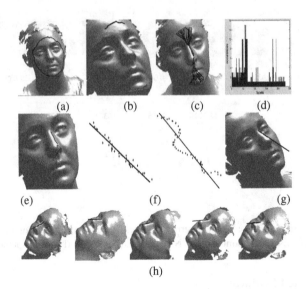

Fig. 18. Nose profile detection. a: Selection of a facet rings. b:Intersection with the approximate estimation of the symmetry plane Γ and generation of two stripes. c: Extraction of sequences of facets following the geodesic paths from the two stripes. to the nose tip. d: For each a group, a geometric histogram is computed to select facets scoring large occurrences. e: The two candidate groups of facets (in blue and yellow in colored images). f: 3D line fitting of two groups of facets and selection of the one having the lowest residual error. g: Display of the valid line passing the nose profile.h: Examples of detected nose profiles.

6   Conclusions and Future Work

In this work, we presented a compact representation of describing 3D facial surface in the form of spiral-facets. The proposed spiral facets framework has resulted in a 3D face representation that is intrinsic to the face surface, more simple, compact, generic and computationally less expensive than other representations. We have demonstrated that the spiral-facets can be adapted to a wide spectrum of application including nose tip detection, frontal face extraction, face shape description, face pose computation, face alignment and nose profile identification. We have also shown that by generating smoothed closed curves from the rings structure it is possible to obtain robust and accurate estimates of the face pose and at the same time be able to perform reliable face alignment of two instances of the 3D face. In the future work we will focus on extending this framework into other application particularly leading to 3D face recognition through the development of a "faceprint" that would uniquely define each 3D face.

References

1. Moreno, A., Sanchez, A., Martinez, E.: Robust representation of 3d faces for recognition. Int. Journal of Pattern Recognition and Artificial Intelligence 20, 1159–1186 (2006)

2. Chua, C., Han, F., Ho, Y.: 3d human face recognition using point signature. In: Conf. on Automatic Face and Gesture Recognition, pp. 233–238 (2000)
3. Wu, Y., Pan, G., Wu, Z.: Face Authentication Based on Multiple Profiles Extracted From Range Data. In: Kittler, J., Nixon, M.S. (eds.) AVBPA 2003. LNCS, vol. 2688, pp. 515–522. Springer, Heidelberg (2003)
4. Xu, D., Hu, P., Cao, W., Li, H.: 3d face recognition using moment invariants. In: IEEE Int. Conference on Shape Modeling and Applications, pp. 261–262 (2008)
5. Irfanoglu, M., Gokberk, B., Akarun, L.: 3d shape-based face recognition using automatically registered facial surfaces. In: Conf. Pattern Recognition, vol. 4, pp. 183–186 (2004)
6. Lu, X., Jain, A.: Deformation analysis for 3d face matching. In: IEEE Workshops on Application of Computer Vision, pp. 99–104 (2005)
7. Lee, Y., Park, K., Shim, J., Yi, T.: 3d face recognition using statistical multiple features for the local depth information. In: Conf. Vision Interface, pp. 102–108 (2003)
8. Xu, C., Wang, Y., Tan, T., Quan, L.: A new attempt to face recognition using eigenfaces. In: Asian Conference on Computer Vision, vol. 2, pp. 884–889 (2004)
9. Bronstein, A., Bronstein, M., Kimmel, R.: Expression invariant 3d face recognition. Audio- and Video-Based Person Authentication, 62–70 (2003)
10. Berretti, S., Bimbo, A., Pala, P.: Description and retrieval of 3d face models using iso-geodesic stripes. In: Conf. Multimedia Information Retrieval, pp. 13–22 (2006)
11. Samir, C., Srivastava, A., Daoudi, M., Klassen, E.: An intrinsic framework for analysis of facial surfaces. International Journal of Computer Vision 82, 80–85 (2009)
12. Kakadiaris, I., et al.: Three-dimensional face recognition in the presence of facial expressions: An annotated deformable model approach. IEEE Transaction on Pattern Analysis and Machine Intelligence 29, 1–10 (2007)
13. Pan, G., Wu, Y., Wu, Z., Liu, W.: 3d face recognition by profile and surface matching. In: IEEE/INNS Conf. on Neural Networks, vol. 3, pp. 2169–2174 (2003)
14. Xu, C., Wang, Y., Tan, T., Quan, L.: Automatic 3d face recognition combining global geometric features with local shape variation information. In: IEEE Conf. on Automatic Face and Gesture Recognition, pp. 302–307 (2004)
15. Mian, A., Bennamoun, M., Owens, R.: An efficient multimodal 2d-3d hybrid approach to automatic face recognition. IEEE Transactions in Pattern Analysis and Machine Intelligence 29, 1927–1943 (2007)
16. Cormen, T.H., Leiserson, C., Rivest, R.L., Stein, C.: Introduction to Algorithms, 2nd edn. MIT Press, McGraw-Hill (2001)
17. Sethian, J., Kimmel, R.: Computing geodesic paths on manifolds. Proc. National Academy of Sciences 95, 8431–8435 (1998)
18. Colbry, D., Stockman, G., Jain, A.: Detection of anchor points for 3d face verification. In: Proc. Computer Vision and Pattern Recognition (2005)
19. Heseltine, T., Pears, N., Austin, J.: Three-dimensional face recognition using combinations of surface feature map subspace components. Image and Vision Computing 26, 382–396 (2008)
20. Segundo, M., Queirolo, C., Bellon, O., Silva, L.: Automatic 3d facial segmentation and landmark detection. In: Proc. 14th Int. Conf. on Image Analysis and Processing, pp. 431–436 (2007)
21. Wang, Y., Tang, X., Liu, J., Pan, G., Xiao, R.: 3D Face Recognition by Local Shape Difference Boosting. In: Forsyth, D., Torr, P., Zisserman, A. (eds.) ECCV 2008, Part I. LNCS, vol. 5302, pp. 603–616. Springer, Heidelberg (2008)
22. Ruiz, M., Illingworth, J.: Automatic landmarking of faces in 3d-alf. In: 5th International Conference on Visual Information Engineering (VIE 2008), pp. 41–46 (2008)
23. Romero, M., Pears, N.: Landmark localisation in 3d face data. In: IEEE Conf. on Advanced Video and Signal Based Surveillance, pp. 73–78 (2009)

24. Xu, C., Tan, T., Wang, Y., Quan, L.: Combining local features for robust nose location in 3d facial data. Pattern Recognition Letters 27, 1487–1494 (2006)
25. Frey, P., Borouchaki, H.: Surface mesh quality evaluation. International Journal for Numerical Methods in Engineering 45, 101–118 (1999)
26. Ashbrook, A.P., Fisher, R.B., Robertson, C., Werghi, N.: Finding Surface Correspondence for Object Recognition and Registration Using Pairwise Geometric Histograms. In: Burkhardt, H., Neumann, B. (eds.) ECCV 1998. LNCS, vol. 1407, pp. 674–686. Springer, Heidelberg (1998)
27. Al-Osaimi, F.R., Bennamoun, M., Mian, A.: Integration of local and global geometrical cues for 3d face recognition. Pattern Recognition 41, 1030–1040 (2008)
28. Nair, P., Cavallaro, A.: 3-d face detection, landmark localization, and registration using a point distribution model. IEEE Trans. Multimedia 1, 611–623 (2009)
29. Niese, R., Al-Hamadi, A., Michaelsi, B.: A novel method for 3d face detection and normalization. Journal of Multimedia 2, 1–12 (2007)
30. Piegl, L., Tiller, W.: The NURBS Book. Springer, Heidelberg (2006)

REFA: A Robust E-HOG for Feature Analysis for Local Description of Interest Points

Manuel Grand-brochier, Christophe Tilmant, and Michel Dhome

Laboratoire des Sciences et Matériaux pour l'Électronique et d'Automatique (LASMEA)
UMR6602 UBP-CNRS, 24 avenue des Landais, 63177 Aubière, France
{Manuel.Grand-brochier,Christophe.Tilmant,
Michel.Dhome}@lasmea.univ-bpclermont.fr
http://wwwlasmea.univ-bpclermont.fr

Abstract. This article proposes a Robust E-hog for Feature Analysis (REFA) to describe interest points and their neighborhood. Initially the two most used methods: SIFT and SURF are studied and various advantages (invariances, repeatability) are extracted to create a new approach (detection, description and matching). First, the Fast-Hessian detector is used because it gives the best repeatability rate, however it will be optimized. Secondly the local neighborhood description is based on a histogram of oriented gradients on an elliptical shape. Finally a decision tree, validation threshold and deletion duplicates are used to match interest points. This method must also be as robust as possible for image transformations (rotations, scales, viewpoints for example). All tool parameters (orientations, thresholds, analysis shape) will be also detailed in this article.

Keywords: Elliptical-HOG, Local descriptor, Robustness to image transformations.

1 Introduction

There are a large number of applications based on image analysis, especially 3D reconstruction problems, tracking or pattern recognition for example. These applications need data usually extracted with two tools: the detection of interest points and the local description of these. The detector analyses the image to extract the characteristic points (corners, edges, blobs). The neighborhood study allows us to create a local points descriptor, in order to match them. For matched interest points, the robustness of various transformations of the image is very important. To be robust to scale, interest points are extracted with a global multi-scales analysis, we considered the Harris-Laplace detector [1–3], the Fast-Hessian [4] and the difference of Gaussians [5, 6]. The description is based on a local exploration of interest points to represent the characteristics of the neighborhood. In comparative studies [7–9], it is shown that oriented gradients histograms (HOG) give good results. Among the many methods using HOG, we retain SIFT (Scale Invariant Feature Transform) [5, 6] and SURF (Speed Up Robust Features) [4], using a rectangular neighborhood exploration (R-HOG: Rectangular-HOG). We also mention GLOH (Gradient Location and Orientation Histogram) [8, 10] and

G. Csurka et al. (Eds.): VISIGRAPP 2011, CCIS 274, pp. 225–239, 2013.
© Springer-Verlag Berlin Heidelberg 2013

Daisy [11], using circular geometry (C-HOG: Circular-HOG). To provide the best possible list of points for different applications, we propose to create a system of detection and local description (a Robust E-hog for Feature Analysis: REFA) which is as robust as possible against the various transformations that can exist between two images (illumination, rotation, viewpoint for example). It should also be as efficient as possible as regards the matching rate. Our method relies on a Fast-Hessian points detector, an elliptical exploration and a local descriptor based E-HOG (Elliptical-HOG). We propose to estimate local orientation, with the study of the Harris matrix, in order to adjust the descriptor (rotation invariance) and finally we will normalize (brightness invariance).

Section 2 presents briefly SIFT and SURF, and lists the advantages of each. The various tools, parameters (orientations, thresholds, analysis pattern) and the shape that we use are detailed in Section 3. To compare our approach to SIFT and SURF, many tests have been carried out. Databases and a synthesis of the different results are presented in Section 4.

2   Related Work

In order to suggest a robust method and to give many interest points, Lowe propose a new approach, SIFT [5, 6], consisting of a difference of Gaussians (DoG) and R-HOG analysis. The detector is based on an approximation of the Laplacian of Gaussian [12] and interest points are obtained by maximizing the DoG:

$$D(\mathbf{x},\sigma) = (G(\mathbf{x},k\sigma) - G(\mathbf{x},\sigma)) * I(\mathbf{x})$$
$$L(\mathbf{x},k\sigma) - L(\mathbf{x},\sigma). \tag{1}$$

The descriptor uses an orientation histogram, based on equation 2, to determine the angle of rotation θ at interest point $\mathbf{x} = (x,y)$, to be applied to the mask analysis.

$$\theta(\mathbf{x}) = \tan^{-1}\left(\frac{(L(x,y+1) - L(x,y-1)}{(L(x+1,y) - L(x-1,y)}\right) \tag{2}$$

It then uses R-HOG, formed by local gradients in the neighborhood, previously smoothed by a Gaussian. Finally, the descriptor is normalized to be invariant to illumination changes.

An extension of SIFT, GLOH [8, 10], has been proposed to increase the robustness. It amounts to the insertion of a grid in log polar localization. The mask analysis of this descriptor is composed of three rings (C-HOG), whose two largest are divided along eight directions. More recently, the descriptor Daisy [11] has been proposed. It is also based on a circular neighborhood exploration and constructs convolved orientation maps.

SIFT has not a fast computational speed. SURF [4] proposes a new approach, whose main objective is to accelerate the various image processing steps. The first problem was to choose the detector method. The various tests [4, 13] show that the Fast-Hessian has the best repeatability rate. It is based on the Hessian matrix:

$$H(\mathbf{x},\sigma) = \begin{bmatrix} L_{xx}(\mathbf{x},\sigma) & L_{xy}(\mathbf{x},\sigma) \\ L_{xy}(\mathbf{x},\sigma) & L_{yy}(\mathbf{x},\sigma) \end{bmatrix}, \tag{3}$$

with $L_{ij}(\mathbf{x},\sigma)$ the second derivative in the directions i and j of L. The maximization of its determinant (Hessian) allows us to extract the coordinates of interest points in a given scale. The second step, the local description, is based on Haar wavelets. These estimate the local orientation of the gradient, allowing the construction of the descriptor. Finally, SURF studied the sign of the wavelet transform to increase the quality of results.

The presented methods use similar tools: multi-scale analysis (Fast-Hessian or DoG), local description based HOG, local smoothing and descriptor normalization. For matching they use a minimization of either the Euclidean distance between descriptors (SURF) or the angle between vectors descriptors (SIFT). Many tests [7,8,13] can establish a list of different qualities of each. It follows that SURF, with its detector, has the best repeatability for viewpoint changes, scale, noise and lighting. It is also faster than SIFT, however it has a higher precision rate for rotations and scale changes. It has also a higher number of detected points for all transformations. It might be interesting to combine these two methods.

3 Method

The method we propose is divided into three parts: a Fast-Hessian multi-scale detector, a local E-HOG descriptor and an optimized matching. This section describes the different steps of our method and parameters used. The detector Fast-Hessian provides a list of interest points, characterized by their coordinates and local scale. Our descriptor is based on the Harris matrix interpretation, and the construction of E-HOG. Matching is based on an approximation of the nearest neighbors and removing duplicates. These issues will be detailed below.

3.1 Detection

The Fast-Hessian is an approximated method of a Hessian matrix (equation 3), to reduce the computing time. This detector uses integral images, therefore it takes only three additions and four memory accesses to calculate the sum of intensities inside a rectangular region of any size. The Fast-Hessian relies on the exploitation of the Hessian matrix (equation 3), whose determinant is calculated as follows:

$$\det(H(\mathbf{x},\sigma)) = \sigma^2(L_{xx}(\mathbf{x},\sigma)L_{yy}(\mathbf{x},\sigma) - L_{xy}^2(\mathbf{x},\sigma)), \tag{4}$$

where $L_{xx}(\mathbf{x},\sigma)$ is the convolution of the Gaussian second order derivative $\frac{\partial^2}{\partial x^2}g(\sigma)$ with the image I in point $\mathbf{x}$, and similarly for $L_{xy}(\mathbf{x},\sigma)$ and $L_{yy}(\mathbf{x},\sigma)$. Gaussians are optimal for scale-space analysis and the Fast-Hessian provides an approximation of these second order derivatives (Figure 1).

Fig. 1. Left: Gaussian second order partial derivatives, right: approximation for the second order Gaussian partial derivatives

By looking for local maxima of the determinant, we establish a list of K points associated with a scale, denoted $\{(\mathbf{x}_k, \sigma_k); \ k \in [\![0; K-1]\!]\}$, where:

$$(\mathbf{x}_k, \sigma_k) = \underset{\{\mathbf{x}, \sigma\}}{\mathrm{argmax}}(\det(H(\mathbf{x}, \sigma))). \tag{5}$$

The number of interest points obtained depends on the space scale explored and thresholding of local maxima. We have to find a compromise between scale space exploration and relevance of extracted points. To get the best compromise we use the following curves (Figure 2):

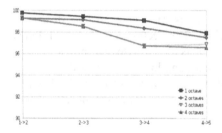 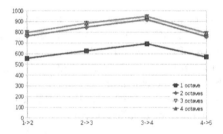

Fig. 2. These graphs represent, for ODB_{vl} images: (left) the correct matching rate according to the number of octave and (right) the number of points that can be matched

It represents, on one hand the matching precision for ODB_{vl} images and on the other hand the number of points that can be matched. The best compromise is two octaves, it has better precision than three or four octaves while keeping an almost identical number of points. One octave has a better precision than two octaves, but loses a lot of points. Therefore we choose two octaves instead of four used by SURF.

3.2 Description

As with SIFT and SURF, our method is based on HOG, yet our analysis window will consist of ellipses (E-HOG). Different tools will also be necessary to adjust and normalize our descriptor.

Determining the Local Orientation Gradient. To be as invariant as possible for rotations, estimating the local orientation gradient of the interest point is necessary. This parameter allows us to adjust the E-HOG, giving an identical orientation for two corresponding points. For this, we use the Harris matrix, calculated for each point $\mathbf{x}_k$ and defined by:

$$M_H(\mathbf{X}_k) = \begin{bmatrix} \sum\limits_{V(\mathbf{x}_k)} [I_x(\mathbf{x}_k)]^2 & \sum\limits_{V(\mathbf{x}_k)} I_x(\mathbf{x}_k)I_y(\mathbf{x}_k) \\ \sum\limits_{V(\mathbf{x}_k)} I_x(\mathbf{x}_k)I_y(\mathbf{x}_k) & \sum\limits_{V(\mathbf{x}_k)} [I_y(\mathbf{x}_k)]^2 \end{bmatrix} \tag{6}$$

where $V(\mathbf{x}_k)$ represents the neighborhood of the interest point, I_x and I_y are the first derivatives in x and y of image, calculated using the Canny-Deriche operator. The properties of this matrix are used to study the information dispersion. The local analysis of it eigenvector ($\overrightarrow{\mathbf{v}_1}$) associated with the highest eigenvalue can extract an orientation estimate:

$$\theta_k = \arctan(\overrightarrow{\mathbf{v}_1}), \tag{7}$$

Descriptor Construction. The initial shape of our descriptor relies on a circular neighborhood exploration of the interest point. The seventeen circles used, are divided into three scales (Figure 3) and are adjusted by θ (equation 7).

This angle allows us to be robust regarding image rotation. The circle diameter is proportional to σ, thus accentuating the scale invariance. To manage the problem of viewpoint changes and anisotropic transformations, we propose to modify the shape of our descriptor. The goal is to get local information more consistently. We forward to use an elliptical exploration to describe the neighbor of interest points (Figure 4).

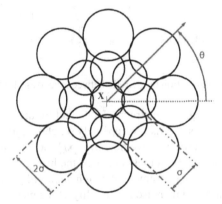

Fig. 3. Initial mask analysis of our descriptor, centered at $\mathbf{x}$ and oriented by θ

An analysis of the properties of affine detectors [2, 14] allows us to determine the ratio r_k between the axes of ellipses. For example for the Harris affine detector, two scales are used to represent local region and are bound by the following equation: $\sigma_D^k = r_k \sigma_I^k$ where σ_D is the differentiation scale, σ_I is the integration scale and r is the ratio. It is noted that r is generally between 0.5 and 0.75. By the parallelism between these two scales and our ellipses, it is possible to determine the best ratio r_k. Based on tests presented in Figure 5, the ratio giving the best result is equal to 0.6. Then, Figure 6 illustrates the construction of our ellipses (for better visualization, we only show the central ellipse of each descriptor).

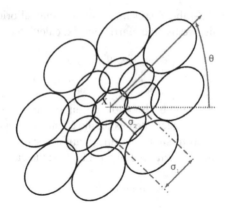

Fig. 4. Final mask analysis of our descriptor, centered at **x** and oriented by θ

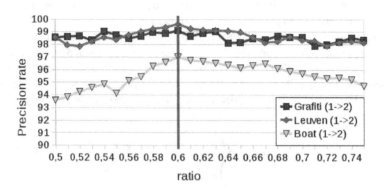

Fig. 5. Optimization of the ratio between the axes of ellipses

In each ellipse, we choose to construct a HOG and Figure 7 details the results obtained in function of numbers of bins. Accordingly we choose to construct a HOG eight bins (in steps of 45). Our descriptor, we note $des_I(\mathbf{x}_k)$, belongs to $\mathbb{R}^{136}$ (17 ellipses × 8 directions). To be robust for brightness changes, the histogram is normalized and we also use a threshold for E-HOG to remove the high values of gradient. This step allows us to remove such outliers and increase the stability of the method.

3.3 Matching

The objective is to find the best similarity (corresponding to the minimum distance) between descriptors of two images. Euclidean distance, denoted d_e, between two descriptors is defined by:

$$d_e(des_{I_1}(\mathbf{x}_k), des_{I_2}(\mathbf{x}_l)) = \sqrt{[des_{I_1}(\mathbf{x}_k)]^T \cdot des_{I_2}(\mathbf{x}_l)}. \qquad (8)$$

The minimization of d_e, denoted d_{min}, provides a pair of points $\{\mathbf{x}_k; \mathbf{x}_{\hat{l}}\}$:

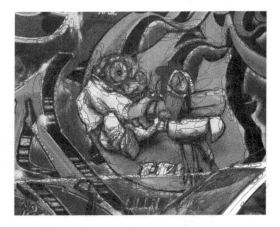

Fig. 6. Example of local description of interest points

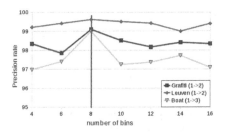
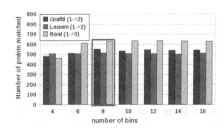

Fig. 7. Precision rate (at left) and number of points matched (at right) in function of numbers of bins

$$\tilde{l} = \underset{l\in[0;L-1]}{\operatorname{argmin}} \left(d_e(des_{I_1}(\mathbf{x}_k), des_{I_2}(\mathbf{x}_l))\right), \qquad (9)$$

$$d_{min} = d_e(des_{I_1}(\mathbf{x}_k), des_{I_2}(\mathbf{x}_{\tilde{l}})). \qquad (10)$$

To simplify the search for this minimum distance, we propose to use an approximative nearest neighbor search method (a variant of k-d tree) [15, 16]. The principle is to create a decision tree based on descriptors components of the second image and to extract the k nearest neighbor(s) that is/are considered potential candidate(s) for matching (Figure 8). So, for each new descriptor of the first image, all components are tested and the nearest neighbor is defined. Research is therefore faster, without sacrificing precision. To have a more robust matching, thresholding is applied to this distance, to find a ``high''minimum. The pair of points is valid if:

$$d_{min} \le \alpha \times min(d_e(des_1(x_k, y_k), des_2(x_l, y_l))), \qquad (11)$$

for $l \in [0; N-1]\backslash\tilde{l}$ and with α the threshold selection which is determinated by analysing the curves of Figure 9. This threshold allows us to increase the selectivity, but the consequence is a reduction in the number of matched points. If the threshold goes away from 1, the matching becomes more selective and therefore fewer points are

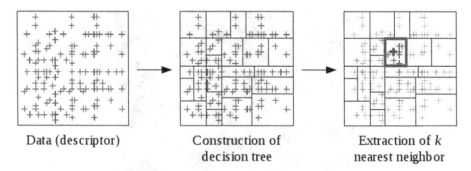

Data (descriptor)   Construction of   Extraction of k
                           decision tree   nearest neighbor

Fig. 8. Example of decision tree to extract the nearest neighbors

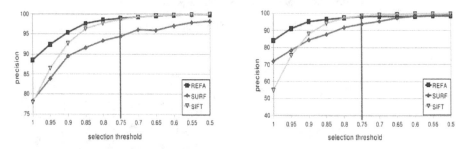

Fig. 9. These graphs represent the correct matching rate according to the threshold selection. Left is for viewpoint changes (grafiti 1 → 2) and right is for rotation + scale (boat 1 → 3).

used. The problem is to find the best compromise between the correct matching rate and the number of matched points. SIFT recommands a threshold of 0.8 and SURF a threshold of 0.7. By analysing the curves of Figure 9, we choose a threshold $\alpha = 0.75$. Finally, we do not allow a point to match with several other points, and a final step is to remove duplicates.

4   Results

We are going to compare our method with SIFT and SURF. These two approachs are the most used and give good results for image transformations such as rotation, scales and illumination changes. We propose to study the matching rate and the precision of each of them. We will also study the *recall* $= f(1 - precision)$ curves and the estimation error of the transformed image.

4.1   Databases

To validate our method, we propose to study the results for synthetic and real transformations. For the first, we generate mathematical changes in the image in order to get the ground truth, and for the second, transformations are created by moving the camera. So we choose two databases:

- The first one, noted *ODB* and extracted from the Oxford [1] database, proposes scene transformations with an access to the matrix of homography. Transformations studied are brightness changes (ODB_b), modified jpeg compressions (ODB_c), blur (ODB_n), rotations and scales (ODB_{rs}), and small and large angle viewpoint changes (respectively ODB_{vs} and ODB_{vl}). Figure 10 illustrates this database.

ODB_b ODB_c ODB_n

ODB_{rs} ODB_{vs} ODB_{vl}

Fig. 10. Examples of images used for transformations: (top: left to right) brightness changes, modified jpeg compressions, blur, (bottom: left to right) rotations + scales, viewpoint changes (small angle), and viewpoint changes (large angle)

- A second database, noted *SDB*, composed of a set of synthetic image transformations (Figure 11 and Figure 12). These transformations are rotations 45 (SDB_r), scales (SDB_s), anisotropic scales (SDB_{as}), rotations 45 + scales (BS_{rs}) and rotations 45 + anisotropic scales (BS_{ras}).

4.2   Evaluation Tests and Results

Matching Rate and Precision Rate. We propose to compare the matching rate T_a, as well as the precision P of every method. T_a is defined by the number of matches divided by the number of possible matches. P is defined by the number of correct matches divided by the number of matches performed. We study the graphs in Figures 13 to 16, detailing the precision curves and the number of points matched for different transformations.

---

[1] http://www.robots.ox.ac.uk/~vgg/data/data-aff.html

SDB_r SDB_r SDB_s

Fig. 11. Examples of laboratory images (board cameras) used for synthetic transformations

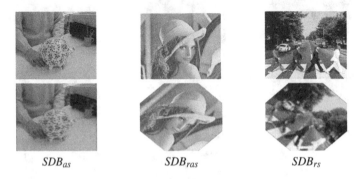

SDB_{as} SDB_{ras} SDB_{rs}

Fig. 12. Examples of internet images (Pig, Lena, Beatles) used for synthetic transformations

These types of transformations are a classic and good robustness is essential for many applications. For scales changes our approach presents the best results, this is due to the scaling adaptation of our elliptical mask. For rotation SIFT is invariant and our goal is to propose results which would be approximate. So we can see (Figure 13.b) that the adjustment of an angle θ allows us to have results similar to SIFT.

These two types of transformations introduce many outliers and we can see that our method presents the best results and good stability. These performances are mainly based on threshold gradients values and the normalization of descriptors.

These transformations use all the tools in our approach (scale, θ, threshold and normalization) and so our performances are better than SIFT and SURF.

These curves show a better precision rate for our method and our number of points matched decreases more slowly. Another observation can be made through the transformations studied, concerning the stability of our method. Indeed, our curves decrease more slowly than SIFT and SURF, implying a more constant precision rates.

To conclude this part of experiment, we propose a synthesis of the results obtained in Figure 17.

Our method presents results whiwh are better than or as good as SIFT and SURF. Our matching rate remains better than the two other methods with the exception of the databases ODB_{rs} and SDB_r transformations. Nevertheless the difference between SURF and our method for this type of transformation is lower than 4%. For other

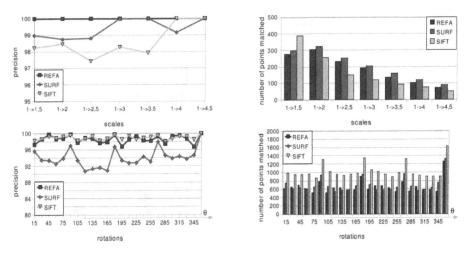

Fig. 13. (Top) Precision rate for scales changes (SDB_s) and (bottom) precision rate for rotations (SDB_r)

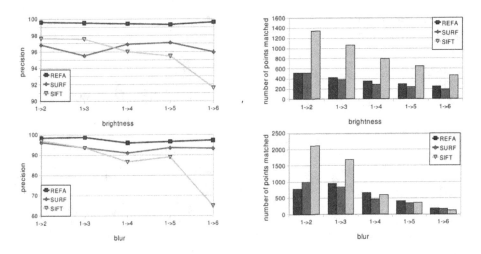

Fig. 14. (Top) Precision rate for brightness (ODB_b) and (bottom) precision rate for blur (ODB_n)

types of transformation, the biggest differences are observed for rotation 45 + scale ($\approx 10\%$ between our method and SURF and 37% with SIFT) and for large angle viewpoint changes ($\approx 18\%$ with SURF and SIFT). Our matching precision is also better and remains constantly above 95%. The biggest difference is obtained for large angle viewpoint changes (4% for SURF and 8% for SIFT).

Influence of Data. To observe the influence of data on different methods, we use the $recall = f(1 - precision)$ curves [8] and we propose to analyse two curves (Figure 18)

We can observe that our method is more stable than SIFT and SURF. Therefore, our method is more robust to the deterioration of data for these transformations.

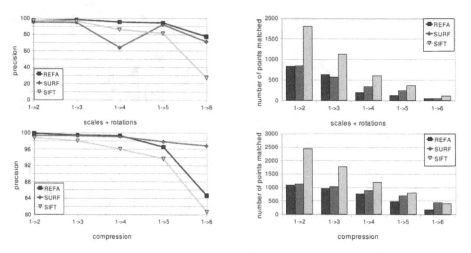

Fig. 15. (Top) Precision rate for rotation and scale (ODB_{rs}) and (bottom) precision rate for compression jpeg (ODB_c)

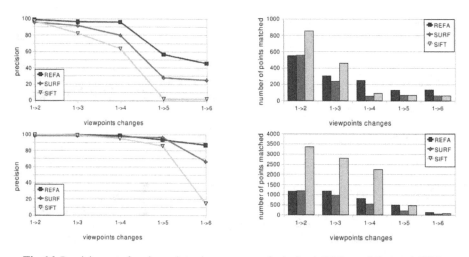

Fig. 16. Precision rate for viewpoints changes respectively (top) ODB_{vl} and (bottom) ODB_{vs}

Estimation of the Image Transformation. We propose a final study on the estimation of the homography matrix. For 3D reconstruction, for example, the estimate of this matrix is very important, and the goal is to have the best estimation (having an error rate as low as possible) with maximum points validating this matrix. The estimation is based on the matches and the Ransac algorithm. We studied three transformations and the results are:

– viewpoints changes (ODB_{vl}):

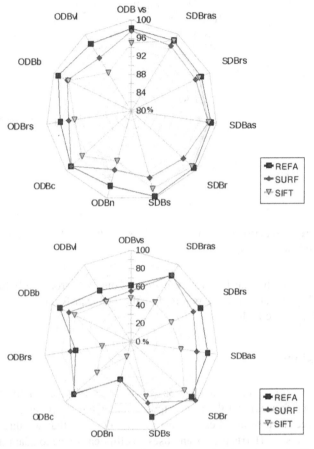

Fig. 17. These graphs represent at top: a matching rate T_a and at bottom: a matching precision P. Matching rate is the ability to match points and matching precision is the match quality. The goal is to have the highest rate of correctly matched points (with better precision).

	error (%)	valid points (%)
REFA	0.06	96.72
SURF	3.46	96.34
SIFT	2.98	92.35

– rotation and scale (ODB_{rs}):

	error (%)	valid points (%)
REFA	0.54	93.23
SURF	1.69	86.03
SIFT	2.06	88.24

– blur (ODB_n):

	error (%)	valid points (%)
REFA	0.61	97.13
SURF	0.66	92.1
SIFT	0.58	96.56

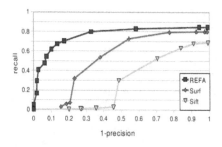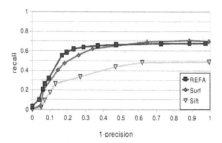

Fig. 18. (left) A recall versus 1-precision for brightness (ODB_b: $1 \rightarrow 4$) and (right) a recall versus 1-precision for rotation + scale (ODB_{rs}: $2 \rightarrow 4$)

Our method obtains, for the first two transformations, an error rate below SIFT and SURF and a higher rate of valid points. For the last transformation, the results are similar for all three methods.

5   Conclusions

In this article we presented a method based on the advantages of SIFT and SURF (repetability, invariances) and the use of tools such as the Harris matrix, the HOG or the decision tree. Detection relies on Fast-hessian detector that we thresholded. Description interprets the Harris matrix and uses an elliptical shape to adapt the descriptor to the image transformation. Finally, matching creates a decision tree and removes duplicates. To validate our method, we compared it to SIFT and SURF. Our method has a better matching rate and better precision for most transformations. It is also robust to data degradation problems and provides a more reliable estimation of homography matrix, keeping good rate of valid points. Therefore data extracted from images are better and will result in an improvement of the applications referred to (3D reconstruction or pattern recognition for example).

Our prospects are a generalization of our method, with application to a spatio-temporal analysis. We will add a temporal variable to the Hessian matrix (equation 3). We will also transform our descriptor shape to obtain an neighborhood exploration ellipsoidal (for tracking for example). The first results are very convincing, we have obtain a precision rate equal to 95% for on-board camera video sequences.

References

1. Harris, C., Stephens, M.: A combined corner and edge detector. In: Alvey Vision Conference, pp. 147–151 (1988)

2. Mikolajczyk, K., Schmid, C.: Scale & affine invariant interest point detectors. International Journal of Computer Vision 1, 63–86 (2004)
3. Mikolajczyk, K., Schmid, C.: An Affine Invariant Interest Point Detector. In: Heyden, A., Sparr, G., Nielsen, M., Johansen, P. (eds.) ECCV 2002, Part I. LNCS, vol. 2350, pp. 128–142. Springer, Heidelberg (2002)
4. Bay, H., Tuytelaars, T., Van Gool, L.: SURF: Speeded Up Robust Features. In: Leonardis, A., Bischof, H., Pinz, A. (eds.) ECCV 2006. LNCS, vol. 3951, pp. 404–417. Springer, Heidelberg (2006)
5. Lowe, D.: Object recognition from local scale-invariant features. In: IEEE International Conference on Computer Vision, pp. 1150–1157 (1999)
6. Lowe, D.: Distinctive image features from scale-invariant keypoints. International Journal of Computer Vision 60, 91–110 (2004)
7. Choksuriwong, A., Laurent, H., Emile, B.: Etude comparative de descripteur invariants d'objets. ORASIS (2005)
8. Mikolajczyk, K., Schmid, C.: A performance evaluation of local descriptors. IEEE Pattern Analysis and Machine Intelligence 27, 1615–1630 (2005)
9. Bauer, J., Snderhauf, N., Protzel, P.: Comparing several implementations of two recently published feature detectors. Intelligent Autonomous Vehicles (2007)
10. Dalal, N., Triggs, B.: Histograms of oriented gradients for human detection. In: IEEE Conference on Computer Vision and Pattern Recognition, pp. 886–893 (2005)
11. Tola, E., Lepetit, V., Fua, P.: A fast local descriptor for dense matching. In: IEEE Conference on Computer Vision and Pattern Recognition, pp. 1–8 (2008)
12. Lindeberg, T.: Feature detection with automatic scale selection. International Journal of Computer Vision 30, 79–116 (1998)
13. Juan, L., Gwun, O.: A comparison of sift, pca-sift and surf. International Journal of Image Processing 3, 143–152 (2009)
14. Mikolajczyk, K., Tuytelaars, Schmid, C., Zisserman, Matas, Schaffalitzky, Kadir, Gool, V.: A comparison of affine region detectors. International Journal of Computer Vision 65, 43–72 (2006)
15. Arya, S., Mount, D.: Approximate nearest neighbor queries in fixed dimensions, pp. 271–280. ACM-SIAM (1993)
16. Arya, S., Mount, D., Netanyahu, N., Silverman, R., Wu, A.: An otimal algorithm for approximate nearest neighbor searching in fixed dimensions, pp. 573–582. ACM-SIAM (1994)

Mutual On-Line Learning for Detection and Tracking in High-Resolution Images

David Hurych, Karel Zimmermann, and Tomáš Svoboda

Center for Machine Perception, Department of Cybernetics
Faculty of Electrical Engineering, Czech Technical University in Prague
Prague, Czech Republic
{hurycd1,zimmerk,svoboda}@cmp.felk.cvut.cz
http://cmp.felk.cvut.cz

Abstract. This paper addresses object detection and tracking in high-resolution omnidirectional images. The foreseen application is a visual subsystem of a rescue robot equipped with an omnidirectional camera, which demands real-time efficiency and robustness against changing viewpoint. Object detectors typically do not guarantee specific frame rate. The detection time may vastly depend on a scene complexity and image resolution. The adapted tracker can often help to overcome the situation, where the appearance of the object is far from the training set. On the other hand, once a tracker is lost, it almost never finds the object again. We propose a combined solution where a very efficient tracker (based on sequential linear predictors) incrementally accommodates varying appearance and speeds up the whole process. Next we propose to incrementally update the detector with examples collected by the tracker. We experimentally show that the performance of the combined algorithm, measured by a ratio between false positives and false negatives, outperforms both individual algorithms. The tracker allows to run the expensive detector only sparsely enabling the combined solution to run in real-time on 12 MPx images from a high resolution omnidirectional camera (Ladybug3).

Keywords: Detection, Tracking, Incremental, Learning, Predictors, Fern, Omnidirectional, High-resolution.

1 Introduction

This paper focuses on the problem of real-time object detection and tracking in a sequence of high-resolution omnidirectional images. The idea of combining a detector and fast alignment by a tracker has already been used in several approaches [1,2]. The frame rate of commonly used detectors naturally depends on both the scene complexity and image resolution. For example, the speed of ferns [3], SURF [4] and SIFT [5] detectors depends on the number of evaluated features, which is generally proportional to the scene complexity (e.g. number of Harris corners) and image resolution. The speed of Waldboost [6] (or any cascade detector) depends on the number of computations performed in each evaluated sub-window. In contrast, most of the trackers are independent of both the scene complexity and image resolution. This guarantees stable frame rate

G. Csurka et al. (Eds.): VISIGRAPP 2011, CCIS 274, pp. 240–256, 2013.
© Springer-Verlag Berlin Heidelberg 2013

however, once the tracker is lost it may never recover the object position again. Adaptive trackers can follow an object which is visually dissimilar to the training set and cannot be detected by the detector. We propose to combine a detector and a tracker to benefit from robustness (ability to find an object) of detectors and locality (efficiency) of trackers. Ferns-based detector (also used by [2] for 10 fps tracking-by-detection) is one of the fastest object detectors because of the low number of evaluated binary features on detected Harris corners. The speed makes the ferns detector ideal for the purpose of object detection in large images.

One of the most popular template trackers is the KLT tracker [7], which uses the Lucas-Kanade *gradient descent* algorithm [8]. The algorithm has become very popular and has many derivations [9]. The gradient descent is a fast algorithm yet, it has to compute the image gradient, the Jacobian and inverse Hessian of the modeled warp in every frame. For some simple warps, the Jacobian may be precomputed [10], [11]. One may also get a rid of the inverse Hessian computation by switching the roles of the template and image [9]. Nevertheless we always need to compute the image gradients and in general case also the Jacobian and inverse Hessian of the warp. An alternative for template tracking are *regression-based* methods [12], [13]. They avoid the computation of image gradient, Jacobian and inverse Hessian by learning a regression matrix from training examples. Once learned they estimate the tracking parameters directly from the image intensities. If the regression function is linear, it is called *linear predictor*. The training phase is the biggest disadvantage of linear predictors, because the tracking cannot start immediately. Nevertheless, the regression matrix (function) may be estimated only from one image in a short time (few seconds). The training examples are generated by random warpings of the object template and collecting image intensities. This regression matrix may be updated by additional training examples during tracking [2].

Recently, it has been shown [3], [2], that taking advantage of the learning phase, greatly improves the tracking speed and makes the tracker more robust with respect to large perspective deformations. A learned tracker is able to run with fragment of processing power and estimates object position in complicated or not yet seen poses. However, once the tracker gets lost it may not recover the object position.

To fulfill the real-time requirements, we propose a combination of a robust detector and a very efficient tracker. Both, the detector and the tracker, are trained from image data. The tracker gets updated during the tracking. The tracker is extremely fast and as a result of that, faster than real-time tracking allows for multiple object tracking.

1.1 Related Work

We use a similar approach to [2], who also use a fern object detector and a linear predictor with incremental learning for homography estimation. The detector is used for object localization and also for a rough estimation of patch transformation. The initial transformation is further refined by the linear predictor, which predicts full 2D homography. The precision of the method is validated by inverse warping of the object patch and correlation-based verification with the initial patch. The detector is run in every frame of the sequence of 0.3 Mpx images processing 10 frames per second (fps). This approach however, would not be able to perform in real-time on 12 Mpx images. We use the fern detector to determine tentative correspondences and we run RANSAC on detected points to estimate the affine transformation. After a positive detection we apply the learned predictor in order to track the object for as many frames as possible. [2] use an iterative version of linear predictor similar to the one proposed by [12], while we use a sequence of learnable linear predictors (SLLiP). The SLLiP proved [13] to be faster than the iterative version, while keeping the high precision of the estimation. Our tracker is incrementally updated during tracking [2,1]. We validate the tracking by the updated tracker itself (see Section 2.2), which is more precise, than correlation-based verification by a single template in case of varying object appearance.

Recently [14] used adaptive linear predictors for real-time tracking. Adaptation is done by growth or reduction of the tracked patch during tracking and update of the regression matrices. However, this approach is not suitable for our task, because of the need to keep in memory the large matrix with training examples, which is needed for computation of the template reduction and growth. This training matrix grows with additional training examples collected for on-line learning, which is undesirable for long-term tracking.

[1] use linear predictors in the form of locally weighted projection regressors (LWP R) as a part of self-tuning particle filtering (ISPF) framework. They approximate a non-linear regression by a piece-wise linear models. In comparison we use SLLiP similar to [15], which uses the result of previous predictors in sequence as the starting point for another predictor in a row. In [1] the partial least-squares is used for data dimension reduction. We use a subset of template pixels spread over the object in regular grid, which proved to be sufficient for dimensionality reduction, while keeping the high precision and robustness of tracking.

The rest of this paper is organized as follows. In Section 2 you find the formal descriptions of used ferns detector and sequential predictor tracker and in Section 2.3 the outline of our algorithm. In Section 3 we present the general evaluation of our algorithm. A detailed evaluation of the detector and tracker are given in Sections 3.1 and 3.2. In the last two sections we discuss the computational times of the algorithm and conclude the paper.

2   Theory

The method combines a fern-based detector and a tracker based on sequential linear predictors. Both the detector and the tracker are trained from the image data. The tracker has its own validation and is incrementally re-learned as the tracking goes. The detector locates the object in case the tracker gets lost.

2.1   Ferns-Based Detector

Object is modeled as a spatial constellation of detected harris corners on one representative image. In a nutshell: the fern detector first estimates similarity between harris corners detected in the current frame and harris corners on the model. The thresholded similarity determines tentative correspondences, which are further refined by the RANSAC selecting the largest geometrically consistent subset (i.e. set of inliers). In our approach, the object was modeled as a plane. Since we observed that the estimation of full homography transformation was often ill-conditioned, because of both insufficient number of detected corners and non-planarity of the object, the RANSAC searches for the affine transformation, which was showed to be more robust.

Detailed description of the similarity measure is in [3]. In the following, we provide just short description for the sake of completeness. The similarity measures probability $p(\mathbf{V}(\mathbf{v}), \mathbf{w})$ that the observed appearance of the neighbourhood $\mathbf{V}(\mathbf{v})$ of the detected corner $\mathbf{v}$ corresponds to the model corner $\mathbf{w}$. The appearance is represented as a sequence of randomly selected binary tests, i.e. given the corner $\mathbf{v}$ and sequence of n point pairs $\{(\mathbf{x}_1, \mathbf{y}_1), (\mathbf{x}_2, \mathbf{y}_2), \ldots (\mathbf{x}_n, \mathbf{y}_n)\}$, the appearance of the $\mathbf{v}$ is encoded as binary code $V_k(\mathbf{v}) = I(\mathbf{v} + \mathbf{x}_k) > I(\mathbf{v} + \mathbf{y}_k)$, where $I(\mathbf{v} + \mathbf{x}_k)$ is the image intensity.

On one hand, it is insufficient to model probabilities of binary tests independently, i.e. assuming that $p(\mathbf{V}(\mathbf{v}), \mathbf{w}) = \prod_{k=1}^{n} p_k(V_k(\mathbf{v}), \mathbf{w})$. On the other hand, modeling $p(\mathbf{V}(\mathbf{v}), \mathbf{w}) = p(V_1(\mathbf{v}), \ldots, V_n(\mathbf{v}), \mathbf{w})$ is ill-conditioned, since we would have to estimate probability in 2^n bins, where n is usually equal to several hundreds. Therefore, we divide the sequence of n binary tests into $N = n/m$ subsequences with length $m \approx 8 - 11$. Subsequences are selected by N membership functions $I(1) \ldots I(N)$ and we denote $h_k = \text{card}(I_k)$, $k = 1 \ldots N$. Finally, we consider these subsequences to be statistically independent and model the probability as:

$$p(\mathbf{V}(\mathbf{v}), \mathbf{w}) = \prod_{k=1}^{N} p_k(V_{I_k(1)}(\mathbf{v}), \ldots, V_{I_k(h_k)}(\mathbf{v}), \mathbf{w}) \tag{1}$$

The proposed detector requires an off-line training phase, within which the subsequent probabilities are estimated. Once the probabilities are pre-computed, we use them online to determine the tentative correspondences. In the following both phases are detailed, together with the detector on-line update.

Off-line training phase: First n binary tests are randomly selected and divided into N subsequences (note that these subsequences can be viewed as decision trees, which have the same binary for the whole floor, which are often called ferns). The model is estimated from one sample image, where Harris corners are detected within delineated object border. Appearance of each corner's neighbourhood is modeled by N h_k-dimensional binary hyper-cubes, with 2^{h_k} bins, representing joint probability $p_k(V_{I_k(1)}(\mathbf{v}), \ldots, V_{I_k(h_k)}(\mathbf{v}), \mathbf{w})$. To estimate probabilities, each corner neighbourhood is L-times perturbed within the range of local deformations we want to cope with. For each perturbed training sample and each subsequence, binary tests are evaluated and corresponding bin is increased by $1/L$. Note that different Harris corners are modeled via different probabilities but the same binary tests, which allows significant improvement in the on-line running phase, since the computational complexity of the similarity computation is almost independent of the number of Harris corners in the model.

On-line running phase: Given an input image, Harris corners are detected. For each corner $\mathbf{v}$, binary tests are evaluated and similarity to each model corner is computed via Equation 1. Similarities higher than a chosen threshold determine tentative correspondeces. Eventually, RANSAC estimates affine transformation between the model and the given image. Confidence of the detection is equal to the number of inliers.

On-line incremental learning: Re-learning of the detector may be invoked, when the object is not detected and its position is known with a sufficient confidence from the tracker. In such a case, each of k corners from the original model is warped to the current object position. We collect several perturbed image samples from the local neighborhood around each transformed corner. At each training sample binary tests are evaluated. Finally, probability distribution p_{k_a} for all the new training samples are estimated and the original probability p_k is updated by the exponential fogetting $p_k := (1 - w) \cdot p_k + w \cdot p_{k_a}$, where weight $w \in< 0; 1 >$ is forgetting speed. Currently the detector incremental learning is not used in the main algorithm, because of some further research that needs to be done. See Section 3.4 for benefits and drawbacks of the method and first results.

2.2   Sequential Linear Predictors

We extend the anytime learning of the Sequential Learnable Linear Predictors (SLLiP) by [15] in order to predict not only translation but also the full homography transformation. Next extension is the incremental learning of new object appearances also used by [2]. The predictor essentially estimates deformation parameters directly from image intensities. It requires a short off-line learning stage before the tracking starts. The learning stage consists of generating exemplars and estimation of regression functions. We use a simple cascade of 2 SLLiPs - first for 2D motion estimation (2 parameters) and second for homography estimation (8 parameters). The homography is parameterized by position of 4 patch corners. Knowing the corners position and having the reference coordinates, we compute the homography transformation for the whole patch. We have experimentally verified, that this 2-SLLiP configuration is more stable than using just one SLLiP to predict homography. First the translation is roughly estimated by first SLLiP and than a precise homography refinement is done. Because of speed, we opted for least squares learning of SLLiPs similarly, as suggested by [15].

Lets denote the translation parameters vector $\mathbf{t}^t = [\Delta x, \Delta y]^T$, estimated by the first SLLiP, and the homography parameters vector $\mathbf{t}^a = [\Delta x_1, \Delta y_1, \ldots, \Delta x_4, \Delta y_4]^T$, estimated by the second SLLiP which represents the motion of 4 object corners $\mathbf{c}_i = [x_i, y_i]^T, i = 1, \ldots, 4$. The object point $\mathbf{x} = [x, y]^T$ from previous image is transformed to corresponding point $\mathbf{x}'$ in current image accordingly

$$\mathbf{p} = \mathtt{A}\left(\begin{bmatrix} \mathbf{x} \\ 1 \end{bmatrix} + \begin{bmatrix} \mathbf{t}^t \\ 0 \end{bmatrix}\right) \tag{2}$$

$$\mathbf{x}' = [p_x/p_z, p_y/p_z]^T, \tag{3}$$

where $\mathbf{p}$ are homogeneous coordinates. The homography matrix $\mathtt{A}$ is computed from 4-point correspondences, between shifted object corners $\mathbf{c}_i + \mathbf{t}^t$ from previous image and current corners positions $\mathbf{c}_i + \mathbf{t}^t + [\mathbf{t}^a_{2i-1}, \mathbf{t}^a_{2i}]^T, i = 1, \ldots, 4$ estimated by the 2-SLLiP tracker.

Estimation of parameters vectors $\mathbf{t}^t$ and $\mathbf{t}^a$, *learning* and *incremental learning* will be explained for a single SLLiP with general parameters vector $\mathbf{t}$. Equations are valid for both SLLiPs, which we use. SLLiP is simply a sequence of linear predictors. Predictors in this sequence estimate the parameters successively (4), thus each improving the result of previous predictor estimation and lowering the error of estimation. SLLiP tracks according to

$$\mathbf{t}_1 = \mathtt{H}_1 I \left(X_1 \right) \tag{4}$$
$$\mathbf{t}_2 = \mathtt{H}_2 I \left(\mathbf{t}_1 \circ X_2 \right)$$
$$\mathbf{t}_3 = \mathtt{H}_3 I \left(\mathbf{t}_2 \circ X_3 \right)$$
$$\vdots$$
$$\mathbf{t} = \bigcirc_{(i=1,\dots,k)} \mathbf{t}_i,$$

where I is the current image and X is a set of 2D coordinates (called *support set*) spread over the object position from previous image. $I(X)$ is a vector of the image intensities collected at image coordinates X. Operation $\circ$ stands for transformation of support set points using (2) and (3), i.e. aligning the support set to fit the object using parameters estimated by the previous predictor in the sequence. Final result of the prediction is a vector $\mathbf{t}$ which combines results of all predictions in the sequence. The model θ_s for SLLiP is formed by the sequence of predictors $\theta_s = |\{\mathtt{H}_1, X_1\}, \{\mathtt{H}_2, X_2\}, \dots, \{\mathtt{H}_k, X_k\}|$. Matrices $\mathtt{H}_1, \mathtt{H}_2, \dots, \mathtt{H}_k$ are linear regression matrices which are learned from training data.

In our algorithm, the 2 SLLiPs are learned from one image only and they are incrementally updated during tracking. A few thousands of training examples are artificially generated from the training image using random perturbations of parameters in vector $\mathbf{t}$, warping the support set accordingly and collecting the image intensities. The column vectors of collected image intensities $I(X)$ are stored in matrix $\mathtt{D}_i$ and perturbed parameters in matrix $\mathtt{T}_i$ columnwise. Each regression matrix in SLLiP is trained using the least squares method $\mathtt{H}_i = \mathtt{T}_i \mathtt{D}_i^T \left(\mathtt{D}_i \mathtt{D}_i^T \right)^{-1}$.

Incremental learning corresponds to an on-line update of regression matrices $\mathtt{H}_i$, $i = 1, \dots, k$. An efficient way of updating regression matrices was proposed by [2]. Each regression matrix $\mathtt{H}_i$ can be decomposed as follows

$$\mathtt{H}_i = \mathtt{Y}_i \mathtt{Z}_i, \tag{5}$$

where $\mathtt{Y}_i = \mathtt{T}_i \mathtt{D}_i^T$ and $\mathtt{Z}_i = \left(\mathtt{D}_i \mathtt{D}_i^T \right)^{-1}$. New training example $\mathbf{d} = I(X)$ with parameters $\mathbf{t}$ is incorporated into the predictor as follows

$$\mathtt{Y}_i^{j+1} = \mathtt{Y}_i^j + \mathbf{t}\mathbf{d}^T \tag{6}$$

$$\mathtt{Z}_i^{j+1} = \mathtt{Z}_i^j - \frac{\mathtt{Z}_i^j \mathbf{d}\mathbf{d}^T \mathtt{Z}_i^j}{1 + \mathbf{d}^T \mathtt{Z}_i^j \mathbf{d}}, \tag{7}$$

where the upper index j stands for the number of training examples. After updating matrices $\mathtt{Y}_i$ and $\mathtt{Z}_i$ we update the regression matrices $\mathtt{H}_i$ using (5). For more details about incremental learning see [2].

The tracking procedure needs to be validated in order to detect the loss-of-track. When the loss-of-track occurs, the object detector is started instead of tracking. To *validate* the tracking we use the first SLLiP, which estimates 2D motion of the object. We utilize the fact that the predictor is trained to point to the center of learned object when initialized in a close neighborhood. On the contrary, when initialized on the background, the estimation of 2D motion is expected to be random. We initialize the predictor several times on a regular grid (validation grid - depicted by red crosses in Fig. 1) in the close neighborhood of current position of the tracker. The close neighborhood is defined as 2D motion range (of the same size as the maximal parameters perturbation used for learning), for which the predictor was trained. In our case the range is $\pm (patch\_width/4)$ and $\pm (patch\_height/4)$. We let the SLLiP vote for the object center from each position of the validation grid and observe the 2D vectors, which should point to the center of the object, in the case, when the tracker is well aligned on the object. When all (or sufficient number of) the vectors point to the same pixel, which is also the current tracker position, we consider the tracker to be on its track. Otherwise, when the vectors point to some random directions, we say that the track is lost, see Fig. 1. The same approach for tracking validation was suggested in [16].

The next section describes in detail the algorithm used in our system, which combines the ferns detector and 2-SLLiP tracker.

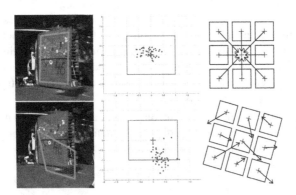

Fig. 1. Validation procedure demonstrated in two situations. The first row shows successful validation of tracked *blue_door*, the second row shows loss of track caused by a bad tracker initialization. First column shows the tracker position marked by green. The third column depicts the idea of validation - i.e. a few initializations of the tracker (marked by red crosses) around its current position and the collection of votes for object center. When the votes point to one pixel, which is also the current tracker position (or close enough to the center), the tracker is considered to be well aligned on the object. When the votes for center are random and far from current position the loss-of-track is detected. In the second column we see the collected votes (blue dots), the object center (red cross) and the motion range (red rectangle) normalized to $< -1, 1 >$, for which was the SLLiP trained.

2.3   The Algorithm

Our algorithm combines the ferns detector and 2-SLLiP tracker together. In order to achieve real-time performance, we need to run the detector only when absolutely necessary. The detection runs when the object is not present in the image or the tracker loses its track. As soon as the object is detected, the algorithm starts tracking and follows the target as long as possible. Since tracking requires only fragment of computational power, computational time is spared for other tasks. The on-line incremental update of the predictors helps to keep longer tracks. When the validator decides that the track is lost, the detector is started again until next positive detection is achieved. To lower the number of false detections to minimum, we run the validation after each positive response of the detector. The pseudo-code shown in algorithm 1 should clarify the whole process.

Algorithm 1. Detection and Tracking

Select object
$model\_fern \leftarrow$ learn fern detector
$model\_tracker \leftarrow$ learn $2 - $SLLiP tracker
$lost \leftarrow$ true
$i \leftarrow 0$
while next image is available **do**
  get next image
  $i \leftarrow i + 1$
  if $lost$ **then**
    $detected \leftarrow$ detect object
    if $detected$ **then**
      initialize tracker
      estimate homography
      $valid \leftarrow$ validate position
      if $valid$ **then**
        $lost \leftarrow$ false
        continue
      end if
    end if
  else
    track object
    if i mod $5 == 0$ **then**
      $valid \leftarrow$ validate position
      if $valid$ **then**
        $model\_tracker \leftarrow$ update tracker
      else
        $lost \leftarrow true$
        continue
      end if
    end if
  end if
end while

---

3   Experimental Results

The foreseen scenario for the use of our method is a visual part of mobile rescue robot navigation system. The operator selects one or more objects in the scene and the robot (carying a digital camera) should navigate itself through some space, by avoiding tracked obstacles to localized object of interest. Several objects were selected in one frame of particular sequence and from this starting frame they were tracked and detected.

Three types of experiments were performed. First we run the ferns detector itself in every frame without tracking. Second we run the 2-SLLiP tracker with validation without the recovery by detector. And finally, we run the combination of both. In all experiments were both the detector and the tracker trained from a single image. The

Fig. 2. Ladybug 3 with 5 cameras placed horizontaly in circle and one camera looking upwards for capturing omnidirectional images

detector and the tracker performed best on planar objects, because of the modeled 2D homography transformation. We tested our algorithm also on non-planar objects (*lying human, crashed car*) to see the performance limits and robustnes of our solution, see Section 3.3. Algorithm was tested on 8 objects in 4 videosequences. The ladybug camera provides 8 fps of panoramic images captured from 6 cameras simultaneously. Five cameras are set horizontaly in a circle and the sixth camera looks upwards, see Fig. 2. The panoramic image is a composition of these 6 images and has resolution of 5400×2248 pixels (12 Mpx). Fig. 3 shows examples of the composed scenes and tested objects. Appearance changes for few selected objects are depicted in Fig. 4. Notice the amount of non-linear distorsion caused by the cylindrical projection. The objects of interest are relatively small in comparison to the image size. In average the object size was 400×300 pixels. The ground-truth homography for each object was manually labeled in each frame. For evaluation of the detection/tracking performance we provide ROC curves for each tested object. The ROC curve illustrates *false positive rate* versus *false negative rate*.

- *False positive (FP)* is a positive vote for an object presence in some position, but the object was not there.
- *False negative (FN)* is a negative vote for an object presence in some position, where the object actually was present.

In ROC diagrams we want to get as close to the point $(0, 0)$ as possible. Each point in the curve of ROC diagram is evaluated for one particular *confidence threshold c*. In our

Fig. 3. Example images with tracked objects marked by red rectangles

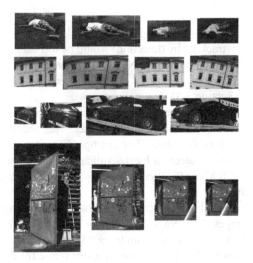

Fig. 4. Four of eight tested objects under different view angles and appearances

system the *confidence r* for one detection is given by the number of affine RANSAC inliers after positive detection. The tracker keeps the confidence from last detection until the loss-of-track. With growing confidence we get less false positives, but also more false negatives (we may miss some positive detections). For one particular c we compute the diagram coordinates as follows:

$$\text{FP}(c) = \sum_{j=1}^{n} (\text{FP}, \text{where } r_j > c) / n, \ \ \text{FN}(c) = \sum_{j=1}^{n} (\text{FN}, \text{where } r_j > c) / n, \quad (8)$$

where n is a number of frames in sequence. To draw the whole ROC curve we compute the coordinates for a discrete number of confidences from interval $< 0, 1 >$ and use linear interpolation for rest of the values.

In Fig. 5 *left* we show three different ROC curves. Each curve corresponds to one method used to search for the object position in sequences. In order to make the evaluation less dependent on a particular object, we computed mean ROC curves over all tested objects for different methods. The green curve depicts the performance of the tracker itself, run on every object from the first frame until the loss-of-track without the recovery by the detector. The blue curve shows results obtained by the fern detector itself run on every frame of all sequences. And finally the red curve shows results, when our algorithm was used. We may observe, that our algorithm performance is better (curve is the closest to point $(0, 0)$) than both individual methods. The separate ROC curves for individual objects may be seen in Fig. 5 *right* and Fig. 6. The experiments are organised as follows. The ferns detector is evaluated in Section 3.1, the performance of tracker is examined in Section 3.2. The algorithm 1, which combines both is evaluated in Section 3.3. And finally in Section 3.5 we provide computation times of all main parts of the algorithm.

3.1 Detector Evaluation

Using only the detector (tracking by detection) would be too slow for desired real-time performance in sequence of large images. Nevertheless we evaluate the performance of the detector itself to see how the adition of SLLiP tracker lowers the false positive and false negative rate (see Section 3.3).

In this experiment the detector was run with slightly different set of parameters than in the experiment which combines it with the tracker. This was necessary in order to achieve the best detection performance. For example here it was not possible to aditionally validate the positive detection by the validator. So we needed to increase the threshold for number of RANSAC inliers necessary for positive detection to lower the number of false positives.

It was also necessary to adjust the detector parameters according to expected object scale and rotation changes. In average the detector was searching for the object in 3 scales and it was able to detect objects under ± 20 degrees rotation. In Fig. 5 *right*, the ROC curves are depicted for detector run in every frame for different objects. The results show that some objects were detected in almost all cases correctly, while some other objects, like the *door*, with poor results. *Door* was the most complicated object for Harris corners-based detector, since only 21 keypoints were detected over the object, which were spread mostly in the central part of the door. That is why there was almost always a low number of inliers comming out of the RANSAC algorithm. This object was lately successfuly tracked by the tracker. Another complicated object was the *car*, due to its reflective surface and vast visual angle changes. Finally, the *human* lying on the floor was also a challenging object due to its non-planarity. As you will see in Section 3.3, the integration of tracking to the algorithm lowers the number of FP and FN and significantly speeds up the algorithm, see Section 3.5.

3.2 Tracker Evaluation

This experiment shows performance of the tracker without the recovery by the detector. The tracker is composed of 2 SLLiPs (for translation and homography). Each SLLiP

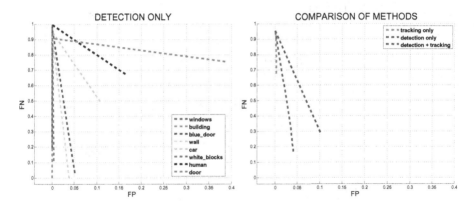

Fig. 5. Left: Each curve corresponds to detection results for one object. Right: Each curve corresponds to results of one method computed as mean ROC curve over all objects.

has 3 predictors in sequence with support set sizes $|X_1| = 225$, $|X_2| = 324$ and $|X_3| = 441$. The support set coordinates were spread over the object in regular grid. The tracker was incrementaly learned and validated during tracking until it lost its track or until the end of sequence. The tracking was manually initialized always in the first image of sequence (different form training image), where the object appeared. Some objects were tracked through the whole sequence. Some objects were lost after few frames, when there was fast motion right in the beginning. In Fig. 6 *left* you may see the lengths of successful tracking until the first loss-of-track. In case of partial occlusion the tracker sometimes jitters or even fails. Nevertheless, when it is incrementally learned, it is able to handle the occlusion as a new object appearance. The estimation of homography is very precise for planar objects.

Tracked objects appear in images as patches in resolutions varying from 211×157 (33 127 pixels) to 253×919 (232 507 pixels). Both SLLiPs work only with the subset of all patch pixels (same subset size for all objects). When tracking, each SLLiP needs to read only 990 intensity values, which is given by the sum of support set sizes of predictors in sequence. This brings another significant speed-up for the learning and tracking process.

3.3 Detector + Tracker Evaluation

Here we evaluate the performance of algorithm described in Section 2.3. The combination of the detector and the tracker improves the performance of the algorithm (lowers FP and FN), as may be seen in Fig. 6 *right* and Fig. 5 *left*. This is caused by their complementarity in failure cases. Tracker is very robust even under extreme perspective deformations, while the detector is not able to recognize these difficult object poses. On the other hand the detector is robust to partial occlusion, where the tracker usually fails and needs to be recovered and re-learned. In comparison with the detector (see Fig. 5 *right*), our algorithm in average significantly improves the results. Only few objects, which were perfectly detected by the detector (e.g. *white blocks* and *blue door*)

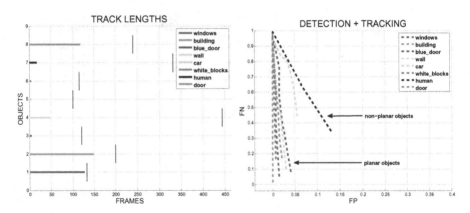

Fig. 6. Left: Each horizontal line depicts the length of track for one object until the first loss-of-track. The red vertical lines show the last frame of particular subsequence, where the object was fully or partially visible. Right: Each curve corresponds to results of one object detection and tracking. The ROC curves fit more to the left side of the diagram. This is caused by the high confidence of detections and tracking. The high confidence is actually valid, because of the very low number of false positives, as we may observe.

have a little worse results with our algorithm. This was caused by the tracking validation, which was running not every frame, but only every 5 frames, which means, that the tracker was lost a few frames just before loss-of-track detection by validation and received a few FPs and FNs. This small error could be eliminated by running the validation in every frame. The extreme efficiency of sequential predictors allows tracking much faster than real-time, which provides enough computational time for validation and incremental learning of the tracker. Running validation after each positive detection allows us to make the ferns detector more sensitive. We lower the threshold which specifies the number of neccessary inliers, which allows more true positive, but also more false positive detections. After each detection, which has small number of inliers, we initialize the tracker in detected pose, let the tracker vote for homography and run the validation. Validation eliminates possible false positive detections and let pass the true positives.

The most difficult object for our algorithm was the *crashed car*, the appearance of which was changing signifficantly during the sequence, due to its reflective surface, non-planar shape and vast changes in visual angle. Detection and tracking of *lying human* was successful in high percentage of detected occurences and low FP and FN. But the precision of homography estimation was quite poor as expected, because of its non-planar geometry. Nevertheless the incremental learning kept the tracker from loosing its track too often. The robust detector and incremental learning of the tracker allows for tracking of more complex (non-planar) objects, but high precision homography estimation can not be expected. Planar or semi-planar objects were detected and tracked with high accuracy.

3.4 Detector Incremental Learning

This last experiment presents our first attempt to incorporate incremental learning of the detector into our algorithm. The way how it is done is described in Section 2.1 part *On-line incremental learning* Here we compare our algorithm with and without detector incremental learning on object *human victim*. This object was particulary difficult to detect, because of its non-planar shape and large view angle changes (see Fig. 4).

In Fig. 7 you may see the ROC curves of our original algorithm and our algorithm with incremental learning of the detector triggered every 5 frames with the weight $w = 0.4$. The incremental learning helped to improve the overall performance of our algorithm. In this sequence it was caused by successful object re-detection after loss of track in a difficult object pose, where the detector, which was not re-learned failed. The detector incremental learning increases the chance to re-detect the object, which appearance is close to the appearance from last incremental update.

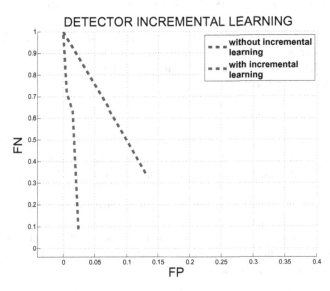

Fig. 7. ROC curves for object detection and tracking without (blue) and with (red) detector incremental learning. Here both methods were tested on one sequence with the object *human victim*. Thanks to the incremental learning the detector was able to detect original object rotated by $90°$ after loss of track, which was not possible without the incremental learning.

On the other hand the exponential forgetting used for detector update changes the histograms of joint probabilities so significantly, that the detector loses its ability to detect the object appearances learned at the beginning. When we run the original detector on each frame of the sequence, it is more successful, than the incrementally learned detector. It is able to detect object only under appearances close to those, used for last few incremental updates and not the previous ones, which is undesireable. Of course this may be reduced by the update weighting constant w, but in principle the update of probability histograms remains an important issue. Last but not least issue is the speed of the detector update, which, implemented in matlab, was running around 2 sec per image for 200 classes (Harris corners) per object and needs to be speeded-up. Because of these two issues we didn't yet incorporate the detector incremental learning into our algorithm.

3.5   Computation Times

The algorithm was run on standard PC with 64 bit, 2.66 GHz CPU. The object detector was implemented in language C and run in the system as MEX. The RANSAC, 2-SLLiP tracker and the rest of the algorithm were implemented in Matlab. When we pretermit the high resolution images, the PC memory requirements were minimal. The computation times for 12 Mpx image sequences are following:

(implementation in language C)

- detector learning: 2 sec for 200 classes, i.e. 10 ms per class (50 ferns with depth 11 and 500 training samples per class).
- detection: 0.13 ms for evaluation of 1 Harris point with 50 ferns and 200 classes. The computational time changes linearly with the number of classes. For one image with 5350 harrises, which passed the quality threshold, it took 0.7 sec. Usually we run the detector in 3 scales.

(implementation in Matlab)

- learning SLLiP trackers: 6 sec for the translation SLLiP with 1500 training samples and 9 sec for the homography SLLiP with 3500 training samples.
- tracking: 4 ms per image. This computational time is summed for both SLLiP trackers.
- validation: 72 ms per one validation. In our experiments, the validation was run every 5 frames during tracking.
- incremental learning: 470 ms together for 10 samples for the translation SLLiP and 10 samples for the homography SLLiP. Incremental learning was triggered every 5 frames after successful validation.

Average amount of Harris points in one image was around 50000, from which around 5300 passed the Harris quality threshold [7] and were evaluated by ferns detector. The use of object detector is neccessary, but its runtime needs to be reduced to a minimum because of the high computational time. The tracker runs very fast, which allows for multiple object tracking, incremental learning and tracking validation.

4   Conclusions and Future Work

In this work we combined ferns-based object detector and 2-SLLiP tracker in an efficient algorithm suitable for real-time processing of high resolution images. The amount of streamed data is huge and we need to avoid running the detector too often. That is why we focused on updating the 2-SLLiP model during tracking, which helped to keep the track even when the object appeared under serious slope angles and with changing appearance. In comparison with the detector run on every frame, our algorithm runs not only much faster, but also lowers the number of false positives and false negatives.

In our future work we want to focus on incremental learning of both the detector and the tracker. The detector is robust to partial occlusion, since it works with Harris corners sparsely placed around the object unlike the patch-based tracker. On the other hand the tracker is more robust to object appearance changes and keeps tracking even signifficantly distorted objects, which the detector fails to detect. This gives the opportunity to deliver the training examples for the detector in cases where it fails, while the tracker holds and vice-versa. We would like to develop a suitable strategy for mutual incremental learning. The tracker incremental learning works well. First experiment with detector incremental learning gives promising results. Yet still some research needs to be done to develop a efficient method for updating the detector's joint probabilities and to speed the detector's incremental learning up for real-time performance.

Acknowledgements. The 1st author was supported by Czech Science Foundation Project P103/10/1585. The 2nd author was supported by Czech Science Foundation Project P103/11/P700. The 3rd author was supported by EC project FP7-ICT-247870 NIFTi. Any opinions expressed in this paper do not necessarily reflect the views of the European Community. The Community is not liable for any use that may be made of the information contained herein.

References

1. Li, M., Chen, W., Huang, K., Tan, T.: Visual tracking via incremental self-tuning particle filtering on the affine group. In: 2010 IEEE Conference on Computer Vision and Pattern Recognition (CVPR), pp. 1315–1322 (2010)
2. Hinterstoisser, S., Benhimane, S., Navab, N., Fua, P., Lepetit, V.: Online learning of patch perspective rectification for efficient object detection. In: Conference on Computer Vision and Pattern Recognition, pp. 1–8 (2008)
3. Özuysal, M., Calonder, M., Lepetit, V., Fua, P.: Fast keypoint recognition using random ferns. IEEE Transactions on Pattern Analysis and Machine Intelligence 32, 448–461 (2010)
4. Bay, H., Ess, A., Tuytelaars, T., Van Gool, L.: Speeded-up robust features. In: Proceedings of IEEE European Conference on Computer Vision, pp. 404–417 (2006)
5. Lowe, D.: Distinctive image features from scale-invariant keypoints. International Journal on Computer Vision 60, 91–110 (2004)
6. Šochman, J., Matas, J.: Waldboost - learning for time constrained sequential detection. In: Proceedings of the Conference on Computer Vision and Pattern Recognition, pp. 150–157 (2005)
7. Shi, J., Tomasi, C.: Good features to track. In: Proceedings of IEEE Computer Society Conference on Computer Vision and Pattern Recognition, pp. 593–600 (1994)
8. Lucas, B., Kanade, T.: An iterative image registration technique with an application in stereo vision. In: Proceedings of the 7th International Conference on Artificial Intelligence, pp. 674–679 (1981)
9. Baker, S., Matthews, I.: Lucas-kanade 20 years on: A unifying framework. International Journal of Computer Vision 56, 221–255 (2004)
10. Hager, G.D., Belhumeur, P.N.: Efficient region tracking with parametric models of geometry and illumination. IEEE Transactions on Pattern Analysis and Machine Intelligence 20, 1025–1039 (1998)

11. Dellaert, F., Collins, R.: Fast image-based tracking by selective pixel integration. In: Proceedings of the International Conference on Computer Vision: Workshop of Frame-Rate Vision, pp. 1–22 (1999)
12. Jurie, F., Dhome, M.: Hyperplane approximation for template matching. IEEE Transactions on Pattern Analysis and Machine Intelligence 24, 996–1000 (2002)
13. Zimmermann, K., Matas, J., Svoboda, T.: Tracking by an optimal sequence of linear predictors. IEEE Transactions on Pattern Analysis and Machine Intelligence 31, 677–692 (2009)
14. Holzer, S., Ilic, S., Navab, N.: Adaptive linear predictors for real-time tracking. In: 2010 IEEE Conference on Computer Vision and Pattern Recognition (CVPR), pp. 1807–1814 (2010)
15. Zimmermann, K., Svoboda, T., Matas, J.: Anytime learning for the NoSLLiP tracker. Image and Vision Computing, Special Issue: Perception Action Learning 27, 1695–1701 (2009)
16. Hurych, D., Svoboda, T.: Incremental learning and validation of sequential predictors in video browsing application. In: VISIGRAPP 2010: International Joint Conference on Computer Vision, Imaging and Computer Graphics Theory and Applications, vol. 1, pp. 467–474 (2010)

Computational Framework for Symmetry Classification of Repetitive Patterns

M. Agustí-Melchor, Á. Rodas-Jordá, and J.M. Valiente-González

Computer Vision Group, DISCA, ETS. Ingenieria Informática
Universitat Politècnica de València, Camino de Vera s/n 46022, Valencia, Spain
{magusti,arodas,jvalient}@disca.upv.es
http://www.disca.upv.es/vision

Abstract. The interest shown recently in the algorithmic treatment of symmetries, also known as Computational Symmetry, covers several application areas among which textile and tiles design are some of the most significant. Designers make new creations based on the symmetric repetition of motifs that they find in databases of wallpaper images. The existing methods for dealing with these images have several drawbacks because the use of heuristics achieves low recovery rates when images exhibit imperfections due to the fabrication or the handmade process.

To solve this problem we propose a novel computational framework based on obtaining a continuous-value symmetry feature vector and classifying it using an NN classifier and a set of prototype classes. The prototype parameters are automatically adjusted in order to adapt them to the image variability. Moreover, a *goodness-of-fit classification* can be applied in the content-based image retrieval context. Our experimental results improve the state of the art in wallpaper classification methods.

Keywords: Symmetry, Symmetry groups, Image retrieval by symmetry, Prototype-based classification, Adaptive nearest neighbour classification.

1 Introduction

Symmetry is an abstract concept that is easily noticed by humans and as a result designers make new creations based on its use. In industrial sectors, such as textiles, ceramics, or graphic arts, the notion of symmetry is always present as an aesthetic element and is indispensable in every new design. When using a symmetrical design, a pattern is repeated to fill the workplane in accordance with strict placement rules. The traditional *Tillings and Patterns Theory* describes the fundamentals of this design creation process. The results are designs such as those shown in Figure 1. These are images of typical woven and mosaic samples, commonly referred to as *regular mosaics*, *wallpaper images*, *wallpaper patterns*, or simply *Wallpapers*. However, little effort has been made in the area of wallpaper image analysis and classification, and so this work explores this direction.

The interest in the algorithmic treatment of symmetries has been recognised by a recent tutorial at the ECCV 2010 Conference [11]. The authors introduce the term *Computational Symmetry* and present several application areas, among which the textile and

G. Csurka et al. (Eds.): VISIGRAPP 2011, CCIS 274, pp. 257–270, 2013.
© Springer-Verlag Berlin Heidelberg 2013

tile design categorisation is one of the most significant. In this sector, many companies have thousands of wallpaper samples accumulated over the years and stored in company storerooms or museums. Fig. 1 shows some examples. In most cases, these collections are digitised and stored in private images databases. These collections are an invaluable asset and are used as sources of inspiration for designers. But designers suffer serious limitations when searching and managing this information because the images are in bitmap format, and designers are accustomed to using abstract terms related with perceptual criteria such as symmetry (but also closeness, co-circularity, co-linearity, overlap, etc.), instead of statistical terms (colour distributions, textures, moments, and so on).

Fig. 1. Details of wallpaper images obtained from [15], [4], and [7] collections. These are images of real textile samples that showi hand-made artefacts and damaged or scratched parts. The geometry of the Unit Lattice is drawn in the centre of each image.

All this information, conveniently organised, can be used to build an Information System that enables all these historical designs to be effectively used. The compact image description obtained can also be used in object detection or Content-Based Image Retrieval (*CBIR*). In this way, CBIR can be used to find images that meet some criteria based on similarity. These systems are oriented towards imprecise searches (the exact match is not the only result that the user expects), and manage the variability of the results in such a way to suggest different possibilities to the final user.

The term *computational symmetry* refers to the algorithmic treatment of symmetries, but as is stated by [11] there are two key points when real world data is used. Firstly, to compute the concepts of group theory from imperfect, noisy, ambiguous, distorted, and often hidden symmetry patterns in real world data. And secondly, the mathematical theory of symmetry groups is applied to algorithms that incorporate/assume the limitations of the representational power of computers.

In this paper, in order to explicitly address each of these statements, we propose a novel computational framework based on continuous measurements of symmetries to classify real and synthetic images of two-dimensional repetitive patterns. These patterns will be formally described through a symmetry group (*wallpaper group*, *plane symmetry group*, or *plane crystallographic group*) based on the symmetries contained. Therefore, we obtain a structural description of the contents of images based on the disposition of a pattern in the image and the computation of its internal symmetries. We solve the inherent ambiguities of symmetry computation by:

- Using continuous symmetry values because total symmetry and totally absent symmetry rarely exist in real images.
- Using an adaptive classifier without learning stages because of the low number of examples for learning we will use prototype based classifiers.

– Obtaining the relative response of the classifier. Thereby enabling similar groups to be considered as the answer of the system, to be useful in CBIR tasks because traditional binary classifiers do not give a ranked list of the class membership of the image, and a symmetry group may be chosen by a small numerical advantage.

2 State of the Art

The symmetry of any 2D pattern can be described through a set of geometrical transformations that transforms it in itself. Those transformations that preserve distances are known as isometries, and the only plane isometries are: translations; rotations (n-fold); reflections (specular); and glide reflections (specular plus lateral displacement). Therefore, up to four different kinds of symmetries can be observed in a pattern, one is external to the pattern (*translational symmetry*), and the other three are internal (*rotation, reflection*, and *glide reflection symmetries*).

Regarding the translational symmetry, a wallpaper pattern is a repetition of a parallelogram shaped subimage, called a Unit Lattice (UL), so that the full pattern can be reconstructed by the replication (displacements) of this UL. A lattice extraction procedure is then needed to obtain the lattice geometry in the form of two direction vectors (L_1 L_2) that define the translational symmetry of the pattern (see Fig. 2). Autocorrelation ([8],[9]) or Fourier approaches have been used, among others, to solve this question. In a previous work [1] we use a wavelet approach for this purpose. In the present work, we assume that the lattice geometry has been already obtained and the UL of each image sample is known in advance.

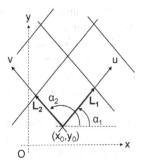

Fig. 2. Lattice geometry

For internal symmetries, we rely on the Symmetry Groups theory [6], which uses the concept of symmetry groups to formulate a mathematical description of complex plane pattern structures. The set of isometric transformations that brings a figure in coincidence with itself is called a symmetry group. In the 1-D case, *Frieze Symmetry Groups* (FSG), the pattern contains one traslational symmetry and several other isometries. In the 2D case, *Plane Symmetry Groups* (PSG), the pattern contains two traslational symmetries (lattice) and several other isometries. For example, the pattern in Figure 1 (left) only has translational symmetry. In contrasts, the other patterns of Figure 1 have more isometries, such as 180° rotations and reflections about two axes, and the last pattern can be reconstructed using 120° rotations.

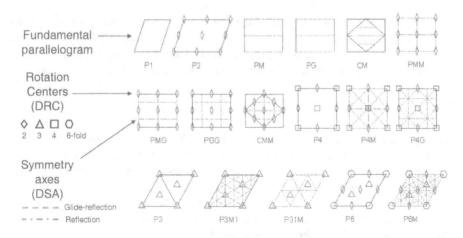

Fig. 3. Visual representation of the 17 Wallpaper Groups including their standard notation, reflection symmetry axes (glide and non-glide), and rotation centres of n-fold symmetries. The UL is referred to as a Fundamental Parallelogram.

It is also known that there is a geometric restriction, called the 'crystallographic constraint', that limits the number of possible rotations that can be applied to a motif or tile to completely fill the plane without holes or overlapping. These rotations are 180°, 120°, 90°, and 60°. Accordingly, the number of PSGs are limited to 17 cases, which is one of the main points that help us to describe the pattern structure. Figure 3 shows the details of each PSG, as well as their standard notation. For example, the patterns in Figure 1 belong (from left to right), to symmetry groups P1, PMM, PGG, and P31M.

Liu et al. [11] reports an extended discussion and comparison of the state of the art of symmetry detection algorithms. A global success of 63% over a test bed of 176 images is reported. The evaluation results show that for all types (synthetic or real, single, or multiple symmetries) of images the best mean sensitivity is 63% and 58% for reflection and rotation symmetry detection, respectively. When considering the detection of multiple symmetries in one image, the best mean sensitivity rates are 42% (for reflection) and 32% (for rotation); while the best values of the overall success rate (including the false positives) are much worse: 25/27% for reflection/rotation symmetry detection in the overall image set; and 16/19% for real images.

Specifically in this context of repetitive images, the classical algorithms for cataloguing wallpapers [6] by symmetry detection are heuristic-based procedures to be used by humans: Alsina [3], Grünbaum & Shepard [5], Schattschneider [10], Rose & Stafford [3]). The best classification result was obtained with Schattschneider's algorithm where a 70% success rate was obtained with a collection of 17 images. These algorithms are proposed in the form of decision trees whose branches are raised as questions to ask when looking at the design. Because of the ambiguities in the computer reformulation of these questions, their implementation is very complex. The main computer autonomous approach of this kind has been made by Liu et al. [9]. This model expresses the Schattschneider algorithm in the form of a *rule-based classifier* (RBC) where each symmetry group corresponds to a unique sequence of yes/no answers. This model can be seen as a kind of *decision tree* classifier with binary symmetry values. Our experience confirms that this method can be tuned to obtain 100% hits for the Joyce [7] dataset, yet this set-up is unsuccessful for other image collections. In addition, the use of RBC obtains only one result without an associate measure of confidence. An enhancement of this solution is necessary, as indicated in [12].

3   Proposed Method for Continuous Symmetry Computation

We propose a novel computational framework based on continuous measurements of symmetries in a distance-based classification of symmetry groups applied to real and synthetic images of two-dimensional repetitive patterns. The use of binary class proto-types describing the PSG mentioned above, adaptively adjusted for image conditions, assumes a high degree of variance of symmetry features, due to noise, deformations, or just the nature of the hand made products. As this classification results in an ordered list of content similarity based on symmetry, it will be used as a result for CBIR.

We started by using a Nearest Neighbour Classifier (NNC) as this enabled us to obtain a measure of goodness for the classification. This kind of method requires the use of continuous-value feature vectors.

3.1   Feature Computation and Symmetry Groups Classification

A close view to PSG description in Fig. 3 reveals that the minimum number of symmetry features needed to distinguish every PSG is twelve: four features (R_2, R_3, R_4, and R_6) related to rotational symmetries; four features (T_1, T_2, T_{1G}, and T_{2G}) to describe reflection symmetries (non-glide and glide) along axes parallel to the sides of UL; and four more features (D_1, D_2, D_{1G}, and D_{2G}) for reflection (non-glide and glide) with respect to the two UL diagonals. We defined a symmetry feature vector (SFV) of twelve elements that identifies the presence/absence of these symmetries as ($f_1, f_2, ..., f_{12}$). To obtain a symmetry feature f_i for a specific isometry, e.g 2-fold rotation, we apply this transformation to the original image $I(x, y)$ and obtain the transformed image $I^T(x, y)$. A piece of the transformed image, of the size of the bounding box of the UL (m), is selected. A score map is then computed as $Map(x, y) = 1 - SAD(x, y)$, where:

$$SAD(x, y) = \frac{1}{m} \sum_{x_0\ y_0} |I(x - x_0, y - y_0) - BBox(x_0, y_0)| \tag{1}$$

If symmetry is present in the image, this map peaks at several positions indicating the presence of that symmetry, while revealing lower values in areas where the symmetry is not held. The $|maximum - minimum|$ difference should then be a good measure to quantify the feature. Figure 4 shows an example. However, there are patterns without internal symmetries, such as P1 (Fig. 1), so that max-min difference should be relative to any other value representing the presence of symmetry. The only symmetry always present in every pattern is the translational symmetry (S_T). So we can obtain S_T by computing the previous score map using the original image and its translated version (following UL sides) and the maximum of this map will represent the upper score level of symmetry S_T present in the image.

 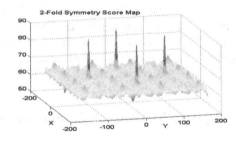

Fig. 4. Original image (left) with the UL overprinted and score map (right) for 2-fold symmetry rotation

$$f_i = \frac{max(Map) - min(Map)}{S_T - min(Map)} \quad 1 \le i \le 12 \tag{2}$$

Finally, we compute the normalised components of the SFV as eq. 2. The higher the value of f_i, the more likely the image contains symmetry. Table 1 (Agustí et al. [2]) shows the SFV vectors obtained for the four wallpaper samples in Fig. 1. As expected, these results confirm high values that indicate the presence of symmetry and low values otherwise. The bold values means those symmetry scores that have to be considered as presence of symmetry when considering the symmetry group the image belongs to. It can see how the proposed symmetry features perform well in most cases and the range between symmetry "presence" and "absence" is, in general, pronounced and the SFV vectors are very discriminatory. These results show that the proposed features behave very well, especially with images collections composed of very geometric, low-noise, and middle level complexity images. However, because these features are computed as grey level differences between image patches, their values strongly depend on the particular arrangements of image pixels - the *image complexity* - so that with strongly distorted and noisy images, the SFV vectors may lose their capacity to discriminate. In general, the errors come from three main sources:

1. **Noise and Distortion:** acquisition noise, bad illumination conditions, holes or breaks due to the age of objects' and hand-made artefacts. Some images are photos of handmade designs, and so show little similarity between the repeated motifs.
2. **Deformations:** some images have changed their aspect ratio, probably due to the acquisition process (e.g. squares become rectangles). In these cases, the translational symmetry remains high, but other symmetries decrease or disappear, and so the original symmetry group (PSG) changes.
3. **Indistinguishability:** in many cases, the presence/absence of certain symmetries is due to small details in the image, so much so that the difference between the original and the transformed image (e.g. reflection) is only a few pixels. In these cases, the computed scores are in the noise level, and so they are indistinguishable from the correct value.

As result some of the computed scores are misleading. For example, the value of 0.8 in the D_1 reflection symmetry of sample 1 must be considered as a symmetry absence, while the lower values of 0.72, 0.74, 0.69 and 0.65, in some symmetry scores of sample

4, denote symmetry presence. It is probably due to distortions and noise artefacts that distort the traslational symmetry of each image. As a consequence, the dynamic range of SFV scores varies from sample to sample, so that the SFV vectors can be used to feature the symmetry structure of an image but not to compare two images because the SFV values are in different ranges. This leads to the use of prototypes that represent the inherent structure of each class, so that each sample can be compared with a set of abstract prototypes and not with other images.

Table 1. Symmetry feature vectors of the four wallpapers shown in Fig. 1

Sample	SFV=$(R_2, R_3, R_4, R_6, T_1, T_2, D_1, D_2, T_{1G}, T_{2G}, D_{1G}, D_{2G})$	PSG
1	(0.62, 0.47, 0.69, 0.34, 0.65, 0.67, 0.80, 0.59, 0.37, 0.43, 0.80, 0.59)	$P1$
2	(**0.82**, 0.09, 0.20, 0.09, **0.88**, **0.83**, 0.20, 0.19, 0.27, 0.26, 0.2, 0.19)	PMM
3	(**0.95**, 0.42, 0.33, 0.46, 0.39, 0.45, 0.31, 0.48, **0.98**, **0.99**, 0.31, 0.48)	PGG
4	(0.46, **0.69**, 0.28, 0.49, **0.74**, **0.65**, 0.48, **0.72**, **0.74**, **0.65**, 0.48, **0.72**)	$P31M$

Table 2. Binary prototypes for the 17 PSG classes

Classes	Prototype Feature vectors	Classes	Prototype Feature vectors
$P1$	(0,0,0,0,0,0,0,0,0,0,0,0)	CMM	(1,0,0,0,0,0,1,1,0,0,1,1)
$P2$	(1,0,0,0,0,0,0,0,0,0,0,0)	$P4$	(1,0,1,0,0,0,0,0,0,0,0,0)
PM_1	(0,0,0,0,1,0,0,0,0,0,0,0)	$P4M$	(1,0,1,0,1,1,1,1,0,0,1,0)
PM_2	(0,0,0,0,0,1,0,0,0,0,0,0)	$P4G$	(1,0,1,0,0,0,1,1,1,1,1,0)
PG_1	(0,0,0,0,0,0,0,0,1,0,0,0)	$P3$	(0,1,0,0,0,0,0,0,0,0,0,0)
PG_2	(0,0,0,0,0,0,0,0,0,1,0,0)	$P31M_1$	(0,1,0,0,1,1,1,0,1,1,1,0)
CM_1	(0,0,0,0,0,1,0,0,0,0,1,0)	$P31M_2$	(0,1,0,0,1,1,0,1,1,1,0,1)
CM_2	(0,0,0,0,0,0,1,0,0,0,0,1)	$P3M1_1$	(0,1,0,0,0,0,1,0,0,0,1,0)
PMM	(1,0,0,0,1,1,0,0,0,0,0,0)	$P3M1_2$	(0,1,0,0,0,0,0,1,0,0,0,0)
PMG_1	(1,0,0,0,1,0,0,0,0,1,0,0)	$P6$	(1,1,0,1,0,0,0,0,0,0,0,0)
PMG_2	(1,0,0,0,0,1,0,0,1,0,0,0)	$P6M$	(1,1,0,1,1,1,1,1,1,1,1,0)
PGG	(1,0,0,0,0,0,0,0,1,1,0,0)		

To classify a wallpaper image, featured by SFV, we need a set of class samples. Fortunately, the number of classes and their structure are known in advance. For the sake of simplicity, we start by proposing the use of binary prototypes representing each one of the 17 plane symmetry group classes. Table 2 shows the resulting 23 prototypes. Some classes have two prototypes because there are two possible places where reflection symmetry can appear. After applying an NNC classifier to several image collections we did not found significant improvements in comparison with the RBC classifier (see the Experiments section). This is probably due to the bias of the feature values: minimum values are not near '0', nor are maximum values near S_t. In this situation, the use of binary prototypes, with inter-class boundaries equidistant to each class, does not fit the problem. However, some advantage have been achieved. Firstly, the Euclidean distance to the class prototype can be used as a measure of confidence. Secondly, the NNC produces an ordered set of outputs describing the class membership of each sample. This latter consideration can enable an automatic adjustment of the prototypes in order to adapt them to the image variability.

3.2 Adaptive NNC (ANNC)

Recent works on NN classifiers have shown that adaptive schemes [14] outperform the results of classic NNC in many applications. In response to the ambiguities in computed symmetry values, we propose an adaptive approach based on establishing a merit function to adapt the inter-class boundaries to the specific image conditions. Fig. 5-a shows a simplified example of a 2D feature space including four binary prototypes. The inter-class boundaries are symmetric with respect to each prototype. In a real context, the $SFV(f_1, f_2)$ vectors never reach certain areas close to the prototypes, Fig. 5-b shows these forbidden areas. The distorted distances force an adaptation of the boundaries between classes.

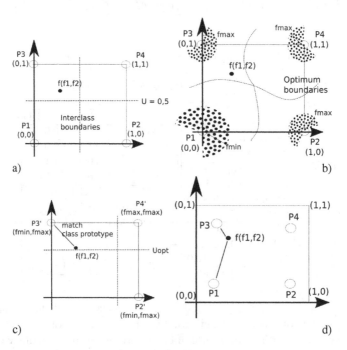

Fig. 5. ANNC algorithm: a) 2D feature space and prototypes $P1$, $P2$, $P3$ and $P4$. b) forbidden areas. c) adaptation of class boundaries. d) final disambiguation.

To achieve this, a transformation of the the feature space can be performed by normalizing these features. In this new space, the null-class $P1$ disappears; and therefore, this class should be treated separately. The new boundaries between classes can be searched in a way that maximises a merit function. We use orthogonal boundaries defined by a single parameter U, the *uncertainty boundary of symmetry*. We studied several merit functions and, finally, propose a distance ratio between the reported first and second classes after classifying the sample with respect to binary prototypes using a

NN classifier. The result is the boundary U_{opt} that best separates the classes. Moreover, instead of moving the inter-class boundaries, the problem is reformulated to modify the class prototypes into new values $(H, L) \in [0, 1]$ that are symmetrical with respect to the middle value U (Fig. 5-c). Finally, the closest class to new prototypes (H, L) and the null-class $P1$ are disambiguated (Fig. 5-d). The algorithm is as follows:

Step 1. The symmetry values are normalised, see Eq. 3, discharging the $P1$ class and resulting in a 16-class problem.

$$SFV' = (f_1', f_2', ..., f_{12}');$$
$$f_i' = \frac{f_i - min(SFV)}{max(SFV) - min(SFV)}; \quad 1 \leq i \leq 12 \qquad (3)$$

Step 2. The original prototypes are transformed into (H, L) prototypes for each of 16 classes. These values are defined with respect to parameter U as: $H = 1$, $L = 2 \cdot U - 1$ for $U \geq 0, 5$ and $L = 0$, $H = 2 \cdot U$ otherwise.

Step 3. For each U, ranging from 0.2 to 0.8, the H and L limits are computed and an NNC is performed using SFV' and the resulting prototypes. Repeating steps 2-3 for all U values, the value (U_{opt}) that maximises the merit function is selected, and the corresponding class is also tentatively selected.

Step 4. Finally, we disambiguate the candidate class from the previously excluded $P1$ class. To achieve this, we again re-classify the SFV but only using the $P1$ and candidate classes.

4   Experiments

As indicated in [11], without a systematic evaluation of different symmetry detection and classification algorithms against a common image set under a uniform standard, our understanding of the power and limitations of the proposed algorithms remains partial. As image datasets reported in literature were not publicly available, we selected several wallpaper images from known websites, to carry out the comparison between the proposed ANNC and the reference RBC methods. We picked image datasets from Wallpaper [7], Wikipedia [15], Quadibloc [13], and SPSU [4], and created a test bed of 218 images. All images were hand-labelled to make the ground truth.

4.1   Results from a Classification Point of View

As the original RBC algorithm source code was unavailable, we implemented it using the original RBC decision tree reported in [9], but using our SFV feature vectors, and binarising the features using a fixed threshold (the average of the best classification results) for all image datasets. The results obtained with RBC, NNC, and ANNC classifiers are shown in Table 3. For the shake of brevity, we only include here the percentage of successful classification, i.e. accuracy or precision.

With respect to the classical algorithms for cataloguing wallpapers, the results are lower: e.g. for Wallpaper image collection, Brian Sanderson gets a 64.71%, Rose & Sttaford a 52.94%, and Schattschneider with a 70.59% of precision as the better result. This last method is the base for RBC that can obtain up to 100% tuning its parameters for that image collection. Note that the RBC method only computes as its answer the group where the image belongs to. The NN classifiers improves the results from RBC. The NNC obtains global results that are 5.98% better than the RBC, and the ANNC obtains a 9.17% when only taking into account the most probable classification result.

Table 3. Experimental classification results from RBC, NNC, and ANNC

Collection name	Number of Images	Sub-set name	RBC precision	NNC precision	ANNC precision
Wallpaper	17		100	82.35	100
Wikipedia	53		54.72	60.38	62.26
	17	WikiGeom	88.24	88.24	100
Quadibloc	46		71.74	69.57	82.61
	29	Quad0102	62.07	75.86	79.31
	17	Quad03	88.24	58.82	88.24
SPSU	102		49.02	62.76	59.80
Global	218		59.18	65.15	68.35

The first image collection is Wallpaper (Figure 6a) shows the entire collection), a standard collection reported in previous works. In this case, both RBC and ANNC methods obtain 100% success. The RBC achieves the same result as reported in [9], which means that our implementation of this algorithm has similar results as the original implementation.

To take into account the varying visual complexity of the images, we separate the next two collections in sub-sets. In the case of the entire Wikipedia collection (see Figure 6b), which includes other distorted images, a decrease in results is evident. In the WikiGeom dataset, which is a sub-set of Wikipedia formed by strongly geometrical patterns, the ANNC and NNC results outperformed the RBC. Figure 6c shows some examples of this collection.

Similar results were obtained with Quadibloc image collection, which is of intermediate visual complexity. The ANNC obtains a near 80% success rate with this collection, clearly outperforming the NNC and RBC methods. We studied it as two subsets: one formed by sketches over a uniform background (Quad0102, Figure 7a), and other (Quad03, Figure 7b) constituted by more visually complex motives with many highly contrasting colours. With Quad0102 we obtain a 79.31% while Quad03 obtains a 88.24%. Instead of obtaining better results with visually simple images (Quad0102), the existence of wide white areas (background) with small black motives (foreground) obtains high values of symmetries for almost every isometry.

The worse results were obtained with the more visually complex images in the SPSU collection. The Figure 7c show some examples of this collection. In this case, all results are below 60%. These lower values are due to the existence of noise and imprecise details (handmade) in the images. Also, these images show several repetitions and illumination artefacts that suggest the need for a pre-processing step. It is remarkable that the ANNC algorithm is still 10 higher than the RBC algorithm for this visually complex dataset.

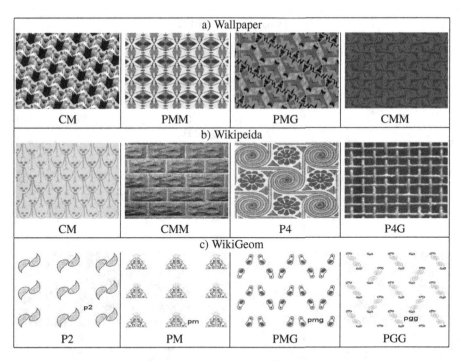

Fig. 6. Examples from wallpaper [7], and Wikipedia [15] (including WikiGeom) collections and their corresponding PSG

4.2   Results from CBIR Point of View

Working with a distance-based classifier offers an additional advantage because it delivers a value defining the degree of proximity to the prototype chosen ($d_i = dist(SFV, P_i)$). Note that the RBC method only computes as its answer the group that the image belongs to. This (P_i, d_i) description, which can be extended to the whole set of prototypes, can be used as a high level semantic image descriptor, and is useful in areas such as CBIR. This is particularly helpful in the presence of complex images that, due to various factors (manufacturing defects, noise, small details, etc.) present an ambiguity about the symmetry group to which they belong. Some of these images are difficult for experts to label. Thus when taking, the first two (NNC2 & ANNC2) or three (NNC3 & ANNC3) classification results, the success rates are considerably higher (see Table 4) and the distances to the second and third candidate are near the first result. This shows that many of the classification errors were due to the above-mentioned factors. This idea can be conveniently exploited in the context of CBIR.

As we are using distance-based classifiers (NNC & ANNC), we can improve the results obtained by the classification process because we now have information about the distance to the rest of the groups. It is now possible to offer a high-level semantic image descriptor for CBIR to deal with ambiguities by exploring the ranking. Considering the entire ordered list of distances to each PSG, two strategies can be undertaken. Firstly,

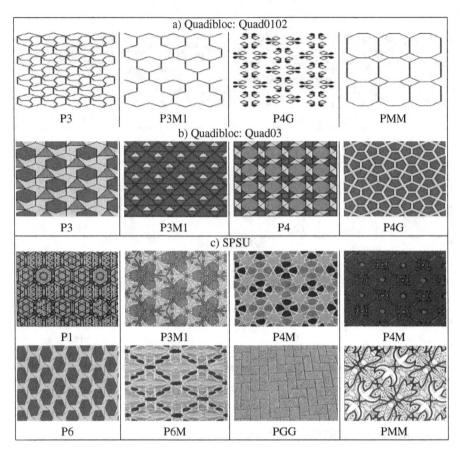

Fig. 7. Examples from Quadibloc [13], and SPSU [4] collections and their corresponding PSG

the user can choose a value of confidence, and the system will respond by listing the groups with less distance that the value entered by the user. Secondly, the system can offer up to a fixed number of entries for the list.

To cope with ambiguities, we can consider the first and second results (columns NNC(2) and ANNC(2) of Table 3) or up to the third result (columns NNC(3) and ANNC(3) of Table 3). There is no a remarkable increase in results when considering a large number of groups to which an image can belong. This is due to the number of symmetries that leads from one PSG to another. In this way, we consider that the system gives a correct answer if the real group the image X belongs to, is between observed K values. A qualitative comparison of the evolution of the result when considering ranking reveals the improvement percentage when considering ambiguities in the results. Taking $K = 2$, NNC obtains a result that is 17.42% globally better than RBC; and ANNC obtains a 23.72% improvement with respect to RBC. ANNC obtains a result that is 25.52% globally better than RBC when $K = 3$ (and NNC obtains a 23.72% improvement).

Table 4. Experimental classification results from NNC, and ANNC, using higher values of rank

Collection name	Number of Images	Sub-set name	RBC precision	NNC2 precision	ANNC2 precision	NNC3 precision	ANNC3 precision
Wallpaper	17		100	100	100	100	100
Wikipedia	53		54.72	73.55	81.13	81.13	83.02
	17	WikiGeom	88.24	94.12	100	100	100
Quadibloc	46		71.74	82.61	91.30	91.3	95.63
	29	Quad0102	62.07	86.21	89.66	89.66	93.10
	17	Quad03	88.24	76.47	94.12	94.12	100
SPSU	102		49.02	71.57	76.47	76.47	82.35
Global	218		59.18	76.60	82.60	82.60	86.70

5 Conclusions

This paper presents a proposal for a novel computational framework for the classification of repetitive 2D pattern images into symmetry groups using an adaptive nearest neighbour classifier (ANNC). The feature vector is composed of twelve symmetry scores, computationally obtained from image grey level values. The procedure uses a Sum-of-Absolute-Differences approach and normalise these values using translational symmetry, the only symmetry that the image certainly contains. A distance-based Nearest Neigbour classifier is then used to classify the image into a symmetry group. A main issue is the use of binary class prototypes to represent the 17 PSG classes.

The absence of symmetry is never computed as '0', nor is the presence of symmetry computed as '1', even assuming perfect image conditions. The dynamic range of the symmetry values (f_i) is extremely variable, depending on the specific conditions of each image. The RBC and the NNC behave poorly, because of ambiguities in symmetry computation. This leads to the use of several adaptive approachs, implemented by an adaptive classifier. The proposed ANNC classifier is based on establishing a merit function to adapt the inter-class boundaries to the specific image conditions, and it is reformulated as an adaptation of prototype feature vectors from binary values $(0, 1)$ to adjusted (H, L) values. This classifier is non-parametric, so there is no need to adjust the parameters involved, and it is also non-supervised, so no learning stages are needed.

The experimental results show the limits of the previous reported method (RBC) when the image conditions are not established. as well as the need to adapt to these conditions. The experimental results show that the ANNC outperforms the other methods, even with very complex image collections. The NNC obtains a 5.98% globally better result than the RBC, and the ANNC obtains a 9.17% improvement over RBC.

The experiments also show how the contents of an image adjust to the definition of a periodic content image, and the type of defects that can be observed influence the final result. In this way, we can observe than geometrical images such as Wallpaper produce optimal results. Also, good results are obtained in the proposed subsets of Wikipedia and Quadibloc collections: WikiGeom and Quadibloc03 are the best adjusted to the definition of a periodic image. These collections show problems such as distorted, illumination artefacts, and noisy and imprecise details due to low image resolution and non-repetitive images. Finally, a new collection as the union of all image sets is considered. This collection is significantly influenced by the nature of the images.

The results are useful in recovery tasks (CBIR systems) using an extended version of ANNC - which produces a list of similarities for every group that can be sorted from highest to lowest values, and so for example, detect images that are near to several groups. This is accomplished by using a rank value on the list of results. ANNC using $K = 2$ obtains a precision improvement of 23.42%. This improvement means that there is a large number of ambiguous classification results. With $K = 3$, precision results from ANNC increase to 27.52%, the small increase of ANNC(3) with respect to ANNC(2) reflects the level of ambiguity that exists.

As future work, we are looking for a new methods of computing the symmetry features, extending the test beds, and colouring images.

Acknowledgements. This work is supported in part by Spanish project VISTAC (DPI20 07-66596-C02-01).

References

1. Agustí, M., Valiente, J.M., Rodas, A.: Lattice extraction based on symmetry analysis. In: Proc. of 3rd. Int. Conf. on Computer Vision Applications (VISAPP 2008), vol. 1, pp. 396–402 (2008)
2. Agustí, M., Rodas, Á., Valiente, J.M.: Computational Symmetry via prototype distances for symmetry groups classification. In: Int. Conf. on Computer Vision Theory and Applications (VISAPP 2011), pp. 85–93 (2011)
3. Alsina, C., Trillas, E.: Lecciones De Álgebra Y Geometría. Gustavo Gili, Barcelona (1992)
4. Edwards, S.: Tiling plane & fancy (2009),
   http://www2.spsu.edu/math/tile/index.html (last visited May 2011)
5. Grunbaüm, B., Shepard, G.C.: Tilings And Patterns. W.H. Freeman and Company, New York (1987)
6. Horne, C.: Geometric Symmetry in Patterns and Tilings. Woodhead Publishing, Abington Hall (2000)
7. Joyce, D.: Wallpaper groups (plane symmetry groups) (2007),
   http://www.clarku.edu/~djoyce/ (last visited May 2011)
8. Liu, Y., Collins, R.T.: A Computational Model for Repeated Pattern Perception using Frieze and Wallpaper Groups. Robotics Institute, CMU, CMU-RI-TR-00-08 (2000)
9. Liu, Y., Collins, R.T., Tsin, Y.: A computational model for periodic pattern perception based on frieze and wallpaper groups. Trans. on PAMI 26(3) (2004)
10. Schattschneider, D.: The Plane Symmetry Groups: Their Recognition and Notation. The American Mathematical Monthly 85, 439–450 (1978)
11. Liu, Y., Hel-Or, H., Kaplan, C.S., Van Gool, L.: Computational symmetry in computer vision and computer graphics. Foundations and Trends in Computer Graphics and Vision 5, 1–195 (2010)
12. Reddy, S., Liu, Y.: On improving the performance of the wallpaper symmetry group classification. CMU-RI-TR-05-49, Robotics Institute, CMU (2005)
13. Savard, J.G.: Basic tilings: The 17 wallpaper groups,
    http://www.quadibloc.com/math/tilint.html (last visited May 2011)
14. Wang, J., Neskovic, P., Cooper, L.N.: Improving nearest neighbor rule with a simple adaptive distance measure. Pattern Recognition Letters 28(2), 207–213 (2007)
15. Wikipedia: Wallpaper group, http://www.wikipedia.org (last visited May 2011)

Author Index

Agustí-Melchor, M.   257
Azernikov, Sergei   69

Bakina, Irina   157
Barth, Peter   105
Bhaskar, Harish   203
Boukadida, Haykel   203
Brusius, Florian   105

Chen, Lili   187

Delmas, Patrice   86
Dhome, Michel   225
Dieny, Romain   172

Ertl, Thomas   142

Glez-Morcillo, Carlos   3
Grand-brochier, Manuel   225

Hurych, David   240

Knoll, Alois   187
Kriglstein, Simone   123

Lal, Brajesh B.   33
Lee, Won-Sook   53
Lutteroth, Christof   86

Madsen, Claus B.   33
Martinez-del-Rincon, Jesus   172
Meguebli, Youssef   203

Naqbi, Mohamed Khamis   203
Nebel, Jean-Christophe   172
Ngo, Hanh T.-M.   53
Nguyen, Minh Hoang   86

Panin, Giorgio   187

Rodas-Jordá, Á.   257

Schäffler, Stefan   19
Schulze, Jörg   19
Schwanecke, Ulrich   105
Svoboda, Tomáš   240

Thevenon, Jerome   172
Tilmant, Christophe   225

Valiente-González, J.M.   257
Vallejo, David   3

Wallner, Günter   123
Werghi, Naoufel   203
Wörner, Michael   142
Wünsche, Burkhard   86

Zhou, Yayun   19
Zimmermann, Karel   240